Public Budgeting

DAVID C. NICE

Washington State University

WADSWORTH

™

THOMSON LEARNING

Australia • Canada • Mexico • Singapore • Spain
United Kingdom • United States

WADSWORTH

THOMSON LEARNING

Political Science Editor: Clark Baxter
Senior Development Editor: Sue Gleason
Assistant Editor: Jennifer Ellis
Editorial Assistant: Jonathan Katz
Marketing Manager: Diane McOscar
Marketing Assistant: Kasia Zagorski
Project Manager, Editorial Production:
Mary Noel
Print/Media Buyer: Tandra Jorgensen

Permissions Editor: Robert Kauser
Production Service: Shepherd, Inc.
Copy Editor: Shepherd, Inc.
Cover Designer: Bill Stanton
Cover Image: © FPG International/
Mark Gottlieb
Cover Printer: Maple-Vail, New York
Compositor: Shepherd, Inc.
Printer: Maple-Vail, New York

ISBN 0-830-41515-7
**Library of Congress Cataloging-in
Publication Data**

Nice, David C., 1952-
    Public budgeting/David C. Nice.
        p. cm.
    Includes bibliographical references and index.
    ISBN 0-8304-1515-7
    1. Budget—United States. 2. Budget. I. Title.

HJ2051 .N46 2001
352.4'8'0973—dc21   2001046519

Wadsworth/Thomson Learning
10 Davis Drive
Belmont, CA 94002-3098
USA

For more information about our products,
contact us:
**Thomson Learning Academic Resource
Center**
1-800-423-0563
http://www.wadsworth.com

International Headquarters
Thomson Learning
International Division
290 Harbor Drive, 2nd Floor
Stamford, CT 06902-7477
USA

UK/Europe/Middle East/South Africa
Thomson Learning
Berkshire House
168-173 High Holborn
London WC1V 7AA
United Kingdom

Asia
Thomson Learning
60 Albert Street, #15-01
Albert Complex
Singapore 189969

Canada
Nelson Thomson Learning
1120 Birchmount Road
Toronto, Ontario M1K 5G4
Canada

DEDICATION

I dedicate this book to my wife, Ruth, who has taught me a great deal about budgeting.

Contents

Preface

Public budgeting is an aggravating enterprise under all but ideal circumstances. We generally want more than we can afford, and we often don't agree regarding what we want. If we are honest and have a reasonable degree of humility, we are also aware that we often don't understand what we are doing. In all these respects, public budgeting bears a close resemblance to other aspects of life.

Unfortunately, democracy (whether direct or representative) does not function terribly well when large numbers of people know very little about public budgeting and when a wealth of inaccurate information about public budgeting is believed by many people. Are we a generous nation when foreign aid decisions are made? Is there a Social Security crisis, and what sorts of proposals might help improve the situation? Would a poor child be better off living in Sweden or in Texas? A better-informed public is in a better position to help guide public decisions regarding budgets.

Budgetary decisions, both public and private, serve as a sort of social lie detector, casting light on the sometimes large gap between what we say and what we do. Reflect on the amount of money that Americans spend on gambling, cosmetics, recreational vehicles, sports, jewelry, or any number of other products and activities. Compare those sums with the amounts that we spend on libraries or the probable cost of extending health care coverage to the millions of Americans who lack that coverage today. These comparisons may not always make us feel comfortable, but they are educational.

THE PLAN OF THE BOOK

I have tried to combine the emphases of budgetary literature from the political/policy side with the literature having more of a public administration and public finance emphasis. These two streams of literature often speak to related concerns and help to place each other in perspective but often seem to function separately. I hope the effort will be of value.

Chapter 1 provides a brief introduction and discusses the various uses of public budgeting along with the most important theories of public budgeting. The chapter will also explore major strategies used by participants in the budget arena and the techniques used to cope with the complexity and conflict associated with budgeting. Chapter 2 discusses the major revenue sources and spending patterns of national, state, and local governments in the United States, and explores changes in revenues and spending over the years. Chapter 2 also explores the implications of some of those changes for public budgeting.

Chapter 3 provides a general overview of the various phases in the budget process, to provide some context for Chapters 4 through 7. Chapter 4 examines the processes involved in developing a budget proposal and how those processes have changed over the years. This chapter describes some of the different formats used for public budgets and what we have learned from using those formats. Chapter 5 provides a brief, nontechnical introduction to some of the analytical techniques used in budgetary analysis. Those techniques include forecasting future revenues and expenses, and analysing the effectiveness and efficiency of programs.

Chapter 6 explores the adoption phase of budgeting, with particular emphasis on the evolution of the budget process in Congress, but also on distinctive features of state and local budget adoption. Chapter 7 discusses the implementation of budgets after they have been approved, as well as some of the major methods for revising a budget after it has been adopted. Chapter 8 examines financial management, which has many facets: decisions regarding major purchases of durable equipment and facilities, public debt, auditing and accounting, and management of funds on hand.

Chapter 9 explores the complex relationships between the economy and public budgeting. As we will see, the economy can affect public budgets in many ways, and budgetary decisions can also affect the economy. Chapter 10 examines the issue of fiscal federalism, which includes such topics as financial aid from one level of government to another, competition among governments for revenues, and the ways in which one government may try to influence the budgetary decisions of other governments. Chapter 11 offers some concluding thoughts on public budgeting with particular attention to the question of why, after more than 100 years of reforming public budgeting, we continue to be less than satisfied with public budgeting in the United States.

ACKNOWLEDGMENTS

I received help from a number of sources as I worked on this book. A research leave from Washington State University provided time to gather materials and to draft portions of the manuscript. Many scholars have helped to develop my thinking on budgetary issues; among those whose contributions are not reflected adequately in the bibliography are Joel Aberbach, Jeff Cohen, Patrick Fisher, Tom Hone, Tom Lauth, Lance LeLoup, Greg Lewis, Nick Lovrich, and Jack Walker. I am deeply in debt as well to the following instructors whose reviews proved invaluable in revising the manuscript: Wes Clarke, University of North Texas; Reed Marlin Davis, Seattle Pacific University; and Rhonda Riherd Trautman, University of Kentucky. And the entire crew at Wadsworth helped in countless ways; among the most important people were Sue Gleason, Clark Baxter, Sharon Adams-Poore, and Jennifer Ellis. Lisa Janowski was a tremendous help in preparing the manuscript and caught an embarrassingly large number of my mistakes. My chocolate lab, Teddy, helped to keep my blood pressure under control while I worked on the book.

Public Budgeting

1

The Nature of Public Budgeting

What Is Public Budgeting?

What Are Budgets Expected to Do?

Theories of Public Budgeting

Budget Strategies

Coping with Complexity and Conflict

Concluding Thoughts

> We have only one person to blame, and that's each other.
>
> BARRY BECK, Hockey Player
> (QUOTED IN FOSS, 1997: 92)

Public budgeting is central to the operation of government in the modern era, yet many citizens and more than a few public officials find budgeting to be a baffling and mysterious exercise. Budgeting is often confusing, in part because it has a language of its own that many people do not understand. In addition, a wealth of inaccurate information about public budgeting circulates through American society. This book is an effort to make budgeting a little less baffling and mysterious. This chapter will offer a definition of public budgeting, discuss the various tasks that public budgeting is expected to perform, and explore some of the major theories about public budgeting. In addition, this chapter will review some of the strategies that are often employed in public budgeting and discuss some of the techniques that decision makers use to cope with the enormous complexity and conflict that budgeting often entails.

WHAT IS PUBLIC BUDGETING?

Although public budgeting can be defined in a variety of ways (see Lee and Johnson, 1994: 1–2; Rubin, 1997: 2–4), for our purposes, public budgeting is making and implementing decisions regarding the acquisition, allocation, and use of resources by government, with a primary focus on money in the modern age. In earlier times, people often were required to contribute labor to public projects, such as road repair, and taxes were sometimes paid with commodities, such as grain. Money obviously presents some great advantages, such as portability and ease of storage. However, even in the modern age, many government programs rely, at least in part, on volunteer labor (see Gowda, 2000), and in-kind transactions, such as trading a section of public land for a section of private land, continue to be important for some programs.

Note that this definition of public budgeting is rather broad; in its broadest interpretation, public budgeting is equivalent to public policy making generally. As we will see later, one issue that underlies some budget reforms centers on precisely how much budgeting and policy making should overlap. Should the budget be the central vehicle for guiding and controlling government, or does that approach create an unmanageable budget process (see Chapter 4)? There do not seem to be any easy answers to that question.

Public budgeting has much in common with budgeting in the private sector; families, like governments, must decide how to generate income, allocate that income across various uses (such as food, clothing, and shelter), and keep track of how the money is actually used. Public budgeting, however, does have some relatively distinctive features.[1]

One somewhat distinctive feature of public budgeting is the frequent occurrence of serious conflict regarding budgetary decisions. How high should taxes be, and how should the tax burden be distributed? How should funds be allocated among different programs; does education need additional funding, or should more money be spent on health care? What restrictions or regulations should accompany the money? Should the budget be used to help manage the economy, and, if so, how? Private budgeting can also involve conflict, as in the case of family members arguing over how much to spend on a vacation or new car, but public budgeting almost always involves conflicts among a large number of groups and individuals who have different views regarding the ideal budget.

Public budgeting is also somewhat distinctive, at least in democracies, in the openness of budgetary decisions to outside influences. Citizens, interest groups, political parties, and the mass media all seek to shape budgetary decisions made by government. Many private-sector budget decisions, by contrast, are made with relatively little direct input from people or groups outside the organization making the decisions. Here, too, the differences are not absolute. Businesses spend large sums of money on advertising in an effort to influence the spending decisions of families, and those family spending decisions in turn may strongly affect the budget situations of individual businesses, churches, and other private organizations.

Public budgeting in the modern era is also distinctive in that it is subject to a large number of rules, regulations, and procedural guidelines that make the process quite complex and sometimes confusing. Budgeting in virtually all formal organizations is subject to rules and regulations, but public budgeting, especially in democracies, is particularly hedged about with rules, restrictions, and complex procedures. Specific procedures are usually required to make government budget decisions; numerous steps in the process may be required. Restrictions on how certain funds can be used, how funds can be raised, and a host of other aspects of the budget may limit the options of decision makers.

WHAT ARE BUDGETS EXPECTED TO DO?

One reason why public budgeting is often controversial and difficult is the fact that we expect it to do a number of different and sometimes incompatible tasks. Improving the budget process' ability to perform one task may erode its ability to perform another task.[2]

Setting Goals and Priorities

One important and difficult budgetary task is the setting of goals and priorities. Because we often want more than we can afford, both in public and in private life, budgeters must decide which services and programs deserve generous support, which ones should receive only modest support, and which ones should receive little or nothing. Is protecting the environment more important than giving more students access to a college education? Should the public sector expand, or would it be better to leave more resources in the private sector? Sometimes goals and priorities are stated fairly explicitly, as in the case of mobilizing for victory during World War II. Financing the war effort left few resources available for other public programs or for private consumption; that effort was supported by campaigns to promote the sale of war bonds to help finance the war and simultaneously take money out of the private sector. Rationing was also used to limit private consumption of materials needed for the war effort. In other cases, goals and priorities emerge in a somewhat back-handed manner. For example, a community may respond to financial problems by cutting back on maintenance of facilities. The mayor of that community is unlikely to state publicly that neglecting maintenance is a good thing to do. The process of setting goals and priorities is a predictably controversial task, particularly in large and diverse political systems, where many different views regarding goals and priorities are likely to exist.

Linking Goals to Actions

A second important budgetary task is translating abstract policy goals into tangible actions. After World War II, the United States embarked on an effort to create a nationwide network of multilane highways. A critical part of that effort was raising and distributing the many billions of dollars needed to construct the Interstate Highway System. Without an effective budgetary process, policy goals may never be reached because the resources needed to achieve the goals are never provided.

Managing the Economy

Managing the economy is another important budgetary task, particularly in the modern era. We will explore that topic in some detail in Chapter 9. According to some observers, the budget can be used to help steer the economy. If it is growing too slowly, budgetary stimulus can help to correct that problem. If the economy is overheated, budgetary actions can help cool it down. This task is often controversial in several respects. First, different people may have different views regarding the performance of the economy; if I am unemployed, I may be more concerned about the unemployment rate, whereas a wealthy investor may be more concerned about inflation. Second, economists disagree regarding the most appropriate ways to guide the economy. Third, not everyone believes that government should try to manage the economy. Finally, if public officials are often unable to make budgetary decisions in a timely fashion, they may be unable to make needed adjustments when they would be most effective.

Promoting Accountability

Budgets also serve as instruments to promote accountability, both to public officials and, particularly in democracies, to the public. A public agency or a private contractor receives public money to perform one or more tasks; part of the budget process involves assessing whether that money was properly and productively used. Citizens can use the budget to assess whether officials have honored their campaign promises and whether government is using tax revenues appropriately. Unfortunately, many Americans are poorly informed regarding many budgetary issues. A 1997 survey found that 63 percent of all Americans incorrectly believed that the U.S. government spent more money on foreign aid than on Medicare (Kohut and Toth, 1998: 22). Many Americans also know little about how their state governments raise or spend money.[3] There appears to be ample room for improvement in using public budgets as an instrument of public accountability.

Controlling the Use of Public Resources

A related budgetary task involves providing control over the use of public resources. If an agency's budget provides it with $325 million to spend in the next 12 months, the budget process needs mechanisms to make certain that the agency does not spend $4 billion instead. If an agency receives $3 million to buy office equipment, an effective budget process needs to ensure that the money is not spent on vacations in the Bahamas instead. Some of the government red tape and inflexibility that cause numerous complaints arise from the need to prevent misuse of public funds.

Promoting Efficiency and Effectiveness

Another important budgetary task, one that is dear to the hearts of many budget reformers, is encouraging greater efficiency and effectiveness in government. Given that we often want more than we can afford, we may be able to narrow the gap between wants and resources if we can accomplish more with a given amount of resources. Increasing efficiency and effectiveness requires officials to assess how well programs are performing and to be constantly looking for alternative strategies that might be more effective. The quest for greater efficiency and effectiveness may sometimes conflict with the desire to prevent misuse of public funds, for the former emphasis may require some amount of flexibility and willingness to experiment and take risks, all of which may increase the danger of misuse of funds.

Social Planning and Reform

Budgets can also serve as instruments to promote social planning and reform in many ways. Governments at all levels in the United States have spent billions of dollars on roads and highways since 1900. That spending has helped to make the United States a very automobile-oriented country and has shaped the physical development of cities, the locational decisions of many businesses and families, and the development of the American economy. Tax incentives may be used to encourage home ownership, modernization of factories, or saving for retirement. Using government budgeting to guide societal development can be controversial, both because people may disagree regarding what type of development should be encouraged and because not everyone is comfortable with government playing that type of role. In addition, budgets may shape a society's development in unintended ways. America's commitment to automobile transportation has helped to make the the country heavily dependent on imported oil, a situation that was almost certainly not intended by most people when the good-roads movement began lobbying for road and highway improvements prior to World War I.

Keeping the Process Manageable

A final concern for budgeters involves keeping the budget process from becoming unmanageably difficult. Beyond some point, if we add more and more conflicts, issues, and information to budgeting, we run the risk of making the job of budgeters completely impossible. If levels of conflict become too high, budgeters may not be able to make decisions or stick by them for any length of time. If the amount of information in the budget process becomes too large, decision makers may not be able to comprehend enough of the information to make reasonable decisions. As we will see later, some budget reforms over the years have run afoul of this problem. Budgeters, then, recurrently face the task of keeping the budget process at manageable levels of conflict and complexity. We will discuss some methods for coping with the problems of conflict and complexity shortly.

THEORIES OF PUBLIC BUDGETING

A basic problem facing anyone trying to make sense of public budgeting is the immense amount of information that is or might be relevant to budgeting. In addition, many people are interested in the question of what factors influence budgetary decisions. There is also the value-laden question of what factors *should* influence budget outcomes. Scholars who have faced these issues have turned to budgetary theories in order to help organize information about public budgeting, explain budgetary outcomes, and, in some cases, suggest guidance for possible improvements in budgeting.[4] Bear in mind that the broader views of public budgeting—views that make it virtually synonymous with public policy making—make theories of budgeting equivalent to theories of public policy making or even politics generally.[5] We will examine several of the most important budgetary theories. As we will see, scholars disagree regarding which of the theories are most valid.

Incrementalism

Probably the single most influential budgetary theory is *incrementalism*. According to this theory, budgeters do not have the time, energy, or analytical capacity to seriously consider a wide range of possible budgets. Even if they had sufficient time and energy, previous commitments and political considerations

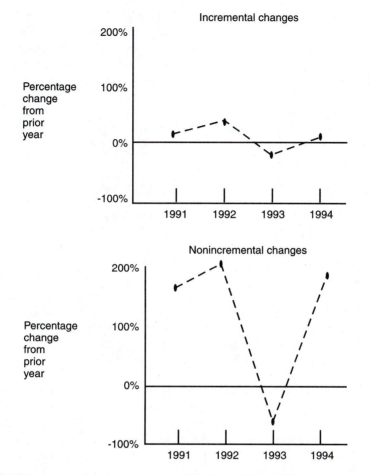

FIGURE 1.1 Incremental and nonincremental budgetary changes.

SOURCE: Hypothetical data.

greatly limit budgetary flexibility. Dramatic spending increases for a large number of programs would probably require a large tax increase, which would
anger taxpayers. Large spending reductions would anger program beneficiaries
and might imply that previous spending decisions were foolish or inappropriate. As a result, decision makers will often use the current budget as a rough
guide to decisions for next year's budget and focus most of their attention on
relatively modest budgetary changes. Budgets, therefore, typically change rather
gradually[6] (see Figure 1.1).

Critics of incrementalism have attacked it on several grounds. If budgets
change gradually, they may not be able to respond to rapidly changing conditions. If some money is not being spent productively, gradual changes will
not be able to correct the situation for some time. In addition, some critics

contend that incrementalism is not a very accurate depiction of public budgeting in many cases. Budgets for individual programs and agencies sometimes
change dramatically, especially in times of crisis (such as the outbreak of a
major war) or for programs that require a large initial commitment of funds
in order to exist at all—such as the U.S. space program. Moreover, incrementalism generally assumes that the various players in the budget process participate on a fairly continuous basis and understand what others are doing. If
some players, however, participate only occasionally or do not understand
what other players are doing, the restraining influence of incrementalism may
break down.[7]

Rational Decision Making

A second important theory of public budgeting depicts it as (ideally) an exercise in rational decision making. In this view, public budgeting should help a
nation (or state or locality) make progress toward important social goals, such
as safer streets or a cleaner environment. Adherents of this perspective are often
critical of public budgeting; they believe that it often fails to allocate money
where it is needed most and wastes money on unproductive programs. This
perspective underlies many proposed budget reforms and is frequently found
in public choice theories and in welfare economics.[8] In this view, budgeters
need precise information on whether programs perform effectively and need
to use that information to guide their decisions. Reforms may be needed to
encourage those actions.

Critics of this theory complain that it often assumes that we know and
agree on what we want to do; in reality, public budgeting struggles with frequent conflicts regarding social goals. In addition, we often lack important
information regarding how well programs actually work or which option
today will yield the best results 10 or 20 years in the future (Lindblom, 1959).
We will return to these issues later. More generally, politics is a human enterprise, and human beings have emotions as well as rational thoughts. Budgetary
decisions may make people feel proud, sad, fearful, relieved, or angry, and sensible decision makers need to consider those emotional consequences as well
as "rational" analyzes of budget issues.

Political Influence

A very different theory of public budgeting sees it as a fundamentally political
process. This perspective comes in many variations. Some of the most common
versions contend that powerful interest groups, public officials in positions of
authority, or anyone else with considerable influence will mold the budget to
fit their preferences. Public budgets reveal who has enough clout to gain what
they want from government. When budget cuts are needed, this view predicts
that programs benefiting people who are politically weak are more likely to be
cut than are programs with well organized, politically active supporters.[9] The
tendency for Social Security benefits to keep pace with inflation since the 1970s
while the purchasing power of benefits for Aid to Families with Dependent

Children/Temporary Assistance to Needy Families declined is consistent with this perspective. Social Security recipients are numerous and politically active, whereas most welfare recipients are not politically active.

Bear in mind, however, that politically weak groups are not always forgotten in budgetary decision making. If they were, many welfare programs would not exist. Compassion, beliefs about fairness, and other political values may help weaker groups advance their interests in the budget arena at times, and procedural safeguards in the budget process may limit the impact of unreasonable demands made by powerful groups. We may need to know, therefore, not only which people or groups are powerful but also what people want or believe is fair, reasonable, or desirable.[10]

Economics Shapes Budgets

A very influential theory of public budgeting depicts it as largely driven by major economic forces. In this perspective, a city with a healthy economy will spend more than a city where almost everyone is poor, regardless of the preferences of public officials, the maneuvers of interest groups, or the results of budgetary analyses of how well programs perform. A wealthy nation will spend more than a poor nation. A rapidly growing economy will produce more revenues for expansion of programs; a declining economy will force cuts in programs and/or borrowing to finance public services. Financial aid from one level of government may shape the budgetary decisions of the level of government receiving the aid.[11] Budgeting, then, is like white-water rafting, and powerful economic currents may sweep budgeters in directions that they would not have chosen otherwise.

Procedures Shape Budgets

A final budgetary theory emphasizes the importance of budgetary procedures, processes, and strategies in shaping the budget. The rules of the process may give some participants advantages over others and may make some budget choices easier to adopt or harder to change. Some people may be baffled by the complexity of public budgeting and unable to make sense of what is happening; they are likely to be at a disadvantage compared to people who understand the process. Some participants may choose poor strategies for pursuing their budgetary goals and may, consequently, fail to reach their goals. One sign of the influence of this theory is the volume of budgetary literature devoted to budgetary procedures and strategies.[12] Another sign of this theory's influence is the recurring tendency for people who are unhappy with budget decisions to call for reforming the budget process in some fashion, such as a balanced budget amendment to the Constitution. We will explore a variety of budget reforms at various points in this book.

Critics of this perspective complain that budgetary rules and procedures sometimes have less impact on budget decisions than reformers often hope. In part this reflects the many forces that shape budgetary decisions, regardless of the rules and procedures. In addition, rules and procedures that stop people from getting what they want in the budget arena are often revised or under-cut, sooner or later (see Chapter 11).

The variety of budgetary theories, including others not examined here, alert us to the need to consider a number of different forces that may be at work in public budgeting. Simple explanations of what is happening and why may have the virtue of simplicity but may miss much of the complexity and richness of what is actually happening.

BUDGET STRATEGIES

Budget decisions affect people's lives in many ways. Can a family afford to send three children to college? Will a community have passenger train service? How high will my taxes be next year? What will happen to someone who falls into poverty? Will my agency be able to afford new equipment soon? All those questions may be answered, at least in part, during the budget process. As a result, people who want to influence budgetary decisions must decide how best to exert that influence. The range of options is as wide as the range of methods for exerting political influence generally, but a number of strategies are common in budgetary politics.[13]

Cultivating Clientele Support

One important strategy is the cultivation of clientele support. Generally speaking, clienteles are groups with a continuing and strong interest in a government program. They may receive benefits from the program, as in the case of Social Security recipients, or they may have a business relationship with the program, as in the case of defense contractors. In some instances, groups that are regulated by an agency may become clienteles. Having a large, organized, and politically active clientele will make gaining the support of the president, state legislature, or county commission a good deal easier. Programs that lack strong clientele support may be vulnerable to budget cuts when funds are relatively scarce and may have a more difficult time competing for added funds when they are available.

Gaining the Trust of Others

Building and maintaining the trust and confidence of other participants in the budget process is another important budgetary strategy. Public budgeting almost always involves a number of participants, many of whom must approve a proposal. Being well prepared, honest, and aware of those participants' expectations and preferences will make things flow more smoothly. Gauging those preferences is not always easy, however, particularly when the number of participants is large, when new participants arrive on the scene, or when some participants conceal their preferences in hopes of gaining a tactical advantage.

Documenting a Need

A third, partly related strategy involves developing and presenting convincing evidence of the need for some course of action and/or evidence that some existing course of action is beneficial. A rising crime rate may help to persuade the city council to increase funding for law enforcement; an analysis showing that an education reform improves student performance may help generate funds to implement the reform more broadly. A major thrust of several budgetary reforms since the 1930s has been to require more systematic analysis of needs and program performance in budgeting. These efforts have sometimes encountered problems when there have been disagreements regarding values and goals, and assessing how well programs work is sometimes very difficult. We will return to those issues in later chapters.

Looking for Sympathetic Decision Makers

Another important strategy, particularly in countries like the United States, makes use of the large number of participants who make budgetary decisions. A group that is ignored by the White House may appeal to Congress; if the national government is not responsive, state governments may be. If the governor and state legislature will not listen, perhaps a court will be more sympathetic. In a number of states and localities, a public vote may enact a budget decision that would not have passed in the legislature. With many decision-making arenas and many decision makers, people may shop around for the decision that they want.

Coping with Painful Actions

When painful budgetary actions are threatened, other strategies may be employed. Officials may try to shift blame to other decision makers, as in the case of President Reagan blaming Congress for the budget deficits during his presidency. If the budget must be cut, officials may try to cut less visible and less painful items, such as cutting back on maintenance or postponing major purchases. Conversely, officials may try to fend off cuts by cutting visible, popular programs in hopes of raising a public outcry that will lead to a restoration of funds. Officials may simply stall, postponing painful actions until they have left office or conditions have improved.

The "Camel's Nose"

People who are seeking funds for a new program may employ the "camel's nose" technique, which involves asking for a small amount of money for the first year and a somewhat larger amount in each succeeding year rather than asking for a huge sum of money in the first year. This strategy assumes that budgeting is relatively incremental; gradual changes are likely to generate less opposition than are large, abrupt changes. After money is spent on some project for several years, decision makers are likely to feel that abandoning the project will mean that the initial funds were wasted. This strategy presents the risk that a project that would have been rejected if policy makers had known its total cost at the beginning may be able to gain approval.

   Two other strategies that resemble the camel's nose may also be employed. A program may be started as a temporary measure in the hope that a temporary program will win approval more easily than an ongoing commitment. After the "temporary" measure has been in place for some time, it may be converted to a permanent program. Alternatively, program advocates may present it as an outgrowth of existing operations rather than as a new initiative; again, this assumes that incrementalism is at work and that current commitments receive less scrutiny than do new programs.

Making the Program Appear Self-Supporting

An important budgetary strategy for some programs is to present them as at least partly self-supporting. For example, a state park may charge an entrance fee that helps cover the cost of maintaining the park. A highway may be financed in part by tolls paid by highway users. This strategy may sometimes be beneficial in requiring people who benefit from a program to help pay for it, but problems may arise if the fees reach a level that poor people cannot afford. In addition, fees, like taxes, must still be paid by people. An expensive program that covers 30 percent of its costs from user fees is still an expensive program.

Capitalizing on Temporary Circumstances

Other budgetary strategies involve taking advantage of favorable conditions that may temporarily improve a program's attractiveness. During a crisis situation, a program may gain funding if it can be presented as a potential remedy for whatever is causing the crisis. Proposals to create a Social Security system in the United States languished until the Great Depression, when elected officials and the public became more interested in programs that might help stabilize the economy and prevent people from falling into poverty. A friendly political environment may enable a program to begin or expand operations, particularly if program supporters are prepared to take advantage of that environment when the opportunity arises (see Kingdon, 1995).

Deception and Confusion

A budgetary strategy that raises troubling ethical questions is the use of concealment, deception, confusion, and even misinformation in order to promote a budget proposal. If people cannot understand what a budget proposal might do or if they are misled into thinking that it might do something that it will not do, they may accept or even support that proposal, even though they would have opposed it if they had more accurate information regarding its effects. People who might object to slashing funds for state mental hospitals might agree to reforms that greatly reduce the number of patients in those hospitals; the reduction in patient load may then be used to justify budget reductions (see Behn, 1980: 336–337). Given the complexity of budgeting and the fact that many people do not know a great deal about public (or private) budgeting, the opportunities for using this strategy are unfortunately frequent. During the 1980s, a number of public officials who certainly should have known better made public statements to the effect that only the federal government was borrowing large sums of money, in contrast to families, businesses, and state governments, all of which were presented as models of financial responsibility and prudence. In point of fact, families, businesses, and state governments also borrow considerable sums of money. Frequent use of this strategy greatly weakens the budget's ability to promote accountability, for accountability requires accurate information.

Minimizing the Risk of Future Cuts

Another family of budgetary strategies seeks to deal with concerns that funding may be withdrawn after it has been committed. An agency may begin the year with $100 million to spend, but revenue shortfalls may bring the threat of reductions in that funding. One method for fending off that threat is spending or otherwise committing the money as quickly as possible. Equipment or supplies will be purchased as soon as money becomes available. Another option is to pad the budget with additional funds to reduce the pain inflicted by a later reduction. If an agency can develop its own revenue sources, it may try to hide some of those funds from the central budget office to provide a cushion against budget cuts.

COPING WITH COMPLEXITY
AND CONFLICT

Public budgeting in the modern era is an enormously complex task in all but the smallest jurisdictions. There are many programs, many organizations, and many demands. The budget for a single program may involve a large number of decisions regarding individual projects, schedules for completion of various tasks, rules and regulations accompanying the money, and coverage of the program, among other things. Officials may need to assess complicated analyses of program effectiveness and sort through numerous claims and counterclaims regarding program needs and accomplishments. The sheer volume and complexity of the information can be overwhelming. In the words of former Budget Director David Stockman, who initially impressed many observers with his apparent command of budgetary issues, "None of us really understands what's going on with all these numbers" (quoted in Greider, 1982: 33).

At the same time, public budgeting often involves considerable conflict. Supporters of a program clash with opponents of the program. People who support a program in general may disagree with one another regarding various aspects of the program's operation. A member of Congress who supports funding for military hospitals may, nonetheless, object to using the funds to pay for abortions. Distributing the costs of government across taxpayers is a perennial source of controversy. If the budget process is to function effectively, officials need to develop methods for coping with the complexity and conflict the budgeting involves. Fortunately, a number of coping devices are available.[14]

Incrementalism

Incrementalism is an important coping device. If officials confine their attention to budget proposals that are similar to what is being done now, they are spared the work of assessing a huge number of more drastic budgetary changes. Moreover, drastic changes often involve considerable uncertainty, both regarding how well a radically different program would work and how the public would react to it. Sticking to familiar ground reduces (but does not eliminate) the amount of uncertainty decision makers must face. At the same time, incrementalism reduces the amount of budgetary conflict by reducing the number and range of proposals that are contending for political support. If we assume that each program will receive approximately the same amount that it is receiving this year, plus or minus a proportionally small adjustment (a common assumption in incremental decision making), we reduce the danger that supporters of different programs will try to take funds away from one another's programs. There is, consequently, less conflict.

Fair Shares

The norm of *fair shares* is another common coping device. This technique calls for giving almost all programs some share (although not necessarily exactly the same share) of additional funding when the budget is growing and giving almost all programs some share of the sacrifice when budget cuts are necessary. When this norm is followed, proposals to give some programs enormous budget increases while other programs are being severely cut will not normally receive serious consideration. Exceptions may occur, as in the case of a major crisis that calls for dramatic action in some policy areas but not others—a major war, for example. This norm will help reduce the number of budget proposals that must be considered; as a result, complexity and conflict are both reduced.

Separate Pools

Dividing various portions of the budget into separate pools that are treated separately from one another can also help reduce complexity and conflict. A particular source of revenue may be earmarked for a specific program; some state constitutions require motor fuel tax revenues to be spent only on road and highway programs. Some programs may be taken out of the budget entirely and handled separately from other programs. A program may be assigned to a public corporation or a special authority, such as an airport authority that has its own sources of money. That program may have little or no contact with the regular budget process of the government that created it.[15] These techniques simplify budgetary decisions by reducing the number of decisions that must be made in the regular budget process and by reducing the range of proposals that must be considered. If motor fuel taxes cannot be spent on any program except roads and highways, then budgeters do not need to analyze or quarrel over proposals to spend that money for education, health care, or welfare.

Division of Labor

The complexity and conflict of budgeting may also be reduced by a division of labor among participants in the budget process. During the "classical era" of federal budgeting, individual agencies were expected to identify which activities needed additional money and bring those needs to the attention of other officials. The White House assessed the total amount of revenue likely to be available, made some effort to set priorities among different programs, and sometimes tried to use the budget to guide the performance of the economy. Congress, generally working through its committees, tried to guard the Treasury against excessive or frivolous demands but also tried to provide needed support for worthwhile programs. Each set of actors depended on the other sets to do their parts of the process, which reduced the amount of work done by each participant and reduced the potential for conflict (Wildavsky and Caiden, 1997: chaps. 2, 3).

Another division of labor in budgeting involves the use of legislative committees that focus on different parts or aspects of the budget. As we will see in Chapter 6, Congress has tried a number of different approaches to using committees in the budget process. For most of our history, Congress assigned revenue decisions to one set of committees, decisions regarding spending to a second set of committees, and decisions regarding the creation and operation of programs to still other committees (with some overlap). Members of one committee were spared the work of detailed review of those aspects of the budget handled by other committees.

Another version of the division of labor involves having two or more levels of government, each of which makes some budgetary decisions. State or local officials may emphasize relatively localized problems, such as fire protection or law enforcement, that might escape the notice of national officials. National officials may focus on relatively broad ranging problems, such as national defense, that cannot readily be handled by state or local governments in many cases. We will return to this issue in Chapter 10.

A division of labor in budgeting presents a number of risks for budgeters. If I depend on someone else to deal with some aspects of the budget that I generally ignore, that other person may shape the budget in ways that I dislike. The other person may make mistakes that complicate my work or cause my decisions to be faulty. I may vote to approve funding for a project on the basis of assurances that enough revenues are available to finance it; I may later regret that decision if revenues are less abundant than I was told. Without some effective mechanism of coordination, a division of labor may produce a group of decisions that, taken together, produce effects that no one wants. For example, if revenue decisions are made by one group and spending decisions by another group, we run the risk of spending more than we can afford unless the revenue and spending decisions are somehow linked. One recurrent theme in the history of public budgeting in the United States is the search for a workable method for dividing the budgetary labor.

Avoiding Programmatic Decisions

Budgeters may try to reduce complexity and conflict in the budget process by avoiding, when possible, making decisions regarding programs within the budget process. The traditional congressional practice of having one set of committees to process bills authorizing the creation of programs and making many of the decisions regarding program operations and another set of committees to handle the spending legislation reflects, in part, an effort to minimize the volume of programmatic decisions that must be made in the budget process. Bear in mind that budget decisions must unavoidably affect programs to some degree, a reality that has sometimes provoked great conflict among congressional committees. We will return to that issue in Chapter 6.

Some budget reformers have complained that minimizing the programmatic aspects of budgeting risks providing funds for programs that are not effective. In addition, this coping method requires considerable self-restraint on the part of decision makers, especially when legislation is difficult to pass. If a policy proposal is unlikely to pass by itself, a legislator may be tempted to offer it as an amendment to a spending bill that must be passed. If many legislators feel that temptation, spending bills may be loaded down with all sorts of provisions that are not directly related to the budget and that create intense conflict (see Pianin, 1998).

Postponement

Another technique for coping with complexity and conflict in public budgeting makes use of the fact that budgeting is a repetitive process, with a new budget being adopted every year or two. As a result, budgeters do not need to deal with every possible issue at any given time. One group of issues can be tackled this year, and another group can be addressed next year. Still others can be faced in future years. Moreover, urgent matters that cannot wait until the next budget cycle can be handled by revising a budget in midyear (see Chapter 7). This technique of dealing with only a limited number of issues in each budget cycle can be highly annoying to impatient people and can mean that a significant problem may not be faced for several years. Still, there are simply too many issues in the budgets of all but the smallest governments to resolve in a single year. The repetitive nature of budgeting also helps soften conflict because people who do not win adoption of their budgetary proposals one year can try again in the near future.

Assumptions behind Coping Mechanisms

The common techniques for keeping complexity and conflict in budgeting at manageable levels generally imply that the current budget is reasonably appropriate and, therefore, that it needs only gradual changes that preserve, by and large, the current allocation of funds across various programs (fair shares make sense only if the current shares make sense). Similarly, dividing the budget into pieces through earmarking, off-budget enterprises, and the like assumes that we do not need to consider the possibility of taking money away from one program for another program. That assumption may not always be accurate.

The division of labor in budgetary decision making also assumes a reasonable degree of agreement regarding budgetary priorities. If members of Congress and the president have drastically different budget priorities, a division of labor is unlikely to work very well. Programmatic conflicts are more easily kept out of the budget if there are not very many or very intense conflicts over program operations.

Finally, the coping mechanisms generally require self-restraint among budgetary decision makers. Incrementalism, fair shares, and the various devices to divide the budget into pieces will work only if the various participants refrain from going after one another's shares of the budget. A division of labor requires the participants to avoid second-guessing one another most of the time. Separating most programmatic conflicts from the budget means that officials who primarily make budgetary decisions refrain from intruding into program decisions and that officials who primarily make programmatic decisions refrain from intruding into budgetary decisions. That self-restraint is not always present.

CONCLUDING THOUGHTS

Public budgeting involves making and carrying out decisions regarding acquisition, allocation, and use of resources, particularly money, by government. Although public and private budgeting are similar in many respects, public budgeting is often more controversial, more open to multiple influences, and more heavily regulated than private budgeting.

People expect government budgeting to accommodate a number of different needs, from setting goals and priorities and managing the economy to promoting accountability and controlling the use of public resources. At the same time, budgeters struggle to keep their work from becoming too complex or too conflictual.

Scholars have tried to explain budgetary decisions in a number of ways. One of the most important budgetary theories, incrementalism, contends that budgeters rely heavily on past experience and are usually reluctant to change the budget very drastically from year to year. Other important theories try to explain budgeting in terms of rational decision making, the exercise of political power, the impact of economic forces, or budgetary rules and procedures.

Participants in the budgetary process employ a number of different strategies, including mobilizing the support of program clienteles, gaining the trust of other participants in the process, documenting a need, and making a program appear to be inexpensive at first and building gradually (the "camel's nose). Other strategies include looking for sympathetic decision makers, capitalizing on temporary conditions (such as a crisis), and trying to deceive or confuse other participants in the process.

Budgeters employ a number of methods in their efforts to keep their decisions from becoming too conflict-ridden or too complex. Incrementalism, the principle of fair shares, a division of labor in making a budget, minimizing the emphasis on policies in the budget process, and postponing some issues to future years are among the more common methods used. Nonetheless, budgeting in the modern era is often controversial and very complex.

NOTES

1. See Allison (1980); Bland and Rubin (1997: 3–6); Lee and Johnson (1994: 2–6); Rubin (1997: 5–6).

2. Axelrod (1995: 7–18); Euske (1983); Lee and Johnson (1994: 6–15); Lynch (1995: 3, 27–31); Makolo (1983); Motza (1983); Schick (1966; 1990: 1–3); Wildavsky and Caiden (1997: 1–6, 259–263).

3. "Oregon and Washington Public Knowledge About Government" (1997); "Trends in Public Knowledge" (1996).

4. Key (1940); LeLoup (1988: 13–19); Lewis (1952); Rubin (1990); Swan (1983); Wildavsky (1986: chap. 1).

5. Dye (1992: chaps. 2, 12); Nice (1994: chap. 2); Isaak (1985: pt. 3).

6. Lindblom (1959); Sharkansky (1968a); White (1994); Wildavsky (1986: chaps. 2, 3).

7. LeLoup (1978); Rubin (1997: 127–128); Schulman (1980); Sharkansky (1970: chap. 10).

8. Buchanan and Flowers (1987: pt. 2); Musgrave and Musgrave (1980: chaps. 3–6, 8, 10, 11); Singer (1976: chaps. 3–8).

9. Caiden and Wildavsky (1997: 57–59); Cozzetto, Kweit, and Kweit (1995: 2–5); Greider (1982: 59); Parker (1983).

10. Nice (1985); Wright, Erikson, and McIver (1987).

11. Campbell and Sacks (1967); Dye (1966; 1990); Lowery (1985); Wilensky (1975).

12. Cozzetto, Kweit, and Kweit (1995: 63–66); Grafton and Permaloff (1983); Meyers (1994); LeLoup (1988: 77–82); Wildavsky and Caiden (1997: 57–66).

13. Behn (1980); Finney (1994: chap. 14); Howard (1973: 27–33, 43–67); LeLoup (1988: 77–82); Meyers (1994); Wildavsky (1986: chaps. 6, 8); Wildavsky and Caiden (1997: 57–66).

14. Axelrod (1995: 13–18); Lindblom (1959); Rubin (1997: 134–144); Wildavsky (1986: chapters 9, 10); Wildavsky and Caiden (1997: 44–49).

15. *Budget Issues: Earmarking in the Federal Government* (1995); *Government-Sponsored Enterprises* (1990).

2

Government Revenues, Spending, and Borrowing: A Brief Overview

> A billion here, a billion there and pretty
> soon you're talking about real money.
>
> SENATOR EVERETT DIRKSEN
> (QUOTED IN GOLDBERG, 1994: 93)

From the beginnings of the American political system, leaders have recognized the importance of public budgeting. Two of the complaints made against England in the Declaration of Independence involved government finances, and many of the provisions of the U.S. Constitution deal with government revenues or spending in some fashion. Public budgets have changed considerably over the years, however. Changes have included the amounts of money raised and spent, the formats of public budgets, and the processes used to make budgetary decisions. This chapter will provide a brief overview of government revenues, spending, and borrowing in the United States and explore the implications of changes in government finances for public budgeting. Later chapters will discuss changing budget formats and processes.

In exploring information on government revenues and spending, bear in mind that different information sources are not always fully comparable. Seemingly minor differences in definitions (e.g., is money considered "spent" when a commitment to purchase something is made or when the item is actually paid for?) or coverage (are all revenues included, or are only revenues raised by the government on its own included?) can lead to large differences in apparent levels of government revenues or spending.

Some of the most common differences in measures of revenues and spending deserve mention. If we compare total revenues with *own-source* revenues (e.g., revenues that a government raises on its own rather than being given the funds by another level of government), state and especially local governments in the United States appear considerably larger and more expensive in terms of total revenues. If we compare total expenditures with *direct* expenditures (e.g., purchases of goods and services and direct payments to individuals but excluding grants given to another level of government), national and state governments in the United States appear smaller and less costly when measured by direct expenditures. *General* revenues and expenditures (which exclude some trust funds, such as pension programs) are generally lower than total revenues and expenditures. In 1996, local governments in the United States had $804 billion in total revenues but only $439 billion in general, own-source revenues (*Statistical Abstract,* 1999: 311). Any discussion of budgetary issues must be clear regarding what sorts of budgetary numbers are used, or considerable confusion may result.[1]

1902
   National   XXXXXXXXXXXXXXXX   (33%)
   State   XXXXXX   (11%)
   Local   XXXXXXXXXXXXXXXXXXXXXXXXXXXXX   (54%)

1996
   National   XXXXXXXXXXXXXXXXXXXXXXXXXXXXXX   (55%)
   State   XXXXXXXXXXXXX   (26%)
   Local   XXXXXXXXXX   (19%)

FIGURE 2.1 Changing shares of own-source revenues.

SOURCES: *Statistical Abstract* (1999: 311–312); *Historical Statistics of the U.S.*
(1960: 711, 722, 727–730).

Table 2.1 The Growth of Government Revenues and Spending

TOTAL OWN-SOURCE REVENUES[a]

	1902	**1996**
National	$562 million (33%)	$1,569 billion (55%)
State	$192 million (11%)	$745 billion (26%)
Local	$914 million (54%)	$533 billion (19%)
Total	$1,694 million (98%)[b]	$2,847 billion (100%)

TOTAL DIRECT SPENDING

	1902	**1996**
National	$485 million (29%)	$1,472 billion (51%)
State	$188 million (11%)	$608 billion (21%)
Local	$959 million (58%)	$786 billion (27%)
Total	$1,660 million (98%)	$2,866 billion (99%)

[a]Excludes duplicative transactions.

SOURCES: *Statistical Abstract* (1999: 311–312); *Historical Statistics of the U.S.* (1960: 711, 722, 727–730).

GROWING REVENUES AND EXPENDITURES

One of the most obvious developments in public budgeting in the United States is the growth of government revenues and spending over the years (see Table 2.1). In 1902, all levels of government combined raised and spent just over $1.6 billion, with most of the money being handled at the local level. By the mid-1990s, government revenues and spending were approaching $3 trillion, with the single largest share being raised and spent by the national government. State revenues and spending, which lagged considerably behind their local counterparts in 1902, actually exceeded local revenues and spending by the mid 1990s (see Figure 2.1). Note, however, that revenues and spending have grown dramatically at all three levels of government. Although a good deal of the increase can be explained by population growth and inflation, government's share of the total American economy has grown considerably, from less than 8 percent in 1902 (Mosher and Poland, 1964: 9–10, 24) to nearly 40 percent in recent years.

ACCOUNTING FOR GROWTH

A number of analysts have tried to explain the growth of government revenues and spending, growth that has occurred in many countries. Not surprisingly, a number of different explanations have been offered, but assessing their relative importance has proven difficult.[2] One perspective, often called "Wagner's Law," contends that social and economic changes encourage government expansion. As a nation's economy shifts from subsistence agriculture to industrial production and high-technology firms, demands on the transportation system multiply and environmental problems increase. As people move from farms to cities, demands on law enforcement, fire protection, and sanitation systems all increase. As the technology of work becomes more complex, people need more education. Governments will be asked to do more and more, and meeting the costs of those growing responsibilities makes budgets expand.

Another explanation for budgetary expansion—one that is especially popular among conservatives—contends that many people underestimate the cost of many public programs and, consequently, demand more from government than they would if they knew the true costs. This will be particularly true where governments rely on revenue sources that are relatively hidden, such as a property tax on rental housing that is passed along to tenants in the form of higher rents. This explanation, sometimes called the "fiscal illusion," assumes that people are much better informed about the benefits of government programs than about the costs, an assumption that may not be dependably accurate (see Downs, 1959–60).

Incremental decision making may also contribute to budgetary expansion. If we begin with the assumption that most programs will receive at least as much money as they received last year and then focus our attention primarily on requests for additional money, funding for most programs will either remain stable or grow. If we do not actively look for places to cut spending, then the total budget will gradually increase.

Yet another explanation traces its roots back to Plato's (1975: 164) observation that "accidents and calamities . . . are the universal legislators of the world." Under normal conditions, people are often opposed to significant tax increases. However, when a major crisis strikes, resistance to tax increases may subside, if only temporarily. Tax revenues expand during the crisis, but after it passes, tax levels do not decline as much as they rose before the crisis. Over time, a series of wars, depressions, and other emergencies will produce larger budgets.

Analysis of government spending relative to the size of the economy for most of the 20th century indicates that crises have played a significant role in expanding public budgets (see Dye, 1992: 244; Mosher and Poland, 1964: 26–36). Some

Table 2.2 War and Federal Spending

TOTAL FEDERAL SPENDING

1860	$63 million
1865	$1,300 million
Increase, 1860–1865: 1,963%	
1916	$734 million
1919	$18,500 million
Increase, 1916–1919: 2,420%	
1940	$9 billion
1945	$98 billion
Increase, 1940–1945: 988%	

SOURCE: *Historical Statistics of the U.S.* (1960: 711)

Table 2.3 General Government Current Receipts (All Levels of Government) as a Percentage of Gross Domestic Product, 1996

Sweden	62
Denmark	60
France	50
Austria	48
Netherlands	47
Germany	46
Canada	43
United Kingdom	37
Australia	35
Japan	32
United States	32

SOURCE: Moody (1998: 348). May exclude some special revenues dedicated to specific programs.

of the most dramatic budgetary effects are produced by wars (see Table 2.2). Spending by the national government rose 10-fold between 1940 and 1945, more than twice that much between 1916 and 1919, and very dramatically from 1860 to 1865. The original costs of America's major wars from the Civil War to Vietnam has ranged from 14 to 188 percent of the total value of all goods and services in the American economy for an entire year at the time of the war. In addition, wars produce later costs, such as spending for veterans' benefits and interest payments on debt incurred to pay for the war (*World Almanac,* 1996: 131, 181).

Although government spending and revenues have grown dramatically over the years, public spending relative to the size of the economy in the United States is actually lower than it is in many other countries (see Table 2.3). America's governments raise and spend enormous sums of money in absolute terms, but relative to the size of the country, the financial scope of our governments is smaller than we find in many other countries. In part this difference reflects the more limited government role in the United States regarding health care.

WHERE THE MONEY COMES FROM AND WHERE IT GOES

Governments raise money in many ways and spend it on a wide variety of programs. A comprehensive review of all the revenue sources and all the individual spending items would exhaust the patience of all but the most fanatically interested in government finances. However, much of the broad contours of government budgets can be presented rather simply.

The National Level

At the national level, total revenues and total spending by the late 1990s were approaching $2 trillion. The single largest federal revenue source in recent years is the individual income tax, with social insurance taxes and contributions (such as for Social Security) coming in a close second. The corporate income tax also provides significant revenue, and during much of the 1980s and early 1990s, borrowing was also a major revenue source, although the rate of new borrowing declined during the mid-1990s. The remainder of federal revenue comes from a variety of relatively minor sources, including excise taxes (such as federal motor fuel taxes), inheritance taxes, and fees (see Table 2.4).

The single largest component of federal spending is the rather broad category of human resources. This includes Social Security benefits, health care, public assistance for the poor, and education. The share of the federal budget devoted to human resource programs has risen dramatically since World War II as the federal government has assumed more responsibility for helping to pay for health care and as the size of the elderly population has increased. The growing federal role in human resource programs has increased the number of people and groups with an interest in federal budgetary decisions and, consequently, increased the amount and variety of political pressures on budgetary decision makers.

Another substantial component of federal spending is defense, although its share of the budget has declined considerably since the 1950s. Since World War II, the national government has been on a relatively permanent war footing, which required higher levels of peacetime defense spending than was normally found before World War II. In addition, the technical sophistication of modern weapons and the skill requirements of modern warfare make military preparedness a costly enterprise.

One other major federal expense is interest payments. As we will see shortly, the national government has borrowed a considerable sum of money,

Table 2.4 Major Federal Revenue Sources and Expenditures, 1998

Revenue sources[a]

Individual income taxes	48%
Corporate income taxes	11%
Social insurance taxes and contributions	33%
Excise taxes	3%
Other	5%

Major expenditures

Human resources	62%
Defense	16%
Physical resources	5%
Net interest	15%

[a]Excludes borrowing.

SOURCES: *Statistical Abstract* (1999: 348); *The Economic and Budget Outlook: Fiscal Years 2000–2009* (1999: 130).

mostly since 1980, and the interest payments on that borrowed money have exceeded the cost of all but a few of the largest federal programs.

Not all federal "spending" involves money that is given to an agency to spend. An important though sometimes confusing aspect of federal budgeting involves *tax expenditures*. Tax expenditures are "revenue losses attributable to provisions of the Federal tax laws which allow a special exclusion, exemption, or deduction from gross income or which provide a special credit, a preferential rate of tax, or a deferral of liability" (*American Almanac,* 1996: 336). A tax expenditure has the same economic effect as raising revenue through taxes and then spending it to support some activity or facility. Politically, however, tax expenditures do not have to go through the budget process every year and are sometimes treated differently from spending programs because, as some observers repeatedly say, a tax expenditure simply lets people keep their own money. Bear in mind that a tax expenditure, in effect, means less money in the federal treasury, just the same as spending money means less money in the federal treasury.

Tax expenditures take a number of forms (see Table 2.5). Two of the largest involve employer contributions for medical insurance and care and provisions regarding pension contributions and earnings. Two tax expenditures that are dear to the hearts of many home owners are the deductions for mortgage interest payments and property taxes on owner-occupied homes. Some federal tax expenditures have important effects on state and local financing: Deductions for property taxes on owner-occupied homes and for nonbusiness state and local taxes and the exclusion of interest on state and local public debt (such as state government bonds) from taxable income all make state and local revenue raising a little less painful. If the property taxes on my home increase, some of sting is relieved because I will receive a larger

Table 2.5 Major Federal Tax Expenditures, 2000

Exclusion of employer contributions for medical insurance and medical care	$78 billion
Net exclusion of pension contributions and earnings (employer plans)	$84 billion
Deduction of mortgage interest on owner-occupied homes	$55 billion
Deduction of property taxes on owner-occupied homes	$19 billion
Treatment of capital gains at death	$27 billion
Deductions for nonbusiness state and local taxes other than on owner-occupied homes	$37 billion
Accelerated depreciation (machinery and equipment)	$35 billion
Charitable contributions (other than education and health)	$20 billion
Exclusion of interest on public state and local debt	$20 billion

SOURCE: *Statistical Abstract* (1999: 352).

deduction on my federal income taxes. In a similar fashion, deductions for charitable contributions make fund-raising for charities somewhat easier; a $1,000 contribution to a qualified charity can produce a federal tax saving of $200 or $300 for the donor, depending on the donor's income tax bracket.

The State Level

Generalizing about state and local revenues is a somewhat risky enterprise, for revenue and spending patterns vary a great deal from one jurisdiction to another, especially at the local level. With that caution in mind, a substantial share of state government revenue comes in the form of aid from other governments, mostly the federal government (see Table 2.6). Another major state revenue source is sales and gross receipts taxes. This group includes relatively general sales taxes, which cover all or almost all sales of products (some states exempt groceries and/or other products, such as some medicines), and selective sales taxes on particular products, such as motor fuels. The typical state also raises significant revenue from income taxes, with most of the revenue being raised by individual income taxes. Another important revenue source is taxes and fees that finance various insurance trusts to support unemployment compensation programs, state employee pensions, and other programs.

A proportionally minor state revenue source that has attracted considerable attention in recent years is state lotteries, which are now found in 36 states. Lotteries have become fairly popular, partly because they raise money voluntarily, in contrast to the relatively mandatory nature of taxes. However, a major shortcoming of lotteries is their very high overhead costs: For every dollar taken in by the typical state lottery, more than 60 cents is spent on prizes and administration, leaving less than 40 cents for the state treasury (*American Almanac*, 1996: 312).

The American states spend a large share of their budgets on social welfare programs, including health care for the poor, public assistance, and other related

Table 2.6 State and Local Revenue Sources and Expenditures, 1995–96

State revenues	
Intergovernmental funds	22%
Sales and gross receipts taxes	21%
Insurance trust revenues	20%
Income taxes	17%
Other sources	20%
State expenditures	
Intergovernmental expenditures	29%
Direct expenditures	
Welfare (including health care for the poor)	19%
Education	12%
Insurance trust spending	11%
Health and hospitals	6%
Highways	6%
General debt interest	3%
Other	14%
Local revenues	
Intergovernmental funds	34%
Property taxes	25%
Charges, fees, and miscellaneous	21%
Sales and gross receipts taxes	5%
Other	15%
Local expenditures	
Education	37%
Health and hospitals	7%
Police, fire, and corrections	9%
General debt interest	5%
Welfare	4%
Highways	4%
Other	38%

SOURCE: Bureau of the Census Web site.

programs. Education is another major expense, for everything from kindergartens to major universities and specialized vocational schools. Bear in mind that a great deal of state spending for education is in grants to local schools rather than direct expenditures. State grants also support many other local programs, from roads to welfare. Insurance trusts for programs such as state employee pensions and unemployment compensation are another major component of state spending, as are health and hospitals and highways.

The Local Level

Local revenue systems vary greatly from one local government to another, but overall the single largest source of local revenue is aid from other levels of government, particularly state governments. Property taxes are another important local revenue source, as are charges and fees for a wide range of things: water and sewer service, trash collection, building permits, library cards for nonresidents, parking—the list is practically endless. Charges and fees seem to have come into favor in recent years, in part because they are more acceptable politically than are property taxes in many localities. A modest amount of local revenue is provided by sales and gross receipts taxes; their contribution to the overall totals is limited because many localities are not permitted to use them and because local sales tax rates are generally quite low.

By far the single largest share of local spending is for education, which accounts for more than one-third of all local expenditures. Bear in mind, however, that the share of local spending devoted to education varies greatly from one local government to another. Some local governments have no responsibility for education and spend little or nothing on it; by contrast, school districts typically have no responsibilities except education and devote their entire budgets to education programs.

Spending for health and hospitals is another major expense for local governments. Many local governments own hospitals or other health care facilities, and many public health programs are administered locally. Two programs that are traditional local government responsibilities, public safety (police, fire, and corrections) and roads and highways, continue to loom large in local government spending. Welfare is another major item in local budgets, as is interest on debt, which in recent years has cost approximately the same amount as welfare or police services.

Intergovernmental Grants

The heavy reliance of states and especially local governments on financial assistance from other levels of government is largely a 20th-century development in the United States (see Table 2.7). In 1902, states and localities raised almost all their revenues on their own. By the mid-1990s, state governments were receiving more than one-fifth of their revenues from intergovernmental grants, almost all of them from the national government. Grants provided about one-third of all local revenues by the mid-1990s, with the bulk of that grant money provided by the states.

The extensive use of intergovernmental grants has many important implications for public budgeting. A government that gives large sums of money to other governments is likely to be the target of considerable lobbying activity by recipient governments, whose officials are likely to want the grant money to continue flowing. At least some of that lobbying appears to be fairly influential. According to a recent study, 7 of the 25 most effective lobbying groups in American state legislatures and 3 of the top 11 groups involved people in local government (Thomas and Hrebenar, 1999: 134–135).

Percentage increase in debt, 1980–96

Total	XXXXXXXXXXXXXXXXXXXX	(472%)
Federal	XXXXXXXXXXXXXXXXXXXXXXXX	(412%)
State	XXXXXXXXXXXXX	(270%)
Local	XXXXXXXXXXX	(235%)

FIGURE 2.2 The growth of government debt.

SOURCES: *American Almanac* (1996: 297); *Statistical Abstract* (1999: 311); *World Almanac* (1999: 110)

Table 2.8 The Growth of Government Debt

	1980	1996
Total	$1,250 billion	$6,394 billion
Federal	$914 billion	$5,225 billion
State	$122 billion	$452 billion
Local	$214 billion	$717 billion

SOURCES: *American Almanac* (1996: 297); *Statistical Abstract* (1999: 311); *World Almanac* (1999: 110)

The most dramatic growth in debt occurred at the national level. Although many explanations for the growing federal debt have been offered, evidence indicates that much of the increase was caused by unexpectedly slow revenue growth during the 1980s and rising interest costs (see Lowery, 1985; Schick, 1990: 6–9, 74–77). The resulting budget deficits produced an outpouring of recommendations to bring the federal budget back into balance.[3]

The substantial growth in state and local government debt between 1980 and 1993 should provide a cautionary note to people who believe that the federal government is the only level of government that borrows money. From 1960 through 1972 and again from 1988 through 1993, all local governments combined in the United States spent more money than their revenues could cover (Moody, 1998: 304). One important difference between national government debt and most state and local government debt deserves mention: The public debt instruments of the federal government, instruments such as Treasury bills and U.S. savings bonds, are backed by the full faith and credit of the U.S. government. When those instruments come due, the national government is legally obligated to redeem them at full value. By contrast, nearly two-thirds of all local government long-term debt and nearly three-fourths of all state long-term debt is nonguaranteed (Moody, 1998: 189, 340).

Nonguaranteed debt is not backed by the full faith and credit of the government issuing it. Instead, the nonguaranteed debt is typically to be paid off by the proceeds from a particular project, such as a toll bridge or some other revenue-producing project, or by the revenues from a single tax type, such as motor fuel taxes. If revenues from the project or revenue source fall below expectations, some of the bonds may not be redeemed at full value. Although

Table 2.7 The Growth of Intergovernmental Aid, 1902–96

AID RECEIVED IN DOLLARS

	1902	1996
State	$9 million	$221 billion
Local	$56 million	$270 billion

AID RECEIVED AS A PERCENTAGE OF TOTAL REVENUE

	1902	1996
State	5%	23%
Local	6%	34%

SOURCES: *Statistical Abstract* (1999: 311); *Historical Statistics of the U.S.* (1960: 727, 729).

A government that receives a large share of its revenues in grants from other governments may find that its spending decisions are influenced by the availability of money for some programs but not for others. In addition, if the level of government providing grant money is unable to complete work on its budget in a timely fashion (a common problem for the national government since the early 1970s) or must revise its budget during the year because of a revenue shortfall or an unexpected crisis, recipient governments may have difficulty in deciding how much they can afford to spend on various programs or in implementing their own budgets after they have been adopted.

The large sums spent and received in intergovernmental grants also mean that, unless we are careful, we may mistakenly overestimate the total scope of public revenues and spending. In 1996, total national, state, and local government revenues from all sources amounted to $3,344 billion, or so it appeared. However, this figure counts revenues raised by the federal government and then given to state or local governments twice (once at the national level and once at the recipient level) and counts revenues raised by state governments and then given to local governments twice as well. If we eliminate these duplicative transactions by focusing only on revenues that each level of government raises for itself, total revenues taken from the private sector amounted to $2,853 billion (*Statistical Abstract,* 1999: 312). If we mistakenly counted revenues twice, we would overstate the true size of government by about 17 percent. Intergovernmental grants also raise a number of other important issues, which we will explore in Chapter 10.

THE GROWTH OF GOVERNMENT DEBT

One other important trend in public budgeting is the growth of government debt (see Table 2.8 and Figure 2.2). From 1980 through 1996, the debt of all U. S. governments more than quintupled, from $1.25 trillion to $6.39 trillion.

that does not happen often, defaults do occur: In 1982, the Washington Public Power Supply System defaulted on more than $2 billion worth of bonds. Nonguaranteed debt has grown much more rapidly than full faith and credit debt at the state and local level since the late 1940s, in part because nonguaranteed debt is often exempt from limits on state and local government borrowing (Aronson and Hilley, 1986: 176–179).

The rise of government borrowing has led to many expressions of alarm, particularly at the national level, and many efforts to limit or stop government borrowing. We will discuss some of those efforts later in this book. The rise of borrowing has also led to substantial interest costs being paid by governments at all levels. If a group of officials decides to borrow large sums of money at one point, officials in later years may find that their budgetary options are narrowed by the interest costs that they inherit.

THE CONSEQUENCES OF MORE SPENDING

Government revenues and spending at all levels of government in the United States have risen dramatically over the years, with the fastest proportional growth occurring at the state level and the slowest growth at the local level. Some of that growth is due to inflation and population increases, but crises and the expanding responsibilities of government in the modern era have also pushed up revenues and spending. Even so, governments in the United States consume a smaller share of the economy than do governments in many other industrialized countries.

The increased volume of government spending, with its proliferation of government programs, has made budgeting much more complex, both because understanding the many programs is difficult and because many more individuals and groups are directly affected by and, therefore, interested in budgetary decisions. The task of budgeters is further complicated by the large number of governments in the United States. By 1997, the United States had 87,504 governments, including 3,043 counties, 19,372 municipalities, 13,726 school districts, and 34,683 special districts (*Statistical Abstract,* 1999: 309). Many of these governments have financial relationships with one another, relationships that include grants-in-aid from one level of government to another and service contracts, which one government may use to purchase services, such as law enforcement or trash collection, from another government.

The growth of government revenues and spending also increases the likelihood that budgetary decisions made by governments may affect the economy. Particularly since the Great Depression, federal officials have tried to use the budget to help improve the performance of the economy. State and local governments have also experimented with using revenue and spending decisions to help improve their economies. We will examine those efforts in Chapter 9.

Although government revenues come from many sources and are spent on many programs, a number of features are very prominent. At the national level, personal income taxes and Social Security taxes are the most important revenue sources. Federal spending supports many programs, but a few loom particularly large: Social Security, health care, defense, and interest payments generated by government borrowing.

At the state level, most revenues come from intergovernmental grants, sales and gross receipts taxes, income taxes, and contributions to various insurance trusts. The most expensive items in state spending are welfare (including health care for the poor), education, health and hospitals, highways, and insurance trust programs. The lion's share of local revenues comes from intergovernmental grants, property taxes, and various charges and fees. By far the largest local expenditure is for education, with health and hospitals, law enforcement, welfare, highways, and interest costs also looming large.

The heavy reliance of state and especially local governments on financial assistance from other levels of government is largely a 20th-century development. One consequence of that development is that the budgetary decisions of each level of government are intertwined with the budgetary dynamics occurring at other levels: Governments that distribute grants are lobbied by governments whose officials hope to receive funds. The budgetary decisions of recipient governments may be influenced by the availability of grant funds and by rules and regulations that come with the grants.

Government borrowing has also risen dramatically over the years. Traditionally much of that borrowing has occurred during wars or recessions: The federal government's public debt rose from just over $1 billion in 1910 to over $24 billion in 1920. Between 1940 and 1945, federal debt rose from $43 billion to more than $258 billion (*World Almanac*, 1996: 131). However, federal borrowing ballooned during the 1980s and early 1990s, even in years when the economy was performing relatively well. A significant portion of national budgetary politics during that period revolved around efforts to reduce or eliminate federal budget deficits without making too many people too angry—a difficult proposition at best.

CONCLUDING THOUGHTS

Government spending and revenues in the United States have risen dramatically for national, state, and local governments. The most dramatic increase since 1900 has occurred at the state level, while local government has displayed the slowest growth. Wagner's Law holds that the development of a modern society and modern economy creates a greater need for governmental action of many kinds and, consequently, leads to higher revenues and spending. Other analysts contend that because government spending has greater visibility than government revenues, a bias in favor of governmental growth is created. Incrementalism and periodic crises may also encourage governmental growth.

The composition of governmental revenues and spending have also changed over the years in many ways. Among the most noteworthy changes are the growing share of the federal budget devoted to social programs since World War II, the growing diversity of state revenue systems since 1900, and the growing importance of intergovernmental grants. Governmental debt has also increased dramatically.

The growth of governmental spending and revenues has helped fuel greater conflict in public budgeting and has made budgeting a much more compex task. In addition, the growth of government revenues and spending has helped increase concern over the economic effects of budgetary decisions.

NOTES

1. Useful glossaries of budgetary terminology are found in Collender (1999: 195–210); *A Glossary of Terms Used in the Federal Budget Process* (1993); Schick (1995: 205–216).

2. See Berry and Lowery (1987), Buchanan and Flowers (1987: chap. 8); Dye (1992: 243–246); Lowery and Berry (1983); Mosher and Poland (1964: 20–36); Musgrave and Musgrave (1980: 142–159); and the studies they cite.

3. See *The Budget Deficit: Outlook, Implications, and Choices* (1990); *Budget Deficit: Appendixes on Outlook, Implications, and Choices* (1990); *Deficit Reduction* (1994); Heilbroner and Bernstein (1989); White and Wildavsky (1991); and the studies they cite.

3

The Budget Cycle:
A Brief Introduction

Preparing a Budget Proposal

Enacting the Budget

Budget Execution

Review and Audit

Linkages across Budget Cycles

Concluding Thoughts

You've got to be very careful if you don't know where
you're going, because you might not get there.

YOGI BERRA

Public budgeting includes a number of different phases that involve a variety of participants. This chapter will provide a brief overview of the different phases and the important participants in each phase. We will also explore
some of the many connections among the steps of the process and the implications of those connections. Chapters 4 through 8 will examine the individual phases in the process in more detail.

The important steps in the budget process resemble several of the components
of public policy making generally. First, someone or some group must formulate a budget proposal or possibly more than one; this phase corresponds to the
formulation of policy proposals or policy options for any type of issue. Second,
a budget must be formally adopted; this stage corresponds to the adoption of
any public policy. Third, a budget must be implemented, just as any policy must
be executed or carried out. Finally, analysts and decision makers need to determine whether budgetary guidelines and policies were faithfully followed and
whether those policies produced satisfactory results; this phase corresponds to
the evaluation phase of policy making in general.[1]

Bear in mind that in the American political system, responsibilities are often
not allocated with great precision or clarity. For any given task or decision, any
number of participants may at least occasionally become involved. Although
some participants are typically more involved in some stages of the budget
process than others, practically anyone may barge into any stage of the process
from time to time. In addition, a participant who is officially involved in a particular phase may devote a great deal of time and attention to the process or
may leave the bulk of the work to other participants.

PREPARING A BUDGET PROPOSAL

The first phase of the budget process is the development of a budget proposal.
In the modern era, the executive branch has normally been responsible, at least
in a formal sense, for this phase of the process, although not all governments use
that approach. Presidents, governors, mayors, city managers, department heads,
and other administrators try to assess the likely amount of revenues to be
expected, the cost of current commitments, and important needs, if any, that are
currently not being met. Given the wide range of government responsibilities,

the complexity of many programs, and the difficulty of predicting the future, preparing a budget proposal is often an enormously difficult job. That difficulty is compounded by the growing expectation, especially since the 1930s, that the budget proposal should include analyses of how much work agencies are doing and how much is being accomplished by each program. As we will see, assessing the linkage between government programs and the condition of the country (or state or locality) is a difficult, complex and often controversial task.

Although the executive branch usually bears the formal responsibility for developing a budget proposal, many other participants are likely to be involved. Interest groups often call for additional funding for their favorite programs, decreased funding for programs they dislike, and reductions in taxes that bear heavily on them. Political parties may propose budgetary changes in party platforms, during election campaigns, or more quietly within the budget process (Budge and Hofferbert, 1990; Nice, 1985). Legislators may recommend budgetary proposals for specific programs but may also be involved in developing an overall budget proposal. In addition, prudent executives are likely to consult with legislators in order to determine whether a particular proposal is likely to receive a friendly reception (Finney, 1994: 145–148, 154–155; Wildavsky and Caiden, 1997: 50–51). Public complaints or demands may create pressures to reshape a budget proposal. A court decision may force modification of a budget proposal in order to comply with a new legal requirement (Cooper, 1999; Straussman, 1986). Taken together, these numerous participants are likely to have many different views regarding the ideal budget proposal. Coping with those conflicting views is a difficult task, especially in larger and more diverse political systems.

The timing of each phase of the budget process varies from one jurisdiction to another and, sometimes, from year to year. At the national level, development of the president's budget proposal typically begins approximately 18 months before the budget is to take effect. In state and local governments, the lead time is typically shorter; the development of proposals usually begins at least 6 to 12 months before the budget takes effect. As a result, a well-prepared proposal requires an accurate prediction of future conditions. If conditions change in unexpected ways—revenues are lower than expected or the workload of a program is higher than expected—the budget proposal may need to be substantially revised. Unexpected changes in the political environment, such as a shift in public opinion or an election that changes party control of the legislature, may have the same effect.

Since the 1930s, decision makers have tried to improve the accuracy of budgetary forecasts in order to reduce the risk of errors that may create later difficulties. At the same time, however, there are periodic complaints that forecasts are being manipulated in order to influence budget outcomes. In a related vein, analysts have developed more sophisticated techniques for assessing the impact of programs. Reformers have repeatedly called for including more of that analysis within the budget process. We will examine some of those analytical techniques in Chapter 5.

ENACTING THE BUDGET

The formal adoption of budgets in the United States is normally the joint responsibility of the legislative branch and the chief executive. Congress must adopt revenue and spending bills, which are subject to presidential veto. At the state level, the legislature adopts revenue and spending bills, which are subject to veto by the governor. A major difference between the national and state levels, however, is that most governors can veto individual items in spending bills, but the president cannot. As we will discuss later, the national government experimented briefly in the 1990s with giving the president a power resembling the item veto of most governors, but that power was declared unconstitutional by the Supreme Court. At the local level, budgets are normally adopted by the legislative branch. Cities with the strong mayor form of government usually give the mayor the power to veto bills, but weak mayors and city managers generally do not have veto powers, nor do most chief executives of special district governments, such as school districts. The courts may become involved in making budgetary decisions, whether by striking down a decision or by requiring some task to be done. Voters may also play a direct role when budgetary decisions are placed on the ballot. Some jurisdictions must have voter approval to exceed a certain tax rate, borrow more than a certain amount of money, or make some other decisions.

Regardless of their formal powers, executives are usually very active in the adoption phase of the budget process. Chief executives try to persuade legislators to approve the budget proposal with relatively few changes, although unexpected developments may lead chief executives to propose modifications of their own proposals. Lower-level executive branch officials also try to influence legislative decisions; those efforts may include trying to get more money than requested by the chief executive. This is a delicate process, for overt disloyalty to the chief executive may be punished. An important exception to this generalization is found in states and many localities, where there are a number of independently elected executives. The state attorney general, who is elected by the voters in most states, may feel little obligation to follow the governor's lead in budgetary matters, for example.

Many informal participants are usually active during the adoption phase of budgeting. Interest groups that are concerned with individual programs will lobby for budgetary policies that conform to the groups' agendas. A political party may try to influence decision makers to put the party's stamp on the budget. Most of the general public will not usually be actively involved in the budget process, but decision makers often try to anticipate the public's reaction to budgetary decisions, especially regarding policies that are likely to be noticed by the public. When the political pressures are numerous and push in many different directions, policy makers may have a difficult time making budgetary decisions. In addition, the sheer size and complexity of many government budgets in the modern era make comprehending the budget a very difficult task.

BUDGET EXECUTION

After the budget has been adopted, it must be implemented. This stage of the budget process is usually invisible to most people and rarely receives much news coverage. Administrative procedures regulate the distribution of money to individual departments and agencies and sometimes allow them to borrow money or sign contracts that will require payment at a later date. Internal departmental procedures and reviews by the central budget office help ensure that funds are being spent according to budgetary guidelines. Major expenditures may also require review and/or approval by a legislative committee.

Because decision makers cannot always predict the future with perfect accuracy and because budgets are generally adopted for a year or, in some states, two years at a time, changing conditions, such as the outbreak of war, may require revisions in the budget while it is being executed. Revenues may be lower than expected or, more happily, higher than expected. Revenue shortfalls may trigger reductions in spending below what was originally approved. Changes in public needs or the costs of vital supplies may produce pressures to give individual programs additional funding or to reduce their funding. In addition, groups whose members are unhappy with the budget as adopted may push for revisions in the budget while it is being implemented. As we will discuss in Chapter 7, there are a variety of methods that can be used to modify the budget in response to changing conditions. Some of those methods are largely controlled by the executive branch, but the legislature will probably be involved in making major changes.

Bear in mind that the funds approved during the adoption phase of a specific budget and the funds spent during the execution phase of that same budget are not necessarily identical. A budget may be approved with funding for a project that will take several years to complete; some of that money will not be spent until after that specific budget is implemented. By the same token, the budget being implemented now will include funds approved during the adoption phase of that particular budget but may also include funds approved one or more years earlier (Schick, 1995: 19–21; Wildavsky and Caiden, 1997: 7–8). For people who are concerned with whether spending is in line with revenues in a particular year, this slippage can be worrisome. Moreover, when funds approved in one budget are spent over several years, the longer time lag may increase the risk of unexpected changes that may force revisions in the original budget decision.

REVIEW AND AUDIT

After a budget has been implemented, the review and audit phase begins. Traditionally this phase of the budget process emphasized determining whether budgetary policies and guidelines had been followed. Was the amount spent for highway construction the amount established in the budget? If the budget required that all construction projects costing more than $1 million receive specific approval from a legislative committee before proceeding, was that approval obtained when needed? If the budget prohibited an agency from spending any money for new equipment, was that prohibition obeyed? Did agencies keep accurate records to enable auditors to determine whether budgetary guidelines were followed?

Since the 1930s, the review and audit phase has expanded in scope to include more emphasis on determining the productivity and effectiveness of government programs. If we spent $12 million to create a new national park, how many people came to see it? Was a job training program successful in helping people improve their job skills and get better jobs? Did money spent on environmental protection produce a cleaner, healthier environment? Did the new highway safety program actually improve highway safety? Was the improvement large enough to justify the cost of the program?

This newer emphasis on productivity and effectiveness has made the review and audit phase a much larger and more complex task and has also made it more controversial. As we will see in Chapter 5, assessing the efficiency and effectiveness of government programs is often difficult, in part because many factors may influence the conditions that government programs are trying to influence. We may use the budget to help stabilize the economy, but many forces shape the performance of the economy. If those other forces are not taken into account, we may reach very misleading conclusions regarding the true impact of programs in the budget.

Analyzing productivity, efficiency, and effectiveness also forces us to examine what we actually want government policies to achieve. For many programs, people disagree regarding what programs should be trying to do. Should welfare programs emphasize protecting the dignity of the poor, or should more effort be devoted to fighting welfare fraud, even if that fight humiliates many welfare recipients? Should the education system emphasize job training or a rich understanding of art and culture? Should transportation policies emphasize personal mobility, even if that produces more dependence on imported oil, or should we emphasize energy independence, even if that requires some changes in individual lifestyles? These and many other questions provoke great controversy, but we cannot meaningfully evaluate the performance of public programs without considering what we expect those programs to do. When our expectations conflict, assessing program performance will generate controversy.

The review and audit phase of budgeting is relatively open-ended, in that people may assess a year's expenditures immediately after a budget has been implemented or several years later. In the 1980s, for example, analysts tried to assess the impact of the antipoverty initiatives of the 1960s and earlier and reached remarkably different conclusions (Murray, 1984; Schwartz, 1988). In some cases, review and audit may begin while the budget is still being executed, particularly if there are signs of mismanagement or fraud.

Many different participants may be involved in the review and audit phase of public budgeting. The most important official participant is usually an official or office that is responsible for reviewing the implementation of the budget. At the national level, the General Accounting Office conducts extensive analyses of agency records and also gathers additional information to determine whether agencies have complied with budgetary guidelines, whether their record keeping is adequate, and whether agency programs are making progress toward their stated goals. State and local government auditors perform the same tasks.

Chief executives, central budget offices, and legislators also assess whether agencies complied with budgetary policies and how much programs have achieved. Interest groups, think tanks, and scholars also analyze program accomplishments, although some of their analyses are heavily colored by the biases of particular groups or think tanks (the same can be said about many public officials). The news media sometimes join in the act, primarily when something of a scandalous or disastrous nature has occurred—a piece of expensive equipment that does not work properly or a project that has fallen far behind schedule. Programs that function effectively are not generally regarded as newsworthy.

LINKAGES ACROSS BUDGET CYCLES

The large number of government programs, the many participants in the process, and the controversy and uncertainty that accompany many budgetary decisions make budgeting a very difficult task in the modern age. That difficulty is compounded by the fact that all the different phases of the budget process are occurring at the same time and because what happens at one phase of one budget cycle may create complications for other phases of other budget cycles (Lee and Johnson, 1998: 53–55).

Within a Government

Budget cycles overlap in that when one budget proposal is being formulated, the budget proposal prepared last year is now in the adoption phase, the budget adopted last year is now being executed, and budgets that were executed in previous years are being reviewed and audited (see Figure 3.1). Chief executives and other participants in the process, therefore, are simultaneously developing a budget proposal, working with the legislature to gain adoption of the proposal that they developed last year, implementing another budget adopted the year before, and reviewing earlier budgets to determine whether they were properly executed.

Information gained from reviews and audits of earlier budgets may affect decisions regarding the development of new budget proposals, the adoption of a new budget, and execution of the budget currently in force. Discovery of mismanagement of funds may lead to stricter controls or budget cuts. If previous expenditures did not accomplish very much, budgets for those programs may be trimmed significantly or may be continued only if the programs are

	Fiscal year 1994 cycle	Fiscal year 1995 cycle	Fiscal year 1996 cycle	Fiscal year 1997 cycle	Fiscal year 1998 cycle
Fiscal year 1994	Implement	Adopt	Formulate		
Fiscal year 1995	Review and audit	Implement	Adopt	Formulate	
Fiscal year 1996		Review and audit	Implement	Adopt	Formulate
Fiscal year 1997			Review and audit	Implement	Adopt

FIGURE 3.1 Overlapping phases and cycles of budgeting.

NOTE: Reading across rows, during Fiscal Year 1995, the budget for Fiscal Year 1994 is being reviewed and audited, the budget for Fiscal Year 1995 is being implemented, the budget for Fiscal Year 1996 is making its way through the adoption process, and the budget proposal for Fiscal Year 1997 is being developed. Bear in mind that the formulation and adoption stages are not necessarily 12 months long and that some states adopt a budget for two years at a time. Also, stages of the budget process are not always completed on schedule, and the review and audit phase can continue for a number of years for a given fiscal year. For a related discussion, see Lee and Johnson (1998: 53–54).

considerably modified. Conversely, if reviews indicate that previous funding levels were inadequate, pressures to increase future funding may arise.

In a similar manner, decisions made during the adoption phase may influence the development of future budget proposals. If the legislature drastically alters proposed funding for a program, the executive may revise next year's request to take into account the likely legislative response. That might mean revising the request to match what the legislature is likely to approve, or the executive might revise the request to offer an initial bargaining position that, after compromise with the legislature, may produce a result consistent with the executive's priorities (Wildavsky, 1974: 45–46).

If the implementation phase of a budget reveals difficulties, such as the discovery that funding for a program is too low or too high or that the program is poorly suited to new conditions, that discovery may lead to changes in the budget being adopted for the following year and the budget proposal being developed for the year after that. Implementation problems may also trigger a more thorough audit and review of that program's funding in earlier years.

Different budget cycles may interact because budgetary decisions made in previous years may shape budgetary proposals and adoption decisions for years to come, not only for the program for which the earlier decisions were made but also for other programs. The national government in the United States has, over the years, passed laws that have given people or organizations a legal right to various benefits if they meet specific requirements; Social Security is a well-known example. Spending for those programs is difficult to control within the budget process, especially if the program has well-organized political support. As a result, rising costs for those mandatory programs (whose expenditures are mandated by law) may take funds away from other programs (whose expenditures are not mandated by law). From 1991 through 1998, inflation-adjusted spending for mandatory federal programs rose by 22 percent, but real spending for discretionary (not mandated) programs fell by 19 percent (see *Congressional Appropriations: An Updated Analysis,* 1999: 7).

In a related vein, different budget cycles may become linked by problems with off-budget programs. As noted in Chapter 1, not all a government's activities are necessarily contained in that government's budget. The decision to create a major off-budget program may come back to haunt decision makers years later if that program generates unexpected costs that leave less money for other programs in the formulation, adoption, and implementation phases of budgetary decision making (see Kirkman, 1989).

Across Different Governments

Different budget cycles also become entangled across different governments. In the United States, state governments receive a significant amount of revenue in the form of federal aid; localities receive much of their revenue from state and, to a lesser degree, federal aid. If the level of government providing the grants-in-aid changes funding for its grant programs or changes the rules accompanying the money, those changes will reverberate through all phases of the recipient governments' budgetary processes. Moreover, the different levels of government may have different budgetary timetables, and budgets are not always adopted on schedule and may be revised after they are adopted. All those dynamics mean that officials at the recipient level may be developing budget proposals, adopting budgets, and implementing budgets on the basis of estimates (some might say guesstimates) regarding how much aid will be available, when, and for what programs. If those estimates are inaccurate, the recipient governments' officials may need to modify their budgets substantially. We will explore the topic of grants from one level of government to another in Chapter 10.

Intergovernmental entanglements may take other forms as well. Officials in the level of government providing financial assistance may learn of implementation problems at the recipient level; those problems may lead to revisions in budgetary decisions at the granting level and reviews and audits of the program. Officials receiving grant money may press the granting level to provide more money in next year's budget or to change the rules and regulations attached to the funding during implementation.

Officials in a state or locality also find that their budgetary decisions are sometimes tied to decisions made by other governments at the same level. One common example of that phenomenon is service contracts, in which a state or locality purchases a service, such as sewage treatment or jail space, from another government. If the government providing the service raises prices to obtain more revenue, the other government must budget more funds for the service or find another provider. If the government purchasing the service decides to shift to another provider, the government formerly providing the service will suffer a loss of revenue.

Externalities or spillover effects, in which people in one state or locality are affected by the decisions of another state or locality, can also produce horizontal linkages. One local government's decision to crack down on illegal drug dealers may cause them to move to surrounding communities. Their law enforcement budgets may require modification as a result. If a city succeeds in luring a major business away from another city, the losing city will have to work with a smaller tax base in the future.

These many linkages across different phases of budgeting and across different governments mean that budgeters working on one phase of one government's budget must constantly try to adapt to developments in other phases of their own budget process and to developments in budgets of other governments. That adaptation works best when those officials have accurate, timely information regarding what other players are doing. Adaptation may sometimes require modification of budgetary decisions or their timing and may mean that a decision made in one phase of one government's budget process may be altered because of adverse reactions to that decision by other governments or by participants in the same government working on other phases of the process (for a related discussion, see Rubin, 1997: 287–291).

The informal participants in the budget process may create additional linkages among different budget cycles and among different governments. A shift in party control of the legislative branch may, within a short time span, lead to revisions in the budget proposal being for prepared for submission to the legislature next January, the budget currently in the process of being adopted, the budget currently being implemented, and evaluations of previous budgets. An interest group whose members are unhappy with budgetary decisions made by one level of government may increase pressures on another level of government to compensate by modifying budgetary decisions made at that level. For example, parents and educators who were unhappy with variations in education funding levels from one school district to another pressured state officials in many states to provide more state aid to help equalize educational opportunities across the state.[2]

At best, the linkages across different budget cycles and across different governments can function fairly effectively. That is particularly likely to occur when officials consult with one another on a regular basis, when differences of opinion regarding budget outcomes are not too great, and when budgetary changes occur gradually. However, when different officials do not communicate with one another very well, when conflicts over budgets are more dramatic, or when budgetary changes are more abrupt, a considerable amount of clashing may occur. Poor communication increases the risk that officials may make decisions on the basis of incorrect assessments of what other officials are likely to do; high levels of budgetary conflict increase the difficulty of reconciling decisions made by different participants in the process. Gradual budgetary changes permit gradual adjustments in other affected arenas, but abrupt changes in one place may trigger painful reactions in other places and will magnify the effect of communication problems. Failing to anticipate a 1 percent reduction in a grant program will produce some problems for recipient governments, but failing to anticipate a 40 percent reduction will produce more painful adjustments.

CONCLUDING THOUGHTS

Public budgeting sometimes resembles a series of construction projects. The architects are not always certain what needs to be built or what the customers want or can afford, and the architects and customers may disagree regarding all those questions. The builders suffer from the same problems and from the architects and customers sometimes changing their minds as construction proceeds. The builders are sometimes asked to do impossible things (e.g., eliminate a huge budget deficit painlessly), and the builders do not always agree with the ideas of the architects and customers. Should the new building be a house, a hospital, or a factory? Some people may not want a new building at all. After construction, the people who live or work in the building may find that it is difficult (or easy) to maintain, too large or too small, or well or poorly suited to the job it must do. The architects, builders, and/or customers may decide to remodel the building one or more times. Disputes may erupt at any time regarding the intent embodied in the original plans, whether builders followed the plans adequately, or regarding who promised to do what, when, and at what price.

The reality of budgeting is much more complex than this. Imagine tens of thousands of construction projects going on at the same time. Some of the customers, builders, and architects are helping to pay some of the costs of other construction projects besides their own. Many of the projects affect one another; construction of a major highway may eliminate an entire neighborhood. Construction of a new subdivision or factory may generate much more traffic. Some of the projects provoke great controversy, from members of a family quarreling over the design of their new home to entire communities battling over which of them will be the site of a new shopping mall or toxic waste dump. Other projects proceed smoothly and quietly, with little conflict.

Formulating a budget proposal is somewhat like trying to design a great many construction projects at the same time and trying to accommodate the needs and wants of thousands or millions of clients. Adopting a budget is similar to building a great many projects while struggling with the numerous problems of conflicts regarding those projects, the difficulty of understanding how the various projects will fit together and how each project can best be completed, and the uncertainty regarding what future needs will be and what customers can afford. Implementing a budget is somewhat like living in and using what has been built. Depending on a number of circumstances, that may be a pleasant experience or an ordeal. The review and audit phase finds parallels in people's assessments of whether they are satisfied with their homes, places of work, roads, and so forth. Indeed, a specialized area of budgeting involves exactly these kinds of decisions regarding physical facilities. The next several chapters will explore each of these facets of budgeting in detail.

NOTES

1. For overviews of the stages of policy making, see Anderson (1994); Dye (1992: chaps. 13, 14); Peters (1996: chaps. 3–5, 7). For overviews of the stages of budget processes and interactions among stages and across budget cycles, see Lee and Johnson (1998: chap. 3); Rubin (1997: 287–292).

2. See *School Finance: State Efforts to Reduce Funding Gaps between Poor and Wealthy Districts* (1997).

4

Budget Preparation

"Any jackass can draw up a balanced budget on paper."

LANE KIRKLAND

(QUOTED IN BAKER, 1990:221)

In the modern era, with governments involved in a wide range of programs and responsibilities, formulating a budget proposal is a difficult and complex task. Given the wide range of theoretically possible levels and combinations of revenues and expenditures for a large number of programs, the budget proposal (to the extent that it is taken seriously) greatly narrows the range of possible courses of action and often frames the debate over the budget. A badly prepared budget proposal increases the risk of poor decisions in the adoption phase of budgeting and increases the difficulty of making sensible decisions at the adoption phase. In any case, developing the proposal is very likely to produce considerable conflict.

In this chapter, we will examine various aspects of the process for preparing budgetary proposals. The formulation process can be conducted in a number of different ways. What format should the proposal follow, and how much information should it contain? Who should participate in the formulation process, and how freely should information circulate? What considerations guide or should guide the decisions and actions of the participants in the preparation process? The answers to all these questions have varied considerably over the years.

When developing a budget proposal, officials do not begin with a blank slate. A number of factors often limit the flexibility of decision makers when they formulate a new proposed budget.[1] Many expenditures are mandated by law, and some revenues may be earmarked for specific program. Although the laws may be changed to alter the legal requirements, that is often difficult when beneficiaries of the programs are politically active and organized. Even without legal requirements, funding for programs protected by strong interest groups is usually difficult to cut very much. Union contracts with workers may generate mandatory costs. The public typically expects major public programs to continue, and the weight of previous commitments and the cost of continuing them will usually consume most of the available revenue. Raising large amounts of additional revenue to launch major new initiatives is often politically risky and, in poorer jurisdictions, nearly impossible. Moreover, when the proposal being developed must be approved by other officials, their preferences must be considered. Failing to do that increases the risk that the proposal will not be adopted or will be dramatically changed during the adoption phase. Taken together, these combined elements often leave officials with limited discretion.

THE FORMAT OF THE BUDGET PROPOSAL

Budgeters have tried a number of different formats for budget proposals. Each approach has advantages and disadvantages, a circumstance that has periodically led to changes in the formats used in many jurisdictions as reformers have tried to improve the budget's performance in one sense or another. Bear in mind, however, that the different formats are not necessarily mutually exclusive; decision makers may use more than one in hopes of gaining the benefits of different approaches. The choice of approach may reflect several considerations, including the amount of effort that budgeters are willing to put into the process, the amount of conflict they are willing to endure, and which aspects of the budgetary decisions they want to emphasize.[2]

Lump Sum Budgeting

A relatively simple budgetary format is the *lump sum budget,* which has only a few broad categories, each of which is covered by a large chunk of money. For example, a nation using a very basic lump sum format might have one budgetary item for defense, another for social programs, and another for physical improvements, such as public buildings and highways. A slightly more detailed version might have one pool of money for each department or agency but would not include much specific information regarding the use of the money within the department or agency. The entire budget might be only a few pages long, possibly shorter.

Lump sum budgeting has a number of attractive features. First, it is a comparatively easy format to prepare, revise, and understand. Second, it focuses attention on relatively broad questions rather than blurring them with a mass of detail and minor issues. Third, by keeping the format simple, the lump sum format helps minimize conflict. If we can agree on the total amount of spending for defense, we have completed that part of the budget. We do not need to argue over specific defense programs or projects. The lump sum format is also appealing to administrators because it gives them some flexibility in implementing the budget as conditions change.

To critics of the lump sum budget, it has deficiencies that more than outweigh its strengths. If budgeters are interested in what would happen to programs or services if the budget is changed, the lump sum format provides little guidance. In a related vein, it provides no information regarding the effects of current spending. Are current programs worth the cost? The lump sum format does not address that type of issue. The lack of "details," some of which might be very large, can mean a disturbingly large amount of discretion in the hands of the bureaucracy. Finally, because the budget contains relatively little information, it is of very limited value as an instrument for coordinating different programs or setting social priorities, except in a very broad way—as in the case of defense versus domestic programs.

Defenders of the lump sum format tend to agree with these criticisms somewhat but point out that assessing the impact of funding changes and the effects of programs, controlling the bureaucracy, and coordination and priority setting can be done outside of the budget process through legislation, investigations, administrative controls, and a host of other devices. Not all important decisions need to be made in the budget process. Viewed in this light, the lump sum format implies that the budget will play a limited role in the broader process of governing, a price that might be worth paying if we want the budget to be easy to develop and understand and not too conflict ridden.

Object-of-Expenditure Budgeting

A second important budgetary format is the *object-of-expenditure budget,* sometimes called the line item budget. In this format, the budget is broken down by department and agency and, within each agency, by what objects the agency spends the money to acquire. For example, an agency's total funding could be divided among categories for personnel costs (salary and benefits), equipment, maintenance, travel, and nonequipment supplies. For a large agency, there could be many individual items, with the various categories subdivided to show even more detail—different types of equipment could have separate items, and personnel costs could be subdivided among different categories of workers and different elements of personnel costs, such as salaries, pensions, health insurance, and so forth (see *Budget Object Classification,* 1994). The object-of-expenditure budget tends to focus attention on where the money goes and so seeks to prevent or minimize frivolous or wasteful spending by agencies. In preparing a highly detailed budget of this type, we might hear questions raised regarding why so much money is being spent on travel to out-of-state meetings, whether an agency needs new equipment, or whether a new building should have carpeting rather than floor tile.

Advocates of the object-of-expenditure format contend that it has a number of significant advantages. If used carefully, it can help reduce unnecessary spending, at least in the sense of unnecessary purchases. This format gives budgeters more information regarding where the money is going, compared to the lump sum format, and gives elected officials more control over the bureaucracy. With lump sum budgeting, an agency might obtain money with the informal understanding that it is for new equipment and then use the money for travel instead (although this would be politically risky with any budget format). That is less likely to occur with the object-of-expenditure budget. Its supporters also contend that the details of a budget can be tremendously important; if officials lack information on the specifics of where the money goes, they may have little meaningful basis for making their decisions.

Critics of the object-of-expenditure format complain that it provides little meaningful information regarding what agencies are actually doing. If we know that a university spent $10 million on personnel costs, that tells us little about whether the money was spent for teaching faculty or administrators or whether the students learned anything. We might need to know more about agencies' activities and accomplishments in order to make intelligent decisions. In a related vein, the object-of-expenditure format tells us little about the programmatic impact of budgetary changes. It can tell us that a cut might mean fewer personnel, but if we know little regarding the activities or accomplishments of agency personnel, we will be unsure regarding the effect on services. An overly detailed object-of-expenditure budget may deprive agencies of flexibility needed to cope with unexpected developments. If a police department is given a set amount to purchase gasoline and gasoline prices later rise dramatically, administrators might prefer to put a freeze on travel and use the travel funds for fuel instead. As we will see in Chapter 7, budgets can be changed after they are adopted, but gaining approval of changes can take time; a lump sum budget can mean quicker adaptation to new conditions. Finally, an object-of-expenditure budget requires a good deal more time and effort to prepare and understand than does a lump sum budget, particularly if the objects are specified in considerable detail. Wading through hundreds of pages of individual line items can be a mind-numbing exercise, and if major, last-minute modifications to the proposal are needed, the effort required can be considerable.

Performance Budgeting

In an effort to improve public budgeting, reformers began to advocate *performance budgeting* early in the 20th century. A performance budget includes an object-of-expenditure budget and supplementary information on the activities and workloads of agency personnel and facilities. The police department's budget could, therefore, include information regarding how many arrests were made by the average officer, the number of convictions that resulted, and the number of calls for assistance that were handled. A state park's budget could include statistics on the number of visitors each month, the length of the average visit, and the use of specific facilities, such as the campground or boat ramp.

By giving officials information on the activities of agency personnel and the use of public facilities, performance budgets provide a clearer guide to the likely effects of budgetary changes than would be the case if they used lump sum or object-of-expenditure formats. In addition, by focusing attention on activities and workloads, performance budgets may encourage efforts to improve productivity in public agencies.

Critics of performance budgeting complain that its preparation requires a great deal more effort than object-of-expenditure or lump sum budgeting. Performance budgets may also generate additional political conflict by raising disputes regarding what agencies and their personnel should be doing. If overly simplistic measures of activity are used or if only some activities are measured, performance budgeting may distort agency operations in unintended ways. For example, if a police department will appear more productive by making more arrests, officers may decide to focus on cases that are more easily solved and devote less attention to more complex or difficult cases. A prosecutor might increase his or her conviction rate by giving more emphasis to cases with defendants who cannot afford skilled legal representation. Finally, performance budgeting usually does not address the question of whether these activities are accomplishing anything. People in an agency may be very active without necessarily making any progress in dealing with poverty, crime, illiteracy, pollution, or other social problems.

Program Budgeting

Although a number of governments adopted some form of performance budgeting during the 1950s, reformers who wanted to improve government performance began pressing for a much more ambitious approach, *program
budgeting* or, as it is sometimes called, the planning-programming-budgeting
system (PPBS). In its most elaborate form, program budgeting has several components. First, it includes information on planned spending for several years
into the future. Reformers hoped that including future years would encourage
officials to consider the full impact of a budgetary decision rather than just the
impact on next year's budget. In addition, covering several years would reduce
the use of the *camel's nose* tactic, which starts an expensive program a little at a
time. If the tactic works, by the time officials realize the full cost of the project, they will feel committed to continue it rather than admit that the earlier
outlays were inappropriate.

Program budgeting called for organizing the budget by programs or activities that were all working toward the same objective, regardless of which agencies or departments were involved in those activities. If we decide that one
program is training people for careers, then all the individual activities of various agencies that teach people job skills should be considered together. In the
process, we may gain a greater appreciation of which approaches work best and
may be better able to coordinate related activities in different agencies and
departments.

Program budgeting also requires systematic analysis of the impact of each
agency's activities on various social goals. Does putting more police on the
street actually influence the crime rate? Does a job training program help people get better jobs? Does the publicly funded sports complex help boost the
local economy? The budget should include rigorous assessments of the accomplishments of each program and each agency's activities. Finally, a program
budget should include a discussion of several alternative strategies for reaching
important social goals, a careful analysis of the costs and benefits of the various
strategies, and a clear explanation of why some strategies are preferable to the
others.

The U.S. Department of Defense tried program budgeting during the
Kennedy administration, and President Johnson extended its use to the entire
national government. A number of state and local government also experimented with program budgeting during the 1960s and early 1970s, as did a
number of other countries.

The reformers hoped that program budgeting would help eliminate government activities that failed to produce significant results and target more resources
to programs that were more effective. Tying assessment of program accomplishments to the budget process would ensure that agency performance would be
evaluated on a regular basis and increase the likelihood that those evaluations
would influence budgetary decisions. Placing more emphasis on goals and priorities would encourage officials and perhaps the public to devote more thought
to what sort of nation (or state or community) we want to create or preserve.

Program budgeting, particularly in its more ambitious forms, began losing popularity in the early 1970s. Rigorous analysis of program impact proved to be more difficult and expensive than some officials expected (we will return to that issue in Chapter 5). Emphasizing goals and priorities and examining alternatives to current programs greatly increased the amount of conflict in the budget process, a development that was possibly exacerbated by the mobilization of new political groups in the 1960s and 1970s. Analysts also realized that some agency activities were expected to pursue a number of different goals at the same time, and allocating shares of those activities to the different goals proved difficult. Officials who were accustomed to more traditional budgetary formats found the new approach clumsy and intimidating, and some officials did not welcome analyses that criticized programs those officials had supported for years. As a result, program budgeting as a complete system was abandoned by many governments that had tried it. However, elements of program budgeting survive in many jurisdictions in the forms of a greater concern for the impact and accomplishments of programs, a greater emphasis on goals, and more attention to the effects of budgetary decisions in future years (see *Performance Budgeting,* 1993).

Zero-Based Budgeting

A somewhat more modest budgetary format is *zero-based budgeting,* which includes some of the same emphases as program budgeting. The more drastic version of zero-based budgeting called for eliminating the assumption that each agency should receive approximately the same amount of money that it received last year. Instead, agencies would begin with an assumption of no money and be required to justify every dollar above that amount. In the less drastic version, agencies would prepare a budget proposal based on the current level of funding (possibly adjusted for inflation) and one or more alternative budgets based on, for example, a 5 percent spending reduction, a 10 percent spending reduction, and perhaps a 5 percent increase. The size of the possible cuts or increases might depend on the condition of the economy and/or the particular agency involved.

In preparing their budget proposals, agencies would break down their activities into relatively self-contained units, called "decision units," that normally could not be further subdivided. One decision unit for a city hospital might be the helicopter ambulance unit. Each decision unit would be analyzed in order to assess its accomplishments, and decision units would be grouped into decision packages, which would include the necessary mix of activities needed to perform vital functions. The proposal would also include analyses of the likely level of performance possible with the different levels of funding. Which decision units or decision packages would be deleted or trimmed with a 5 percent spending reduction? How would performance be affected? What would be added with a 5 percent increase, and how would performance be affected? The decision packages would be ranked from highest priority to lowest in order to indicate the least painful ways to accommodate spending reductions and the most productive ways to utilize increases.

Advocates of zero-based budgeting, which was adopted by the national government during the Carter administration and by a number of states and localities, hoped that it would weaken or even eliminate the inertia produced by incrementalism and encourage spending reductions for less productive activities and possibly higher spending for more productive activities (the name "zero-based budgeting" probably suggests a greater hope for the former than the latter). They also hoped that it would be less burdensome and less conflict prone than program budgeting, in part by reducing the emphasis on considering alternative program strategies.

However, zero-based budgeting still requires a great deal more work than lump sum or object-of-expenditure budgeting. In addition, requiring agencies to propose spending reductions, especially large ones, can generate significant political heat from program clienteles and can damage the morale of agency personnel, some of whom may become anxious about their jobs and their ability to do their work (e.g., if the proposed cut might mean layoffs or the inability to buy needed equipment or supplies). In addition, agency personnel hoping to avoid actual budget cuts may be tempted to propose reductions that would make too many people angry (and so be rejected as possible cuts) rather than proposing reductions in less productive activities.

Some Lessons from Experimenting
with Different Budget Formats

A number of different governments, both in the United States and in other countries, have tried different budget formats during the 20th century. The results of that experience point to several tentative conclusions.[3] First, budget decisions are powerfully constrained by many powerful forces, including political pressures, the weight of past commitments, and the condition of the economy. No budget format can significantly alter or withstand those forces. Second, beyond some point, adding more details, decisions, and analysis to the budget proposal can produce more complexity than officials can comprehend and more conflict than officials can comfortably manage. Many other factors affect the amount of complexity and conflict in the budget process, from the interest group system and the political parties to the responsibilities of the jurisdiction making budget decisions. However, budget formats that require addressing a wider range of issues in a specific way, emphasize values, and require consideration of alternative approaches will tend to bring more of those conflicts into the budget process.

Another probable lesson from experiments with different budgetary formats is that generating additional information and analysis is costly and difficult and may not always be worth the cost unless decision makers are interested in the added information. If there is no noticeable interest in terminating the state highway program, requiring state highway officials to justify the program from the first dollar (as required in the more drastic version of zero-based budgeting) is a largely pointless exercise. If many members of Congress do not care whether poor people have access to health care, as appeared to be the case in 1994, detailed analyses of different methods for expanding access to health care are likely to go unread by those members. Analyses are more likely to be worth doing when there is interest in considering alternatives—although this is admittedly not always easy to assess.

Finally, as noted near the beginning of this section, different budget formats have different strengths, and no single format appears to be ideal from all standpoints. As a result, many jurisdictions use a combination of different formats. Some sections of a budget proposal may be organized by objects of expenditure, but other sections may be organized by program. Some funding may be massed in large chunks, as in lump sum budgeting, while other funds are subdivided more narrowly, as in object-of-expenditure budgeting. Most of an agency's funding may be in narrowly defined line items, but the agency may also be given a pool of emergency funds to provide the flexibility of lump sum budgeting. Officials may analyze the effectiveness of programs and consider alternatives on a selective basis.[4] As budgeting virtually always involves compromises, the choice of formats can involve compromise.

FORMULATING THE PROPOSAL: BOTTOM-UP VERSUS TOP-DOWN PROCESSES

Because a budget proposal is often a strong influence on ultimate budgetary decisions and because the proposal often frames the debate over the budget, two key issues in budget formulation are the questions of who participates in the process and how much influence the various participants have.[5] In bottom-up budget formulation, many participants will be involved in the process, and many of them will have significant influence over at least some aspect of the proposal. The budget proposal will emerge from a great many, fragmented decisions on different parts of the budget, and much of the focus will be on individual programs rather than the entire budget. Individual agencies will usually press for more money for their programs, and agencies that ask for more will often receive more. Legislative committees and subcommittees will exert significant influence over proposal development, either directly or indirectly, and numerous interest groups will try to influence the budget proposal, usually with an emphasis on individual agencies and programs.

Top-down processes, by contrast, are much more centralized. A chief executive, such as the president, governor, mayor, or city manager, determines the broad outlines of the budget proposal and sometimes makes specific decisions for individual agencies and programs. A powerful legislative leader or leadership group may play the same role. Many agencies, interest groups, and legislative committees will find that they have little or no influence over the budget requests for their programs.

Bottom-Up Processes

Bottom-up formulation helps to disperse the workload of preparation, which is a very burdensome task in jurisdictions with a wide of range of responsibilities. No one is forced to understand all the many programs, needs, and issues in great depth. People who have the most thorough understanding of each program—the people in the agency, the responsible legislative committee, and the relevant interest groups—will have substantial influence over the budget proposals for their programs. Bottom-up processes are also politically realistic in political systems where power is relatively dispersed; in those systems, such as the United States, proposals that fail to consider a wide range of viewpoints will often encounter difficulty. Bottom-up formulation also seems more democratic to some observers, for many more people have a voice in the process.

Bottom-up formulation also presents a number of risks. It requires a certain amount of mutual trust and respect among the various participants. If I focus my attention on one agency and its programs, I need to trust the other participants to play fairly in developing their proposals (which I normally will not examine in detail, if at all). If trust erodes, bottom-up formulation becomes more difficult.

In a related vein, bottom-up processes require a significant amount of self-restraint among the various participants. Agencies may push for additional money, but demands must be kept within bounds, possibly by informal principles such as "fair shares" or agencies not trying to take away one another's budget bases. If participants become too greedy or if they fail to anticipate what will appear reasonable at the adoption stage, considerable time and effort may be wasted on requests that have no chance of gaining adoption, and budgetary conflicts will escalate.

Some critics of bottom-up formulation also complain that it is poorly suited to setting priorities or coordinating decisions across different programs and agencies (for dissenting views, see Lindbloom, 1959; Wildavsky, 1974). People in each agency will push for more money, regardless of the availability of revenues or the needs of other programs. Coping with a large budget deficit or slow revenue growth will be difficult with bottom-up formulation.

Finally, some critics of bottom-up formulation or any decentralized budgeting system contend that the appearance of democracy may be misleading. If the formulation process is driven largely by agencies, interest groups, and legislative committees, who often share similar views within individual policy areas, many ordinary citizens, who are not part of any of those organizations, may be largely ignored (see Lowi, 1979; McConnell, 1967).

Top-Down Processes

Advocates of top-down formulation, with its more centralized approach, contend that it is better able to provide coordination across agencies, set priorities, and provide greater emphasis on large-scale budgetary issues, such as the overall size of the budget and the appropriate size of the budget surplus or deficit, if any. A strong, visible leader, such as the governor, can offset the power of interest groups, who may place more emphasis on their own parochial concerns than broader interests. If the formulators at the top are in close touch with the officials who must approve the proposed budget (in fact, the two groups may overlap), the top-down approach may also reduce the amount of effort wasted on proposals that have no realistic chance of passage—although the assumption of the two groups being in close touch does not appear to be consistently true.

Critics of top-down formulation contend that in large government units with many responsibilities and programs, loading too many decisions and responsibilities on the shoulders of a small number of officials may overwhelm them with too much political conflict and too much information for them to comprehend. Early in the Reagan years, when the administration tried to impose top-down budgeting on the formulation process, David Stockman, the president's budget director, impressed many people with his apparent knowledge of budgetary issues. His reputation eroded, however, after a series of interviews in which he made the often-quoted admission, "None of us really understands what's going on with all these numbers," along with other remarks that undercut the credibility of some of the administration's budget analyses (Greider, 1982: 15–16, 33, 65).

If the small group of top formulators does not have thorough knowledge of many of the programs and issues covered by the budget proposal, they may resort to simple decision rules, such as across-the-board increases or cuts for all programs. While that approach is consistent with the principle of fair shares, it risks cutting vital and not-so-vital programs equally. Conversely, the political biases of the top leadership group may be given free rein, or budgetary pain may be inflicted primarily on the politically weak (Greider, 1982: 59). Even high-ranking leaders often want to retain their offices and, consequently, the goodwill of powerful interest groups.

Critics also worry that top-down formulation places a great deal of political influence in the hands of a small number of people, possibly just a single leader. Given that many citizens do not seem very well informed regarding budgetary decisions, how democratic is formulation that is controlled largely by a small group, especially if little of their work receives much attention from the mass media or the public? Those concerns are especially relevant if the top leaders try to increase their influence by restricting the flow of information—for example, by leaving some agency positions vacant so that those agencies will have few people to speak for their concerns (see LeLoup, 1988: 75). We will return to that issue shortly.

Choosing a Process

As with budget formats, the choice of top-down or bottom-up formulation is not necessarily an either/or decision; the relative emphasis on each can vary from one agency to another and over time. Prosperity and growing revenues may make bottom-up formulation more practical; a recession or tight revenues may increase the appeal of a more top-down approach. A top-down process may be feasible for programs with weak interest group support, but few officials may want to lock horns with the most powerful interest groups in the jurisdiction regarding funding for their favorite programs. Note, too, that the formal process may have informal dynamics that pull it in a different direction; a strong governor may direct an apparently centralized formulation process but, by considering the possible reactions of various legislative committees or interest groups, may produce a proposal that reflects many decentralized concerns.

ADMINISTRATIVE AGENCIES
IN THE FORMULATION PROCESS

In most political systems, administrative agencies are important actors in the formulation of budget proposals. The rules governing their formal involvement vary considerably from place to place and over time, but they are often involved in one way or another. Agency personnel must, therefore, decide what to do in order to advance their views in the budget process. A number of considerations may shape their decisions.[6]

One of the most important elements that administrators must consider is the likely response of the officials that must approve the budget. Agencies that appear too greedy or extravagant risk losing their credibility. Agencies that request a low level of funding risk getting a low level of funding, for other participants will not often push additional money on an agency, although it does happen at times. Administrators try, then, to appear realistic, although determining what will appear realistic is not always easy. The agencies will often receive formal guidance from higher executives and formal or informal guidance from legislators. Quiet consultation and years of working together may provide additional guidance. However, when a large number of new officials have recently taken office, administrators may be uncertain regarding the newcomers' preferences, and even veteran officials may sometimes shift their positions in response to public pressure or changing conditions.

Agencies that are more aggressive in seeking new funds are more likely to have their requests cut but are also more likely to win increased funding (Sharkansky, 1968; Thompson, 1987). If agencies do not seek additional funding, other participants are likely to conclude that no added funding is needed.

Not all agencies are equally aggressive in pressing for increased funding. Administrators in an older agency with stable relationships with program clienteles and legislative committees and a stable workload may decide that the safer course is to preserve the existing budget base, with adjustments for inflation. Pushing for large funding increases may mean tackling new responsibilities that may produce controversy or require skills that agency personnel do not currently possess. Working on unfamiliar tasks or dealing with new groups may yield mistakes or strained relationships with established clientele groups. Sometimes caution is a safer course.

Sensible administrators seek to build and maintain a positive reputation with budget decision makers. When there is uncertainty regarding budgetary decisions (a common phenomenon), agency personnel who are regarded as honest, knowledgeable, well prepared, and responsive are likely to fare somewhat better, other things being equal. Administrators who are caught making inaccurate statements in their budget requests or are poorly prepared in their budget presentations can lose credibility rapidly.

Other important agency strategies include mobilizing the support of clientele groups, providing evidence of unmet needs and/or agency successes, bolstering the agency's public image, and providing decision makers with opportunities to impress the public. For example, a member of Congress might be asked to announce the construction of an important new facility that will create many new jobs in his or her district.

A delicate problem for administrators occurs in systems where the chief executive has considerable formal control over the final budget proposal. If the chief executive's proposal recommends little or no money for an agency or at least considerably less than people in the agency want, what can they do? If they are openly disloyal to the chief executive's proposal, they may be punished in a variety of ways. If they are too loyal to the proposal, they will be disappointed in the funding they receive. One option is to call on clientele groups to push for more money. Another option is to leak information to friendly legislators who will make the case for additional funding while people in the agency appear at least nominally loyal to the chief executive's guidelines (Wildavsky, 1974: 88–90).

The widespread involvement of agencies in formulating budget proposals seems to conflict with basic democratic principles when many agency employees are career personnel covered by civil service systems. This conflict is sometimes very real, but administrators who ignore public sentiments do so at their peril. For many agencies, many citizens will not have very clear ideas regarding the agency's current level of funding or what funding would be suitable for next year; there may be limited potential for conflict in those situations. In addition, elected officials must normally approve budget proposals in democratic countries, a requirement that will provide some accountability to the public.

THE PRESIDENT AND BUDGET PROPOSALS

The Changing Presidential Role

The president's role in formulating budget proposals has changed considerably over the course of the 20th century.[7] For most of American history, presidents did not have a regularized role in developing revenue and spending proposals.

Presidents sometimes pressed for additional money for some programs, called for spending restraint, or proposed changes in revenue policies, but presidential involvement was sporadic and often selective, focusing on a limited number of issues. Agencies submitted their budget requests to the Treasury Department, which compiled and relayed them to Congress. Agency personnel operated on the premise that they had the right to ask Congress for whatever level of funding they believed was appropriate. The risk of a presidential veto encouraged agency officials to pay some attention to presidential sentiments, however, in preparing their budget proposals.

Beginning in the 1890s, the original system came under increasing strain. Between 1894 and 1914, the national government ran budget deficits roughly half the time, and the costs of World War I added to financial worries. The federal income tax was declared unconstitutional in 1895, a decision that triggered a prolonged effort to amend the Constitution. The national government adopted several programs to provide financial assistance to the states. The amounts of the grants were initially small, but they created new financial commitments that were difficult to withdraw. The size of the federal budget and its long-term growth (with large fluctuations largely due to wars) led to increasing concern that the fragmented, decentralized process of formulating budget proposals was no longer suitable.

Reformers at all levels of government called for stronger executive leadership in policy making generally and often with particular emphasis on budgeting. The reformers believed that a strong executive could overcome the parochialism created by agencies, interest groups, and legislative committees as well as the local interests with considerable influence in America's legislatures. A strong executive would provide a broader perspective and could coordinate budgetary proposals across different agencies, stand up to aggressive interest groups and party bosses, and, as a result, curb wasteful spending. A visible executive official, such as the president, must answer to the general public and would provide greater public accountability for the budget process.

Many members of Congress were skeptical of these arguments. They recognized that the power of the purse has traditionally been a foundation of legislative influence, and some pointed to the constitutional provisions involving financial matters. Most of those provisions are in the constitutional article dealing with Congress. Stronger presidential influence might come at the expense of Congress.

The Bureau of the Budget

The pressures to reform the process continued to build, however, and in 1921, Congress passed the *Budget and Accounting Act*. The act required the president to submit a budget proposal to Congress each year. The proposal would include recommendations for both revenue and spending decisions. Because this would be a large job and because presidents might not be experts at (or terribly interested in) budgeting, the act also created the *Bureau of the Budget*[8] to assist the president in developing the budget proposal and in implementing the budget after it was adopted. The Bureau of the Budget was initially housed in the Treasury Department.

Under the new process, agencies would submit their budget proposals to the Bureau of the Budget, along with supporting information to justify their requests. The Bureau would provide agencies with guidance regarding what might be a reasonable proposal and the appropriate format for the request.

To reduce the very real danger that agencies might try to ignore the president's budget policies and seek whatever level of funding agency officials wanted, the Bureau of the Budget began a review process known as *central clearance.* This process required that any agency proposals for legislation and any agency expressions of viewpoints regarding legislation must, if the proposals or expressions involved money, be submitted to the Bureau of the Budget for review. Only proposals consistent with the president's budgetary policies could be submitted to Congress. Expressions of agency viewpoints could be submitted to Congress even if they were not consistent with the president's programs, but views that were not consistent would be accompanied by comments from the Bureau of the Budget. Submitting testimony that conflicted with the president's policies also risked angering the White House, a risk that must be weighed carefully. Central clearance was not always enforced consistently, but it reflected an effort to make the formulation process somewhat more top-down.

Some members of Congress and some agency personnel were not very comfortable with a system that might, in effect, allow the president to conceal information from Congress, although central clearance can also help shield Congress from excessive financial pressures, at least to a limited degree. Bear in mind, however, that central clearance has not proven to be very effective in blocking informal communications between federal agencies and Congress. A discrete telephone call, a letter sent from one person's home to another, a "chance" meeting at a party, restaurant, or other location—these and many other methods can be used to bypass the central clearance process when the inclination is present. Especially when the president and most members of Congress have differing budgetary preferences, some agencies may benefit considerably by back-channel communications with Congress.

In 1939, the Bureau of the Budget was transferred from the Treasury Department to the newly formed Executive Office of the President. That move was, in part, to underscore that the bureau was the president's agent in the budget process. The bureau's responsibilities also expanded somewhat to include formulating proposals for administrative improvements and monitoring agency performance.

The Office of Management and Budget (OMB)

Further changes followed when the Bureau of the Budget was reorganized and renamed in 1970. The new Office of Management and Budget (OMB) retained all its former duties but gained additional responsibilities in improving the management of the federal government. In the ensuing years, OMB came to play a larger role in selling the president's budget proposals to Congress. In addition, political appointees gradually came to have more influence within OMB, a development that led to complaints of declining expertise and credibility.

Critics also complained that OMB continued to focus primarily on relatively short term budgetary issues at the expense of longer-term management concerns. A series of reforms and reorganizations, culminating in the OMB 2000 reorganization (announced in 1994), have tried to strengthen OMB's management efforts, with somewhat mixed results (*Office of Management and Budget: Changes Resulting from the OMB 2000 Reorganization,* 1995).

Since the mid-1970s, the formulation phase of the federal budget lasts approximately 9 to 10 months. The OMB, the Council of Economic Advisors, and high-ranking officials in the Treasury Department, sometimes accompanied by other advisers, develop forecasts of future economic conditions, the costs of current programs, future revenues, and the costs of new administration initiatives. The OMB sends departments and agencies guidelines for preparing their budget requests.

Agencies then prepare their proposals, which are revised during departmental hearings. Updated information regarding economic projections and policy changes that might affect agency budgets may arrive during this process. Agency and deparmental personnel sometimes must walk a fine line in trying to obtain what they feel their programs need while not appearing too disloyal to White House policies.

Further hearings will be held within OMB, often with an eye to bringing the agency requests more closely in line with White House policies. Although the final decisions regarding the proposal rest with the president, OMB officials will normally be closely attuned to presidential preferences. Consequently, appealing OMB decisions to the president will not often succeed.

Any central budget office, including OMB, faces conflicting pressures on a regular basis. If agency personnel believe the office is a threat, they may respond by concealing information, leaking to the press, rallying interest group allies, or seeking protection from the legislature. If the office appears too friendly toward the bureaucracy, the chief executive may lose confidence in the office's work. If the office is not sufficiently responsive to the chief executive's priorities, he or she may place greater reliance on other staff units, at least on important decisions. If the office appears too subservient to the chief executive, other actors, such as members of the legislature, may begin to doubt the accuracy of the office's budgetary presentations.

By January or February, the president's budget proposal is usually completed (at least for initial purposes) and will be sent to Congress. Since the 1970s, the proposal has been accompanied by a *current services budget,* which indicates the projected cost of continuing current programs into the next fiscal year. Although this seems like a fairly straightforward exercise, it may not be. How much should we allow for inflation? How much should we adjust for changes in program workload—more retirees on Social Security, for example? Seemingly minor differences in the assumptions used to project future costs may make a large difference in the current services budget for an agency for the coming year. That current services projection, in turn, may help shape whether the president's proposal for an agency appears to be a funding cut or an increase. We will explore the issue of forecasting future revenues and spending in the next chapter.

CONGRESS AND BUDGET FORMULATION

Congress is involved in the development of budget proposals in a host of ways, both formally and informally. The legislation authorizing a program may, in a number of ways, make funding for that program virtually immune to control within the budget process by making the spending legally required. Unless the authorization legislation is changed, the money must continue to flow.

Congress may also influence the development of budget proposals whenever the president or agency personnel anticipate the likely congressional reaction to the proposal. In some cases this may involve trimming back (or increasing) a request to make it more acceptable to members of Congress. In other cases, however, a request may be modified strategically in hopes of countering expected congressional changes. For example, an agency might pad its request a bit in anticipation of likely congressional cuts, or the president might recommend less than he actually wants for a program if Congress appears likely to add funding to the request (see Schick, 1995: 60–61; Wildavsky, 1974: 21–24).

Of course, members of Congress may realize or suspect that strategic behavior and adjust their decisions accordingly, with deeper cuts for agencies suspected of padding their requests and greater generosity for programs with unrealistically low budget requests. Presidents and agency personnel generally try to avoid proposals that will appear too unrealistic to members of Congress and, therefore, not be taken seriously, although President Reagan's budgets sometimes ran afoul of that problem during his second term (Schick, 1995: 60–61).

The congressional role in formulating budget proposals expanded with the adoption of the *Congressional Budget and Impoundment Control Act* in 1974. The law required Congress to pass a budget resolution with targets for overall spending and revenues, the desired deficit or surplus, and the allocation of spending across a number of broad categories.[9] The resolution is much less detailed than the president's budget proposal but provides a statement of congressional sentiments regarding the desired broad contours of the budget. As a result, it may sometimes be a rival to the president's proposal.

The budget resolution has often been controversial, particularly in the House. The traditional (pre-1974) congressional budget process enabled members of Congress to avoid making explicit decisions regarding the overall level of revenues and expenditures and the size of the deficit or surplus. Trying to make those decisions, particularly in an environment of slow economic growth since 1970, increasing polarization between the parties in Congress, frequently divided party control between the White House and Congress, and more and more interest groups making demands, has often been difficult and painful. In 1998, Congress was unable to pass a budget resolution because of the many disagreements over budgetary issues (Ornstein, Mann, and Malbin, 2000: 168).

FORMULATING BUDGET PROPOSALS
AT THE STATE AND LOCAL LEVELS

The process of developing budget proposals in state and local governments has some distinctive components, although their importance varies from place to place.[10] One of the most important features is the presence of independently elected executives in many jurisdictions. In almost all the states, the attorney general, treasurer, and secretary of state are elected independently of the governor; many states also have independently elected education officials as well as other officials. At the local level, many jurisdictions have a number of executives who are elected by the voters. The various, independently elected executives often feel free to push for their own funding preferences in the budget process, regardless of what the governor, mayor, or other official may propose.

Intergovernmental revenues provide another important complication for state and local officials trying to develop their proposals. With state governments receiving from 15 to more than 20 percent of their revenue in intergovernmental aid, and with local governments even more reliant on intergovernmental grants in recent years, a reasonable budget proposal at one level depends in part on budget decisions made by the granting levels of government. In addition, most intergovernmental aid is usually targeted for specific programs; officials at the recipient level must either spend the money for the designated program or else forfeit the money, at least in the short run (but see the discussion of fungibility in Chapter 10). Intergovernmental aid may make administrators of the favored programs feel bolder in pressing for spending increases, in part because some of the cost of spending increases is borne by another level of government (Hedge, 1983; Thompson, 1987).

A major complication for developing budget proposals in states and localities is provided by laws adopted by higher levels of government. Those laws, often called mandates (see Chapter 10), may require a state or local government to provide a service or modify a facility without providing adequate funding to cover the costs. State mandates may also regulate local revenue decisions and budget processes.

State Formulation

As with the national government, reformers during the 20th century pushed for giving chief executives in states and localities a larger role in preparing budget proposals. In most states, the governor's role in budget formulation in the modern era is similar to the president's role, with an office or officer who is appointed by the governor or who is a career professional given a major role in preparing the budget proposal. In a number of states, however, the legislature is also involved in the formulation process, whether through informal consultation, participation in a joint executive/legislative committee that develops a proposal, or the development of a legislative budget proposal that is formally independent of the governor's. Professional staff support to assist the governor and legislature in the development and analysis of budget proposals, along with other aspects of budgetary decision making, has increased considerably in most states since the 1920s.

Most states permit agencies to submit their original budget requests to the state legislature, along with the governor's budget recommendation. That practice probably gives agency personnel more opportunities to be advocates for their programs, in contrast to the national government's use of central clearance. Nevertheless, the governors' budget recommendations are usually a good predictor of the final provisions of the budget, although it is difficult to determine whether the similarity reflects the governors' influence over the legislatures, accurate assessments of what the legislatures would approve, or powerful forces, such as the economy, that shape the decisions of both the governors and the legislature.

In some states, particularly those with low legislative salaries, legislative turnover tends to be high. Anticipating the legislature's likely reaction to a budget proposal is likely to be more difficult when large numbers of new members arrive with each new term. Those state legislatures also tend to have short sessions, which makes modification of proposals (if the legislators' preferences were not correctly anticipated) a difficult enterprise.

Local Formulation

In some cities and counties, an elected chief executive prepares the budget proposal, but many localities assign responsibility for the proposal to an appointed official, such as a city manager or a school superintendent. Other jurisdictions, however, use a committee, which may include people from the legislative branch and/or the bureaucracy. Local governments serving large and prosperous populations will usually have considerable professional staff support for developing the budget proposal, but local officials in smaller and poorer jurisdictions often have little staff assistance.

The structure of local government in the United States includes an important feature that almost certainly encourages agency personnel to be advocates for their programs. Special district governments, such as school districts, have responsibility for one or, at most, a few programs. The United States now has more than 48,000 special district governments. If the participants developing a budget proposal have only one program, such as education, to consider, they do not need to compare its needs to the needs of law enforcement or transportation programs.

Anticipating the likely reaction of the legislative branch in local budgeting is made easier than at higher levels by the small size of most local legislatures; many have only a dozen or fewer members. However, gauging the legislature's probable reaction is made more difficult by the high rate of turnover on many local legislatures. Further difficulties may arise if a proposal must be approved by the voters, for officials must try to assess public sentiment as well as which citizens are likely to vote.

At first glance, requirements for public hearings on the budget should further enhance the importance of possible public reactions to the proposal, but in practice this does not necessarily occur. Many public hearing on local budgets generate little public involvement and attract little media coverage.

CONCLUDING THOUGHTS

Developing a budget proposal in the modern era is a difficult task. A government with a wide range of responsibilities will have many programs; understanding all of them to a reasonable degree is an extremely difficult task, and coping with the many political forces in the budgetary arena is at least as difficult.

During periods of discontent with government finances (a seemingly chronic phenomenon in the United States), proposals to revise the formulation process almost inevitably surface. Should we change the format of the proposal to provide more and different kinds of information and focus attention on matters that seem to be neglected? Should we give some people a larger role in preparing the proposal, and/or should we give other people a smaller role?

For much of the 20th century, budget proposals have gradually become more detailed and complex and have placed more emphasis on agency activities and accomplishments. Those developments have helped make budgeting more controversial, both by increasing the range of possible disagreements and by placing more emphasis on questions that touch more directly on social goals and priorities.

The 20th century also witnessed a gradual, though erratic, tendency to give chief executives a larger formal role in the development of budget proposals. At the local level, this has often meant that an unelected official, such as a city manager, plays a vital role in the budget process, a development that may be troubling to people who want the budget to be a instrument for democratic governance. At the national level, the use of central clearance to stop agencies from officially requesting funding that is inconsistent with the president's budgetary policies is also somewhat inconsistent with democracy, which seems to require that information circulate freely (see Mill, 1974). Legislatures, however, appear to have considerable difficulty in developing full-fledged budget proposals on their own, especially in larger jurisdictions.

NOTES

1. Axelrod (1995: 13–18); LeLoup (1988: 50–54); Rubin (1997: chap. 5); Wildavsky (1986: pt. II).
2. For discussions of budget formats, see Bland and Rubin (1997: chap. 5); Hyde and Shafritz (1978: secs. II–IV); Lee and Johnson (1989: 77–87); Novick (1992); *Performance Budgeting* (1993); Schick (1966); Seckler-Hudson (1952); Taylor (1977). Note that not all authors use the same terminology, particularly regarding performance and program budgeting.
3. *Performance Budgeting* (1993); Wildavsky (1986: chap. 10).
4. *Budget Account Structure* (1995: 6–10, 16–18); Fisher (1975: chap. 3).
5. Bland and Rubin (1997: 42–44); LeLoup (1988: 15–18); Pitsvada (1988).
6. Axelrod (1995: chap. 3); Hedge (1983); LeLoup (1988: chap. 3); Rogers and Brown (1999); Sharkansky (1968); Thompson (1987); Wildavsky (1974: 18–35).
7. Axelrod (1995: chap. 4); Fisher (1975: chaps. 1, 2); LeLoup (1988: chap. 5); Schick (1995: chap. 4); Shuman (1992: 16–58).

5

Techniques of
Budgetary Analysis

Forecasting: A Vital Task

Methods of Forecasting

Types of Policy Analysis

Concluding Thoughts

> Predictions are difficult, especially about the future.
>
> YOGI BERRA
>
> (Quoted In Foss, 1997: 29)

One of the most dramatic developments in public budgeting since the early 1900s (if "dramatic" is an appropriate term in public budgeting) is the growing emphasis on using more sophisticated analytical techniques in the budget process. Budget reformers have encouraged the use of these techniques in order to enable decision makers to make more informed budgetary decisions. Some reformers have also hoped that improved analytical techniques would produce budgetary decisions that were more "rational" and less "political"—although that distinction includes the assumptions that political decisions are inherently not rational and that politics (and irrationality) do not influence the analyses. Neither assumption is dependably accurate. In any case, public budgeting has become significantly reliant on analytical techniques that many people do not understand very well, a troubling development for friends of democracy. In this chapter we will examine two major groups of analytical techniques: forecasting and policy analysis, broadly defined.

FORECASTING: A VITAL TASK

One of the most important bundle of analytical methods in public budgeting includes various techniques for predicting the future. In the short run, forecasting is important because, in many jurisdictions, preparation of budget requests begins 6 to 18 months before the new budget will begin and another year (or two years, with biennial budgeting) before the budget ends. Failure to predict future conditions may mean that much time is wasted on proposals for which no money is available and on proposals that prove to be unnecessary. Failing to predict future needs may also mean that the budget does not provide adequate funding for schools, law enforcement, defense, or other vital programs or provides unnecessarily large funding for some programs. Budgeters must, therefore, try to assess how much revenue will be available, the likely level of need for various programs, and the likely cost of programs necessary for dealing with those needs.

Predicting the future over the longer run is also critically important in a number of respects. Budgetary decisions influence public expectations for the future. If we commit to having an extensive state university system with relatively low tuition, parents may plan their children's futures with the expectation that the university system will still exist when their children graduate from high school. If we build an extensive highway system, businesses may build new factories in the belief that the highways will still be in good condition 20 years from now. If we make poor decisions now, correcting or coping with them later may make people very angry if they have planned their lives on the basis of the budget decisions that, in future years, must be drastically changed. Although many budgetary deliberations focus on relatively short term considerations, the failure to consider the long-term consequences of budgetary decisions can lead to great difficulty in future years (see *Budget Issues: Analysis of Long-Term Fiscal Outlook,* 1997). Uncertainties regarding long-term budget projections led some members of Congress in 2001 to fear making enduring budget commitments, such as major tax cuts or spending increases, that might require painful modifications later if predicted budget surpluses prove to be smaller than expected (Kessler and Pianin, 2001).

In a related vein, many budgetary decisions create legal commitments that extend years into the future. If we borrow money using full-faith-and-credit bonds, which we are legally required to repay, we may encounter serious problems if we overestimate our future ability to pay. Similar problems may occur with entitlement programs that guarantee people the legal right to a service or benefit and with contracts for projects that extend over a number of years, such as the construction of a major airport. If we underestimate the future cost of a program or overestimate future revenues, those legal commitments may bring great difficulty in future years. For example, one study of state and local government pension programs estimated their unfunded liabilities at approximately $200 billion in 1992, although that was a large improvement over the situation in the mid–1970s (*Public Pensions,* 1996).

Some budgetary decisions involve projects that will be worthwhile only if they provide benefits for a considerable number of years. Especially if those projects are expensive and cannot be readily converted to some other use, budgeters who fail to anticipate future conditions may waste enormous sums on unnecessary projects, such as a highway that few people use, or may approve a project that is inadequate to meet future needs, as in the case of a city water plant that is too small to provide enough water for the city 10 years after completion. We will examine the special case of these capital projects more closely in Chapter 8.

Failing to predict the future may also create difficulties in the form of deficiencies that cannot be remedied very quickly or easily after they are detected. Neglecting research and development may cause a nation to fall behind other countries in such diverse fields as medicine, manufacturing, and defense. Neglecting maintenance of basic infrastructure, such as roads, water mains, and public buildings, may lead to massive expenses later. Correcting for years of neglect may take years and be very costly, not only in terms of money but also in lives, public inconvenience, and environmental damage.

Because of these various considerations, as well as the desire not to look foolish or incompetent, budgeters try to anticipate the future as they struggle with budgetary decisions. Trying to predict future conditions is not a new idea by any means. Human beings through the ages have tried to foretell what will happen by means of astrology, oracle bones, cracks in turtle shells, and visions, among other methods. In the modern era, however, budgeters use a number of forecasting methods in hopes of casting some light on future conditions.[1] These forecasting methods are particularly important when budgetary proposals are being formulated and during the adoption phase of the budget process, but forecasting can also be important during the implementation phase, particularly if updated forecasts indicate that revenues or program costs are likely to be different than expected when the budget was adopted.

METHODS OF FORECASTING

Naive Projection

One of the simplest approaches to forecasting is to assume that the future will be essentially the same as the present—the "what's past is prologue" or *naive projection* (Gupta 1994: 161) technique. If we have $25 million in revenues for our county this year, this method predicts that we will have about the same amount next year. If snow removal cost the city $173,000 last winter, it will cost approximately that much this coming winter. If we allow for the possibility that each year has minor variations, we can refine the technique by taking an average of the last several years rather than relying on a single year. This approach to forecasting has the advantages of being easy and inexpensive to do and easy to understand, unlike some of the more complex methods. In addition, this type of forecasting is relatively difficult (though not impossible) to manipulate, unlike some of the more complex methods. Under relatively stable conditions, naive forecasting is also reasonably accurate. In many jurisdictions, revenues are fairly stable from one year to the next, as are needs for many programs.

The chief flaw of the "what's past is prologue" technique is that under rapidly changing conditions, current revenues or program needs or costs may not be a very good predictor of the future. If the economy is falling into a major recession, next year's revenues may be considerably lower than this year's revenues. A local economic boom may bring many new residents to the city and, over the course of two or three years, produce a large increase in the number of children in school, many new public safety problems, and much higher demand on the city transportation, water, and sewer systems. Technological innovations may produce a massive increase in the cost of fighter planes. A war may trigger huge increases in military expenses. Under changing conditions, more complex forecasting methods are necessary.

Simple Extrapolation

A slightly more complex forecasting technique is *simple extrapolation*. This approach seeks to identify simple trends in revenues and spending and to incorporate those trends into the forecast. For example, we might determine that revenues have increased, on average, 4 percent each year in the last five years. On that basis, we forecast that revenues next year will be 4 percent higher than this year. The average can be determined by calculating the revenue increase each year and then computing the mean or by using bivariate regression analysis (see the sources in note 1).

Simple extrapolation is a relatively easy method to use and will be more accurate than naive projection when a relatively consistent, long-term trend is present. However, when conditions are changing erratically, simple extrapolation may not be very accurate.

Time-Series Techniques

A more complex approach to forecasting utilizes *time-series techniques,* which range from the relatively simple to extremely complex. A basic time-series forecasting model will try to break down a series of revenue or spending figures into four components: a long-term trend, seasonal variation, cyclical (longer-term) variation, and irregular (unexplained) variation. The long-term trend tells us whether, on average, revenues or spending show a general tendency to increase or decrease, other things being equal. Assessing seasonal variation tells us whether revenues (or spending) vary with the time of year. For example, a community that attracts many summer tourists may generate 75 percent of its sales tax revenue during June, July, and August. Snow removal costs in most jurisdictions will normally be concentrated in the winter months. Knowing the distribution of revenues or costs over the course of a year can give us early warning of some unexpected change. Checking for longer-term, cyclical variations can alert us to broader dynamics affecting revenues or outlays. The most important example of that phenomenon for public budgeting is the business cycle: When the economy slumps, revenues typically fall, and the workload of some programs, such as welfare, increases. Once we understand these dynamics, we will be in a better position to forecast the future.

The proportion of variation that is irregular (i.e., unexplained) tells us how well our model performs. A large amount of unexplained variation means that our model does not account for what is happening very well. Its predictions, therefore, will not be very accurate. Many factors may cause prediction errors, including inaccurate record keeping, poor administrative control over program operations, and external factors that influence revenues or program needs and are difficult to predict (see *Budget Issues: 1991 Budget Estimates: What Went Wrong,* 1992; *Credit Reform,* 1998).

Other relatively simple time-series techniques try to smooth out minor fluctuations in the revenue or expenditure numbers before developing a forecast or check to see whether previous trends are better captured by a curved line rather than a straight line, as in the case of revenues that are growing but have grown more slowly in recent years. The relatively simple time-series techniques are not very difficult to master.

Multivariate Time-Series Analysis

A more sophisticated and complex approach to time-series forecasting utilizes *multivariate time-series analysis.* Although the techniques used in multivariate time-series analysis are beyond the scope of this book, the basic principles are fairly straightforward. Analysts using this approach explore the recent past in hopes of finding factors that help predict revenues or expenditures or, in more complex models, finding factors that help predict other factors that in turn influence revenues or spending. For example, the number of students in high school in the state is a fairly good predictor of future enrollment in the state university system; university enrollment, in turn, affects both the revenues generated from tuition and fees and also the cost of operating the university system. Population growth will normally mean higher revenues (depending somewhat on the sources of population growth, wealthy people moving to the jurisdiction being especially helpful) but also higher demand on the transportation system, more students in school, and more needs for water, health care, and many other services.

If the analysts are successful in finding variables that predict future budgetary changes, then decision makers will have some advance warning if revenues are likely to rise or fall substantially or the need for or cost of some program is likely to change significantly. If the forecasts are accurate and if decision makers are willing to pay attention to the forecasts, many budgetary problems can be avoided or at least minimized.

However, multivariate time-series forecasting presents a number of potential difficulties (Bretschneider and Gorr, 1999: 319–320; Hoaglin, et. al., 1982: 230–231). First, developing an appropriate battery of models can be difficult and expensive. We will need one model for total revenues and a number of separate models for individual revenue sources, especially if some of those sources are earmarked for specific programs. We will also need a number of separate models for the expenditure side; the factors affecting law enforcement needs may be very different from the factors affecting educational needs. Analysts without specialized training and good computer support will find the task overwhelming, and even the best efforts may not produce great accuracy at times.

In addition, even if we are able to develop an accurate set of forecasting models, fundamental changes in the economy or in public policies may greatly erode the accuracy of our forecasts (see Mansfield, 1983: 549). Major tax reforms may bring completely new dynamics to revenues; changes in the rules governing a social program may alter the factors that affect program costs. Past patterns are not always a good guide to the future. Note, too, that for completely new programs, there may not be any past to analyze, although the experience of other jurisdictions that have had the program for some time may provide some guidance. Revenues and program costs may be affected by idiosyncratic events, such as the 1973 oil embargo, that are almost impossible to anticipate but that may undercut the accuracy of any forecasting effort (Pearlstein, 2001).

Complex forecasting models may give an impression of precision that is deceptive at times. Given that many people do not understand the intricacies of multivariate time-series analysis, analysts or officials may be tempted to tinker with the estimates in order to advance their political agendas. Seemingly minor changes in some features of a forecasting model may produce large changes in the results. Especially in the case of longer-term forecasting, which often requires estimates of factors that are unknown (How much will the economy grow in the next six years? How rapidly will prices rise?), forecasts may be manipulated in ways that undercut the accuracy of the predictions (see Schick, 1995: 20–27). Opponents of more spending may try to produce low revenue estimates to undercut calls for more generous funding for programs. Advocates of a program may try to produce low cost estimates to make the program appear more economical. Opponents of the program will do the opposite. According to one study, nearly one-fourth of state budgeting and/or finance offices reported that they considered the wishes of political leaders when developing revenue forecasts. This consideration did not, however, appear to have much adverse effect on the accuracy of the forecasts (Grizzle and Klay, 1994: 149–150).

When past conditions are not likely to be a useful guide to the future, as in the cases of completely new programs or drastically changing conditions, such as the outbreak of a major war, analysts may utilize forecasting methods that rely more heavily on expert judgment in hopes of getting some sense of future conditions.[2] Bear in mind that judgment is also involved in the development of time-series forecasting models, but so-called judgmental forecasting methods rely more heavily on personal opinion and intuition in developing predictions. Several approaches are used.

The simplest judgmental method is to rely on a single, well-informed and experienced person who, on the basis of years of practice and effort, develops a sense what revenues or costs will be for the coming year without using any formalized forecasting system. This approach is simple and inexpensive and, under fairly stable conditions, may produce reasonably accurate results. However, under rapidly changing conditions, the expert's past experience may not be a very accurate guide, and the informality of the system provides little assistance regarding how to cope with the new conditions. Reliance on a single expert's judgment may sometimes produce forecasts that are biased by that expert's personal beliefs. Also, if the key expert retires or resigns, the forecasting system breaks down.

Delphi Technique

A more complex judgmental method is the *Delphi technique*, which tries to utilize the expertise of a number of participants to develop a forecast. In this method, a coordinator or manager (or, in some cases, a committee) contacts a number of experts and asks each of them to offer an individual prediction of whatever is being forecast. The experts do not discuss the matter with one another initially but instead send their individual assessments to the coordinator. Avoiding discussion at this stage reduces the risk that peer pressure or the prestige or forceful personality of one or more of the experts might influence the judgments offered by the others. In some instances the experts are not even told which other experts are involved in the process.

The coordinator then compiles the responses and prepares a summary of them. Depending on the situation, the responses might involve a range of values (How much would putting a man on the moon cost?), an assessment of probable outcomes, or other answers. The summary will usually include information regarding the average or most common responses but also responses that diverge from the usual answers. This summary is then sent to the experts for another round of assessments; those experts whose responses were different from most other responses may be asked to provide additional information to explain or justify those points of view. The experts will not usually be told who developed which predictions. Some of the experts may modify their forecasts after seeing what others have predicted. These new responses are again compiled and summarized, and the new summary is again sent to the experts. Several rounds of this process may be needed to reach a reasonable degree of agreement on the forecast.

The Delphi technique was developed primarily for situations in which there is a reasonable degree of agreement among the participants or at least a hope of approximate agreement. In some cases, however, value conflicts among the participants may be so great that no realistic hope of agreement exists. In those situations, the *policy Delphi technique* may be more appropriate.

The policy Delphi technique retains the coordinator (or committee) managing the process and a group of expert judges, although the criteria for "expert" may be more diverse. Some of the judges may be selected on the basis of their professional training or work experience, but other judges may be policy activists, interest group leaders, or other individuals chosen to represent various points of view. The panel members will be asked to offer their predictions individually, as in the regular Delphi technique, without knowing about the responses of other panelists and often without even knowing their identities. The coordinator prepares a summary of the responses and circulates the summary to the panel members again. They in turn provide new assessments, which are again summarized and distributed.

At some point in the policy Delphi technique, individual participants and their assessments may be identified to other participants. The process will not usually produce a consensus, given the serious value conflicts involved, but may help clarify particular clusters of assessments and the strengths of the arguments and evidence supporting each point of view.

In both versions of the Delphi technique, a careful specification of what needs to be forecast is vital to the success of the process—as is true of all forecasting methods. In addition, the coordinator or manager of the process must be careful not to bias the process by the wording of questions or the feedback given to panel members. Choosing the right panel members is also critical and can be politically sensitive as well as difficult, especially in the case of forecasts for specific programs. Individuals who are knowledgeable are not always well known, and individuals who resent being excluded from the process may not be receptive toward the results. Some people may also be reluctant to offer a prediction without knowing who else is involved in the process and without having some opportunity to gauge their thinking.

Another judgmental method involves convening a meeting of knowledgeable people who sit down together and try to develop a forecast from their collective expertise and experience. This approach can be modified in a number of ways. The experts may be given a body of background information prior to the meeting in order to give them updates on recent developments and trends. The experts may be asked to submit individual, preliminary assessments prior to the meeting and then convene to discuss and debate those assessments. The experts may be drawn from a single specialty or organization, such as the state revenue office, or the panel may include people from several fields and institutions.

A face-to-face meeting may be a faster method for developing a forecast than the Delphi technique, especially if several rounds of feedback are needed for that approach. However, group meetings may yield inaccurate forecasts if one or more members of the group have higher rank than others, if forceful personalities dominate the discussion, or if some members of the group feel reluctant to offer assessments that seem out of step with the others (see Janis, 1982).

Studies of revenue forecasting indicate that revenue projections in many jurisdictions often fall somewhat below actual revenues. Although there is some disagreement regarding why that occurs, some studies indicate that revenue forecasters try to estimate on the low side because having more revenue than expected is less painful than having less revenue than expected. A revenue shortfall may lead to traumatic, last-minute cuts in programs, while "extra," unexpected revenues beyond what was forecast may permit spending on a few additional projects or some new equipment. At the same time, however, low revenue forecasts may be used to fend off demands for higher spending for various programs (see Brettschneider and Gorr, 1999: 320–321).

Because all forecasting methods have shortcomings of some sort and because poor forecasts can yield painful consequences, budgeters may be wise to follow the old advice about not putting all the eggs in one basket. If we use several different forecasting methods and then pool the results together, we may have greater accuracy than if we rely on any one approach exclusively. In a similar manner, having more than one organization preparing forecasts (e.g., one in the executive branch and another in the legislature) and then combining the results can lead to greater accuracy than having only one organization responsible for developing the forecasts.[3]

Regular updating of forecasts can also reduce the risk of errors as the budget process proceeds. Incorporating new information regarding the economy, program needs, and/or program costs into revised forecasts can enable budgetary decision makers to modify their plans earlier in the process, when modifications are often less painful, rather than later.

TYPES OF POLICY ANALYSIS

During all phases of the budgetary process, public policy questions recurrently surface despite efforts to treat the budget as if it had few policy ramifications (see Chapter 1). What are the country's (or state's or locality's) needs? What goals do we want to pursue, and what values do we prize most highly? What is a fair distribution of costs and benefits? Does a program achieve enough to justify its costs? These are the kinds of questions that policy analysis seeks to answer or at least help answer.[4] Reformers since 1900 have recurrently tried to improve the amount and quality of policy analysis being done and, especially beginning in the 1930s and even more since the 1950s, have tried to bring that analysis to bear in the budgetary process. The reformers have hoped to improve the quality of budgetary decisions by providing officials with better information regarding public needs and the performance of public programs. Policy analysis takes a number of forms.

Needs Assessment

One important type of policy analysis is *needs assessment,* which seeks to determine the nature, severity, and extent of a problem or group of related problems.[5] Needs assessment is an important part of building (or assessing) a case for a budget proposal. Is a problem serious enough to warrant spending scarce tax dollars in hopes of reducing or eliminating the problem? Where is the problem? Who is affected by it? Is the problem likely to persist or worsen unless budgetary action is taken?

Needs assessment presents a number of difficulties for policy analysts. Some problems are difficult to detect for a variety of reasons. An unfriendly foreign government may conceal its intentions or capabilities from us. People breaking the law may try to hide their actions, and victims may be reluctant to notify the authorities. People may conceal problems that they find embarrassing, problems such as poverty, illiteracy, or mental illness. People may also have problems without recognizing them; many people with high blood pressure, diabetes, or other health problems are apparently unaware of the fact. Poor record keeping may lead to the loss of much information regarding a problem. Pollution of an underground aquifer may be difficult to detect without sophisticated equipment.

Needs assessments may also encounter difficulties if analysts focus on only one aspect of a problem rather than the entire problem or if the problem is treated in isolation when it is actually linked to other problems. Individual poverty is linked to neighborhood poverty (poor people tend to live in poor neighborhoods where there are few good jobs available). Welfare reformers in the 1990s, therefore, discovered that moving people from welfare to employment required attention to their transportation needs, which had not traditionally received much attention in debates over poverty (*Welfare Reform,* 1998). America's defense needs are linked to our transportation system's great appetite for oil. Overlooking some aspects of a problem or its relationships with other problems may make a problem appear much less severe than it is and may also create unrealistic expectations regarding how readily the problem can be solved or reduced.

Needs assessment can be complicated by problems of forecasting whenever we try to anticipate future needs. Especially when a budgetary decision is likely to produce a long-term commitment, policy makers will want to know how severe a problem will be 10 or more years from now. If the forecasts of future needs are inaccurate, we may fail to prepare to meet those needs or waste funds and effort on an unnecessarily large response. Much of the debate over Social Security during the 1990s was fueled by a forecast of financial problems in the system some time around the years 2029 to 2032. Although the Social Security system's trustees had actually prepared three different forecasts, only one seemed to receive much attention. One of their other forecasts indicated little danger of financial difficulty, but that prediction seemed much less newsworthy (see Skidmore, 1999). In addition, updates of the forecast predicting difficulties found that the year of the crisis moved eight years into the future when the 1996 forecast was updated in 2000 (Berry, 2000).

Needs assessment, like other aspects of policy analysis, can be a politically charged task. Calling attention to a problem that appears to be very large and severe may stimulate demands that something be done about it. That prospect will not be pleasing to people who, for whatever reason, oppose action on that problem. Conversely, a needs assessment that depicts a problem as minor and affecting few people may undercut proposals for dealing with that problem, a development that will probably anger proponents of action. By defining a problem narrowly, using measures that omit many aspects of the problem, and other techniques, analysts may manipulate a needs assessment to make a problem appear unrealistically small. Analysts who define a problem overly broadly; try to link it to other, very large problems; and use other methods may make a problem appear larger or worse than it actually is.

Specifying Goals and Values

Specifying or clarifying goals and values is another important task for policy analysts.[6] This task overlaps somewhat with needs assessment, partly because needs are defined in terms of values. Additional overlap sometimes results because a problem may not be completely solved, but decision makers may establish a goal of keeping the problem at a specified level, such as keeping unemployment at a level of 5 percent or lower.

Specifying goals is difficult for many reasons (Lindblom, 1959). First, virtually all major public programs have multiple goals that sometimes conflict with one another. We expect the education system to train people for the job market, promote good citizenship, communicate culture, encourage independent thinking (and, sometimes, conformity), and solve a variety of social problems. We want the national forests to provide wildlife habitat, recreational opportunities, lumber, grazing for livestock, and watershed protection, among other things. Keeping track of the multiple goals and establishing priorities among them can be difficult and politically sensitive, for no group wants to be told that their concern is a low priority. In addition, comparing the value of many program benefits and costs is very difficult. Most of us think that fairness, privacy, peace of mind, freedom, and human life are valuable, but how valuable are they, and how can we compare them? How much freedom would be worth the sacrifice of 10,000 lives?

Setting goals is also difficult because many public goals are relatively vague and subject to conflicting interpretations. We may want the national park system to protect an area, but "protect" may mean a variety of different things. Should the area be preserved in a relatively wild state, or should we provide numerous paved roads, lodges, restaurants, and other amenities for visitors? We may all want people to have a fair trial, but "fairness" is subject to a variety of interpretations. Trying to develop goals that are specific enough to provide meaningful guidance may generate serious conflict.

Specifying goals can be politically delicate when one goal of a program—perhaps the only goal—is to provide symbolic reassurance to people. When officials do not know what to do about a problem or do not want to attack the problem, they may create a program largely or even entirely to create the impression of action to mollify people who are concerned about that problem (see Edelman, 1988). Those officials will not appreciate an analysis that calls attention to the substantially symbolic function of the program.

Setting goals is likely to be particularly difficult in large, diverse political systems because they are likely to have people with many different views regarding societal and government goals. Emphasizing goals within the budget process will, consequently, generate great controversy. However, failing to consider the importance of goals in the budget process risks wasting scarce funds on relatively unimportant goals while more crucial priorities are neglected. In any case, program analysts must always be alert to goal concerns and recognize that the goals a program is expected to serve may not always be self-evident.

Program Evaluation

Another important branch of policy analysis seeks to evaluate the impact of public programs. *Program evaluation* has been a growth industry since the 1950s, but one of the most important lessons that has been learned (to varying degrees, admittedly) is that valid assessment of program impact is a very difficult enterprise.[7] As a result, some program evaluations tell us much more about the political beliefs of the people doing the evaluations than they tell us about the actual impact of the program.

Multiple Factors One key difficulty in program evaluation arises from the fact that public policies are almost never the only factors affecting the conditions that we want the policies to influence. A new law enforcement program may influence the crime rate, but so may the condition of the economy, the stability of families, and the proportion of the population between the ages of 14 and 30. The skill of school teachers and the instructional methods they use may influence how much a child learns, but the child's innate abilities and family environment may make a great deal of difference, too. An evaluation that fails to consider the role of those other factors may reach profoundly misleading conclusions regarding the program's impact. Identifying those other factors and gathering accurate information about them can be very difficult. Failing to consider them, however, may greatly bias the results of the evaluation.

Evaluations of programs that pursue several goals at the same time (i.e., practically all programs) must also consider the program's performance regarding all those goals. Whenever we ask a program to serve several goals, each goal serves as a limitation on the program's ability to reach the other goals. If the national forest system is asked to provide timber for the many wood products that we use, meeting that goal will limit the system's ability to protect pristine wilderness areas. Our expectation that the criminal justice system should protect individual rights may sometimes conflict with our desire to have the system minimize crime. We expect the Social Security system to provide income support for retirees, the disabled, and the dependents of workers who have died, but one other important job of the Social Security system is to help stabilize the economy by continuing to provide a steady flow of income to recipients during economic recessions. Neglecting the multiple goals of most programs will almost always produce misleading evaluations, with the usual effect being to make the program appear less effective than it actually is (because much of what the program does is being ignored).

Costs and Benefits   Another sensitive aspect of program evaluation explores the distribution of a program's costs and benefits. A program may provide substantial benefits to some people, small benefits to some people, and no benefits at all to other people. The costs of a program may also be unevenly distributed. Program evaluators may try to assess whether those distributions are fair or appropriate, according to one or more criteria. For example, a 1999 proposal to reduce license tag fees in the state of Washington offered the largest reductions to the owners of very expensive cars—the owners of which are likely to be wealthy. Supporters of the proposal were generally silent on the question of why wealthy people needed a particularly large benefit, especially in a state where the state tax system bears especially heavily on poorer people. Discussing the distribution of benefits and costs is likely to be controversial, particularly for programs with a very uneven distribution of costs or benefits. An even distribution of benefits may also be controversial, however, if some benefits are going to people or areas that do not appear to need them.

Timing   Program evaluations must also consider the role of timing in a number of respects. Many programs appear to go through an initial shakedown phase, during which the program does not function very well. Employees may be learning new skills. Relationships with other programs and organizations must be worked out. Initial expectations regarding the pace of progress may have been unrealistic, and some aspects of the program may need revision. If a program is evaluated during this initial phase, an unfavorable evaluation is likely. With time and effort, however, the program's performance may improve (see Peterson, Rabe, and Wong, 1986), and a later evaluation of the same program may be much more positive.

Another important timing issue arises when we try to evaluate a program that produces costs and benefits at different times (e.g., we must pay for the facility now and enjoy the use of it later) or compare programs that generate costs and/or benefits at different times, as in the case of two building designs, one of which is more expensive to build but less expensive to maintain. We can cope with this problem by *discounting* (McKenna, 1980: 135–142). To take a simple example, if we are evaluating a flood control program that will cost $100 million next year and will produce $100 million in benefits five years after that, is it worth the cost? At first glance, the cost and benefit appear equal, but if we invested the $100 million in bonds that earned 5 percent simple interest for the five-year interval, the $100 million would grow to $125 million. The present value of a given amount of money is not equal to the same number of dollars at some later date, then.

Although discounting enables us to do a better job of comparing costs and benefits that arise at different times, it also presents an awkward problem: How do we know what discount rate to use? Should we use the prime interest rate, the current interest rate that the government making the decision would have to pay to borrow money, or some other rate? The choice of interest rates is particularly important for costs and benefits that extend a considerable number of years into the future. Using a higher interest rate makes future benefits appear less valuable, but using a lower rate has the opposite effect.

Another important timing problem in evaluations centers on variations in program impact over time. A new weapon system may perform very effectively, but two years later, a new countermeasure may reduce the weapon's effectiveness dramatically. A park facility may be perfectly adequate for meeting current visitor traffic, but a 50 percent increase in visitor traffic may overwhelm it. A new program may have significant impact, in part because it is new and noteworthy and because of the enthusiasm of agency personnel. Over time the novelty wears off, and the enthusiasm of personnel may decline; the result may be a loss of effectiveness. Conversely, a new program's impact may emerge gradually, with the result that an early evaluation will miss a significant amount of the program's effect. A new compound for melting ice from roads or airport runways may work very well but may, over time, cause the pavement to deteriorate. Evaluations must, therefore, be repeated periodically.

For many programs, the timing of the program's action is itself an important consideration. How quickly do the police or firefighters respond to an emergency call? How long must builders wait for the processing of a building permit application? How often are the city buses on schedule? How quickly can a destroyer's antiaircraft systems be activated after a threat is detected? For some tasks, if they are not performed at the proper time, an otherwise successful performance may be worth a great deal less and in some cases worth nothing at all.

Determining Total Cost A program evaluation issue that is particularly sensitive in public budgeting is determining the full cost of a program. A number of those costs may be borne by other programs, and some may not appear in the budget at all. The total cost of U.S. transportation policies, for example, includes outlays for roads and highways, public airports, Amtrak, and local public transportation but also thousands of fatalities caused by traffic accidents, the cost of medical care for accident victims, environmental damage, the time people spend waiting in rush-hour traffic, and a large portion of America's entanglements in the Middle East. When decision makers want to minimize the apparent cost of a policy, they are sometimes tempted to select budgetary options that have a larger proportion of their costs outside the budget they are drafting. A program that appears cheaper in its on-budget costs may not be cheaper when all costs are considered. As we will see in Chapter 10, officials at one level of government sometimes adopt mandates that require a lower level of government to provide a service but provide no funds to cover the costs. The mandate appears to be inexpensive as far as the adopting government's budget is concerned but may be very costly at the lower level of government.

Opportunity Costs Another difficult aspect of determining program costs involves the concept of *opportunity costs*. In selecting one course of action, we may be forfeiting the opportunity to do something else. The national government's commitment to the space shuttle to launch satellites has probably pulled money away from development of single-use rockets. That cost did not seem very great until a major accident led to the suspension of shuttle launches for an extended period. Assessing the value of forgone opportunities is often difficult, especially over the long term. How much would people use a nonexistent facility in the next 10 years if it did exist? Gauging opportunity costs is also tricky because they may be implicit or uncertain; we might commit to the space shuttle program in the expectation that there will be enough funding in future years for single-use boosters as well. We may not learn until years later that the cost of one approach precludes the other approach.

Evaluating program costs also raises the issue of distribution again. The costs of many programs are quite unevenly distributed, and evaluators may try to determine whether that distribution is reasonable or fair, according to one or more criteria. A new environmental regulation may cost some workers their jobs—a high cost to most people. The noise generated by landings and takeoffs at a new airport or the odor generated by a recycling center will affect nearby residents more than other people. Destroying a scenic area or a historic landmark deprives future generations of the use of that area or landmark.

Other Problems of Program Evaluation Years of experience with program evaluations reveals that there are recurrent problems of bias creeping into the analysis (Gupta, 1994: 445–453: Quade, 1975: 304–306). The personal beliefs of evaluators can shape an evaluation in many ways, some of which are not easily detected. By selecting only certain cases or time periods to analyze, an evaluator may make a program seem effective or ineffective. One measure of program performance may indicate progress, but another measure may indicate failure; the choice of measure may affect the evaluation greatly. An evaluation may include various assumptions (that may or may not be made clear) that may affect the results of the evaluation. Problems of bias can be minimized by having several evaluators with different political views, but that remedy will make evaluations more expensive. Alternatively, having other experts review an evaluation to check for possible biases may minimize their impact or at least aid in their detection. Comparing the evaluation's procedures and results with other evaluations of the same program or of similar programs in other jurisdictions can also cast light on a biased evaluation.

A careful evaluation must consider the possibility that the program on paper is not necessarily an accurate portrait of the policy in the field. A state may have a death penalty law on the books but not sentence anyone to death. A city may have a law against gambling, but police may overlook violations as long as the violators are orderly and discreet. A university may have an affirmative action program on the books but make little genuine effort to recruit female or minority staff. In addition, a program that is officially uniform may in fact vary considerably from one part of the state or country to another in response to localized political pressures. If an evaluator assumes that the program in the field is the same as the program on paper, the resulting evaluation may be profoundly misleading.

Evaluators sometimes have difficulty getting decision makers to pay attention to the results of their evaluations. An elected official who has publicly supported a program for many years may not be receptive to a critical evaluation of that program. Employees in charge of the program may be similarly unreceptive. Officials who are ideologically hostile to a program may be inclined to ignore a positive evaluation of a program. These difficulties may be reduced somewhat by consultation between the evaluator and other interested parties from the beginning of the evaluation process, recognition of the specific needs of officials (e.g., how soon the results of the evaluation will be available), adherence to shared professional standards regarding evaluations methods, and diplomacy (Rossi and Freeman, 1982: 311–318). The difficulties are likely to persist, however, in many cases. Consequently, evaluators may sometimes need to consider whether a specific evaluation is likely to be worth its cost if officials do not appear receptive to the results.

As many program evaluations have become increasingly technical and sophisticated, another potential problem emerges: The average citizen has a very difficult time understanding many program evaluations. If the budget should promote accountability to the public, injecting complex evaluations that many people cannot understand into the budget process presents the danger that people may be manipulated into thinking a program is (or is not) worth its costs and the danger that many people may pay little or no attention to a process that they find impossible to understand. At the same time, however, failing to evaluate programs may mean that substantial funds are spent on ineffective programs, a result that is hardly beneficial to the public.

CONCLUDING THOUGHTS

Analytical techniques used in budgeting have grown increasingly complex over the years. Analysts use forecasting to predict future revenues and program outlays. Forecasting methods range from very simple approaches relying on one expert's judgment or the assumption of current conditions continuing to complex statistical models with numerous equations and many variables. Inaccurate forecasts can lead to money being wasted on unnecessary programs, unmet future needs, or unexpected gaps between revenues and spending.

Policy analysis is used for a number of purposes, such as assessing the need for a program and gauging the effectiveness of a policy. Policy analyses are likely to be more informative if they consider all the goals of a program and take into account all factors that influence the conditions that a program seeks to affect. Even the most accurate analyses, however, may be ignored if they conflict with the political beliefs of officials.

The increasing complexity of forecasting methods and policy analyses has given budgeters more accurate information on which to base their decisions. At the same time, that complexity makes budgeting more difficult for citizens to understand, a development that undercuts the budget's value as an instrument for democratic control.

NOTES

1. For overviews of forecasting, see Bretschneider and Gorr (1999); Grizzle and Clay (1994); Hyde and Jarocki (1978); Levenbach and Cleary (1981); Moore (1989); Schroeder (1996).

2. See Gupta (1994: 133–146); Moore (1989: 268–281); Quade (1975: chap. 12); Schroeder (1996: 102–103).

3. See Bretschneider and Gorr (1999: 325–326); Grizzle and Klay (1994); Moore (1989: 292–294).

4. For overviews of various aspects of policy analysis, see Gramlich (1998); Gupta (1994); Mohr (1988); Nachmias (1979); Quade (1975); Rossi and Freeman (1982); Royse and Thyer (1996).

5. Mohr (1988: 10–24); Rossi and Freeman (1982: 93–121); Royse and Thyer (1996: chap. 2).

6. Gramlich (1998: chap. 4); Quade (1975: chaps. 6, 7, 9).

7. Gramlich (1998); Mohr (1988); Nachmias (1979); Rossi and Freeman (1982).

6

Budget Adoption

Some Important Aspects of Budget Adoption

Budget Adoption in the National Government

Budget Adoption in the States

Budget Adoption at the Local Level

Accounting for Adoption Decisions in Budgeting

Concluding Thoughts

Before we give you billions more, we want to know
what you've done with the trillion you've got.

U. S. Representative LES ASPIN (Quoted In Baker, 1990: 222)

After the development of a budget proposal, officials turn to the task of gaining formal adoption of the budget. In practice these two stages may overlap because officials developing a budget proposal will usually try to anticipate the reactions of the participants at the adoption stage. In addition, previous budgetary decisions may limit the options available to officials who are developing proposals for future years. Moreover, many of the participants at the adoption stage are also involved in the development of budget proposals.

In the United States, the legislative branch is typically the central arena for adoption of budgets, but chief executives are also heavily involved. In addition, the courts are occasional participants in budgetary decisions. At the state and local levels, the voters are sometimes involved in the enactment of specific budgetary policies, such as approving a school tax levy or a bond issue to finance street improvements. Many informal participants, particularly interest groups, are also active in the adoption process.

SOME IMPORTANT ASPECTS
OF BUDGET ADOPTION

Broadly speaking, budget adoption involves three main components: authorization decisions, appropriations, and revenue decisions.[1] One of the recurring issues of budgeting involves establishing an effective linkage among the three components. Not all observers agree on what would constitute "effective linkage" or how it could best be achieved.

Authorization is one key facet of budgeting. Authorization involves the creation of an agency or program and the definition of its powers, responsibilities, and programs. As traditionally practiced, authorization did not provide agencies with money, although authorization legislation sometimes included limits on the scope of agency activities (such as a limit on the number of personnel an agency could employ or the number of aircraft carriers the Navy could have). Beginning in the 20th century, however, authorization legislation sometimes included provisions that, in one or more ways, tried to control the flow of funds to agencies. We will return to that issue later in this chapter.

Appropriation, a second key facet of budgetary adoption, gives an agency the legal power to incur financial obligations and make payments from the treasury or from a specialized funding source in the case of some programs. Traditionally, appropriations followed authorizations; that is, officials needed to create an agency and give it legal power to carry out its responsibilities before appropriating funds for the agency. Unfortunately for people who are easily confused, the federal government's budgetary terminology labels the legal power to enter into financial obligations as *budget authority,* of which appropriations are one major type. Although "authorization" and "budget authority" appear to be similar terms, they are not the same (review the preceding two paragraphs).

Revenue decisions are a third major facet of budgetary adoption. If government is to spend money, the money must be raised in some fashion, usually through taxes, fees, or borrowing. Officials must decide what types of revenue sources should be used and decide whether the various revenues should be put into a common pool to fund all programs or earmarked for specific programs. Most states, for example, earmark motor fuel tax revenues for road and highway programs; some states earmark state lottery revenues for education. Revenue decisions may also include various exemptions or deductions that reduce some taxpayers' tax bills.

In designing a process for budgetary adoption, budgeters try to strike a balance between giving detailed examination to individual programs on the one hand and devoting adequate attention to the overall size of the budget and the relative allocation of resources across different programs on the other. As with bottom-up formulation of proposals (see Chapter 4), a process that emphasizes close scrutiny of individual agencies and programs may neglect consideration of the total cost of government and questions of whether the funds spent for one purpose might be more productively employed elsewhere. As with top-down formulation, an adoption process that overemphasizes budgetary totals may give too little scrutiny to individual programs. The result may be overly generous funding for programs that are not very effective and/or inadequate funding for individual programs that are successful.

As the scope of government activity has increased over the years and as more groups mobilize to press their demands on the government, adopting a budget has become an extremely complex and difficult task in many jurisdictions. Officials struggling with conflicting priorities and increasing complexity have modified budget processes at all levels of government. We will begin with an overview of adoption processes at the national level, then turn to the state and local levels.

BUDGET ADOPTION IN THE
NATIONAL GOVERNMENT

Early Developments

In the early years of federal budgeting, Congress was the dominant player in budgetary adoption. Most of the constitutional provisions dealing with financial matters are found in Article I, the article dealing with Congress. Some presidents tried to influence congressional decisions on some budgetary issues, but presidential involvement tended to be sporadic and often limited to a few issues rather than the dealing with the overall budget.

By today's standards, the early budget process[2] in Congress was comparatively simple. Members of Congress decided to divide budgetary decisions into two pools. Authorization decisions were assigned to one set of committees, which were usually temporary committees in the earliest Congresses. Appropriations and revenue bills were the responsibility of the House Ways and Means Committee (created in 1802) and the Senate Finance Committee (created in 1816). Assigning revenue and appropriations bills to the same committees was a sensible strategy for people who wanted a strong link between revenue decisions and spending decisions (e.g., to minimize the risk of budget deficits). During this early period, Congress gradually shifted to greater use of standing (i.e., relatively permanent) committees for authorization bills. For the first few years, Congress used a single bill to cover all appropriations decisions, but by 1794 it began using several appropriations bills.

The simplicity of the early process reflected, in part, the limited number of federal programs and their simplicity. In addition, there were relatively few interest groups trying to influence budgetary decisions. As the federal budget grew and as political pressures gradually became more complex, the congressional budget process changed.

In the 1860s, Congress created two new committees, the appropriations committees (one for each house of Congress), to handle appropriations decisions. The separation of revenue and appropriations decisions reflected, in part, a desire to distribute political influence within Congress more broadly. In addition, members who were concerned with the rising cost of government and the growing complexity of the budget apparently believed that having a committee in each house with an exclusive focus on appropriations would reduce unnecessary and wasteful government spending (Fenno, 1966: 8–9, 504).

The appropriations committees began trimming spending for a number of programs, but their frugality angered many supporters of those programs. Among the angry people were many members of the authorization committees, who felt that their decisions were being undercut by the appropriations committees' failure to recommend adequate funding. As a result, a series of congressional decisions in the 1870s and 1880s reassigned responsibility for some appropriations bills to the authorization committees responsible for those programs. This arrangement helped provide a stronger link between authorization and appropriations decisions. Higher funding for some programs resulted (Stewart, 1987: 587–600).

Members of the appropriations committees recognized that their committees would cease to have any influence if all the appropriations bills were taken away from them. They began to provide more generous funding for the programs remaining under their jurisdiction. This greater generosity reduced the pressure to reassign those remaining appropriations bills to the authorization committees.

The Middle Phase

As noted in Chapter 4, pressures for change began to build in the 1890s. Rising spending, budget deficits, and battles over revenue sources led to adoption of the Budget and Accounting Act of 1921, which substantially increased presidential involvement in the budget process. In a series of decisions between 1920 and 1922, the appropriations committees regained jurisdiction over appropriations bills, a move that disturbed some members of the authorization committees. They feared that the appropriations committees would repeat the earlier practice of funding programs at a lower level than the authorization committee members preferred.

The Recent Experience

By the late 1960s, the budget process showed increasing signs of strain. Congress was sometimes unable to complete action on the appropriations bills by the beginning of the fiscal year (July 1). A series of budget deficits, initially of relatively modest proportions, raised concerns about excessive spending. Critics complained that the congressional budget process was too fragmented to make coherent budgetary decisions. Frictions between the White House and Congress erupted, particularly during the Nixon administration.

Critics became increasingly concerned about the problem of *uncontrollable spending.* "Uncontrollable spending" is spending that cannot be controlled within the appropriations process. An authorization bill may give qualified people a legal right to a benefit; if that bill becomes law, funds to provide that benefit must be provided, regardless of the preferences of members of the appropriations committees. Medicare, veterans' benefits, and interest on the federal debt are important uncontrollable items. Bear in mind that the "uncontrollables" can be controlled by changing the authorization legislation, but that is usually very difficult if the program has powerful interest group support. By the early 1970s, roughly two-thirds of all federal spending was relatively uncontrollable. Making spending uncontrollable reduced the danger that a program would be financially cut by an unfriendly appropriations committee or future Congress or president.

In a related vein, critics were concerned about *backdoor spending,* which created financial obligations without going through the appropriations process. An agency might be given authority to sign a contract for the purchase of services or supplies or to borrow money that must be repaid later. A loan guarantee might be offered to financial institutions that make loans for a specific purpose, such as financing a college education. The loan guarantee obligates the federal government to compensate those financial institutions for any losses that they incur from participating in the program. Tax expenditures (deductions, tax credits, and exclusions from taxable income) have the same economic effect as spending revenues from the Treasury but do not go through the appropriations process.

Budget Reforms Congress responded to these concerns by reforming the budget process in several ways.[3] *The Congressional Budget and Impoundment*

Control Act created three new organizations in Congress. The Congressional Budget Office, a staff agency, was created to analyze the condition of the economy, forecast future revenues and program costs, and evaluate the effectiveness of federal programs. The office was created, in part, because many members of Congress felt that they could not trust the budgetary and economic analyses provided by the White House. Some reformers also believed that expert budgetary advice would help Congress make better decisions, particularly in light of the growing complexity of the budget and the economy.

The law also created two new committees, the House Budget Committee and the Senate Budget Committee. These committees were to focus their attention on the "big picture" aspects of budgeting: How high should total revenues and spending be? Should we have a surplus, a deficit, or a balanced budget? How should we allocate resources across the major areas of federal government activity? The budget committees were created because of mistrust of and disagreement with the White House's budgetary recommendations and because some members felt that Congress needed to do a better job of integrating its various budgetary decisions.

The creation of new committees with responsibilities in the budgetary arena was a sensitive issue for members of the appropriations and revenue committees, especial in the House of Representatives, where committees are generally more influential than in the Senate. Many members of the House Appropriations and Ways and Means Committees saw the proposed Budget Committee as a threat to their power and influence. As a result, the House Budget Committee had two unusual features. First, no member could serve on the House Budget Committee for more than four years (later increased to six) in any 10-year period. Second, of the 25 members of the committee, five must be members of the Ways and Means Committee, and five must be members of the Appropriations Committee. Both of these provisions were designed to minimize the threat posed by the House Budget Committee to the power and influence of the Ways and Means and Appropriations Committees.

The Budget Calendar Because Congress had often failed to pass all the appropriations bills by the beginning of the fiscal year on July 1, the new law changed the budgetary calendar. The new fiscal year would begin on October 1, a date that gave Congress three additional months in which to complete action on the spending bills each year. Reformers who hoped that Congress would be able to keep on schedule with this new fiscal year were disappointed.

The Budget and Impoundment Control Act required Congress to pass a budget resolution in the spring (see Chapter 4) to guide and coordinate the decisions of the authorization, appropriations, and revenue committees. A second resolution, passed shortly before the beginning of the new fiscal year, would update those guidelines. If the second resolution did not match the authorization, appropriation, or revenue decisions (which presumably were completed by this time), Congress would pass a *reconciliation bill*. This bill could revise the resolution or make changes in the appropriations or revenue decisions. The reconciliation bill could also direct authorization committees to propose revisions in authorization legislation for mandatory (uncontrollable) spending programs.

Since the passage of the 1974 law, Congress has repeatedly tinkered with the budget calendar. The second budget resolution has been discarded, and the reconciliation bill has sometimes been passed earlier in the year. The most famous example of this practice occurred in 1981, when the Reagan administration pushed through a number of budgetary provisions in a reconciliation bill passed in July. The earlier passage was needed in order to give other committees time to develop bills carrying out the directions of the reconciliation bill before the beginning of the new fiscal year.

If Congress fails to pass an appropriations bill by the beginning of the new fiscal year, a *continuing resolution* is used to provide funding for the affected agencies and programs until an appropriation bill can be adopted. The continuing resolution may expire within a few days if enactment of the spending bill is expected soon. If more time is needed, the continuing resolution may last considerably longer—sometimes for an entire year.

Adoption of the budget did not become any easier after passage of the 1974 reforms. Several factors continued to make budgeting very difficult. The increasing mobilization of interest groups with many different priorities, the frequent division of party control between the White House and Congress, and the growing polarization of the parties all helped increase levels of political conflict over many budgetary issues. The erratic performance of the economy, beginning in the early 1970s, and slow revenue growth made accommodation of conflicting demands difficult, and the rising cost of some of the larger uncontrollable spending programs made funding other programs difficult. Growing budget deficits in the early and mid-1980s led to increasing concerns about the budget. Congress and the White House were often unable to complete action on all the spending bills before the beginning of the new fiscal year.

More Recent Budget Reforms All these difficulties led to a series of budget reforms and innovations, beginning in the mid-1980s.[4] In 1985, Congress passed the Gramm-Rudman-Hollings Act, which established a series of gradually decreasing budget deficit targets for 1986 through 1990 and a target of a balanced budget in 1991. If the budget deficit exceeded the target for the year by more than a limited amount, a process called *sequestration* would automatically trim spending according to fixed rules until the target was met. After a Supreme Court ruling struck down some features of the law and members of Congress decided that the deficit targets were unrealistic, a new bill, passed in 1987, established a slightly revised process and a new set of deficit targets, ending with a balanced budget in 1993. The early targets were officially met, in large measure, through the use of unrealistic forecasts and a variety of devices— critics called them "gimmicks" or "smoke and mirrors," such as one-time sales of government assets, that did little or nothing about the underlying deficit.

By 1990, the deficit targets established in 1987 were widely regarded as unrealistic, but concerns over the large deficits continued. Congress and the

White House responded with the *Budget Enforcement Act of 1990* (BEA). The new law included revenue increases and projected expenditure reductions. The new law incorporated somewhat more flexibility than did Gramm-Rudman-Hollings. For example, BEA excluded emergency spending from its controls; this provision led to several arguments regarding what constitutes a legitimate emergency. In addition, BEA did not try to control changes in the costs of entitlement programs if the changes were due to increased workload, as in the case of more retirees receiving Social Security benefits.

The BEA established spending limits for discretionary programs (i.e., the relatively controllable spending items), but those limits could be adjusted for inflation and changing program workloads. This provision led to numerous arguments regarding whether individual programs were actually being cut (as traditionally viewed) or were receiving spending increases that were less than predicted by the adjustment factors. The law provided separate pools of funding for defense, international aid, and domestic programs for the first three years in order to prevent supporters of those different program areas from fighting with one another over funds. Spending caps were established, subject to the adjustments noted previously. In addition, the law provided that any policy changes in revenues or "direct spending" (primarily spending that is controlled largely outside the appropriations process, such as entitlements) could not increase the deficit. Spending increases for programs covered by this provision would have to include revenue increases as well or spending reductions for other programs. Revenue reductions must be accompanied by comparable spending cuts or increases in other revenue sources.

The BEA did not create a smoothly functioning budget process, largely because it could do nothing about the political and economic pressures on the budget. One symptom of those pressures is the series of budget "summits" involving the White House and congressional leaders to hammer out budget agreements since 1990. A more dramatic symptom was the budget confrontation that occurred in the winter of 1995–96. After Congress sent President Clinton two bills with provisions that he regarded as unacceptable, he vetoed the bills. One included a number of appropriations items, and the other dealt with borrowing by the U.S. Treasury. The vetoes led to a series of meetings and confrontations, with accusations hurled in many directions. Conflicts erupted between the White House and Congress, between Democrats and Republicans, and within both parties. The intense conflicts made reaching agreement very difficult, and a lack of funding and borrowing authority led to several partial government shutdowns during the winter (Maraniss and Weisskopf, 1996: 146–205; Meyers, 1997). The disputes were eventually resolved, but the confrontation underscored the problems that are likely to arise when officials with a variety of different political beliefs are struggling to accommodate a wide range of demands in a context of rising costs for a number of major programs and difficulty in raising additional revenues.

A less noticed symptom of continuing difficulty, in the eyes of some observers, is the fact that Congress has exceeded the discretionary spending

Table 6.1 Spending Levels Approved in Congressional Budget Resolutions and Enacted in Spending Bills (Discretionary Spending Only)

FISCAL YEAR	BUDGET RESOLUTION	SPENDING BILLS	GAP
1997	$528 billion	$538 billion	$10 billion
1998	$531 billion	$533 billion	$2 billion
1999	$533 billion	$583 billion	$50 billion
2000	$540 billion	$587 billion	$47 billion
2001	$600 billion	$634 billion	$34 billion

SOURCES: Fram (2000); Pianin (2000); Senate Budget Committee.

levels outlined in its budget resolutions a number of times in recent years (see Table 6.1). In some years the difference between the resolution and approved spending has been relatively small, but for fiscal years 1999 through 2001, the gaps have ranged from $34 billion to $50 billion. Bear in mind that there may be good reasons for spending to be somewhat higher than the budget resolution provides if conditions change between adoption of the resolution in the spring and final enactment of the spending bills in the fall or later. However, some critics have charged that the recent budget resolutions have been politically unrealistic, and the development of budget surpluses may have weakened the desire to control spending (Fram, 2000; Planin, 2000).

By fiscal year 1998, a seeming miracle was accomplished: The federal government ran a modest budget surplus, after a dramatic series of budget deficits in the preceding two decades, along with smaller deficits reaching back to the late 1960s. Moreover, budget analysts projected a series of budget surpluses for future years. That prediction has led to a series of arguments regarding how best to spend the predicted surplus. At the same time, however, longer-term forecasts indicated rising costs for Social Security, Medicare, and Medicaid as the size of the elderly population increases in the next few decades. Those forecasts have triggered a series of debates regarding how best to save or reform Social Security and Medicare, although some skeptics contend that the problems have been somewhat overblown by people who are ideologically hostile to those programs.[5] Budget adoption at the national level is likely to remain a contentious task for the foreseeable future.

BUDGET ADOPTION IN THE STATES

The process of adopting a budget at the state level has changed considerably over the years, with some developments resembling the national level but with a number of distinctive state components as well.[6] In addition, budgetary adoption varies somewhat from state to state.

Major Developments

After the United States gained independence from England, state governments were relatively small operations, with few programs, limited revenues, and very modest expenses. The governors in most states had relatively limited powers, and the state legislature was generally the most powerful branch of government. As late as the early 1900s (even later in some states), the legislature was very much a part-time institution. Because of the modest workload, legislative sessions were often short—as little as 30 days in some states.

During the 1800s and 1900s, governors gradually gained power and influence, with longer terms of office, more staff assistance, stronger veto authority, and more control over state administration. Especially during the 1800s, however, many states also adopted provisions to elect other state executives, such as the attorney general and state treasurer, independently of the governor. During the 20th century, state government responsibilities expanded greatly, as did state revenues and spending. Budgeting became an increasingly complex task, and governors became more active in all phases of budgeting. More interest groups became more active in state politics (Thomas and Hrebenar, 1999), a development that produced more pressures on budgeters and more conflict.

As the work of state government grew, reformers called for reforming state legislatures in hopes of improving their capacity for dealing with complex issues, including the budget. The reformers called for holding legislative sessions every year, longer sessions, more legislative staff support, and higher legislative salaries to permit members to spend more time on the job. However, the reformers were much more successful in the more populous, wealthier states, in part because of the cost of the reforms.

Like Congress, most state legislatures assign responsibility for authorization legislation to one set of committees, appropriations bills to another committee, and revenue bills to yet another committee, although some states have one committee in each house with jurisdiction over both appropriations and revenue bills. A number of states utilize joint committees, with members from both the state house and the state senate, to coordinate budgetary decisions. Some states use a single appropriations bill to cover all agencies, but other states use several bills—a few states will pass a hundred or more.

Complications in State Budgeting

State budgetary adoption is complex in a number of respects. The average state receives several billion dollars in federal grants each year, and federal mandates may generate significant costs for state governments. As a result, state officials try to influence federal government decisions and are affected by those decisions. State governments also provide many billions of dollars in financial assistance to local governments each year and adopt mandates affecting local governments. Both circumstances encourage local officials to be involved in state budgeting and state officials to be involved in local budgeting.

State adoption has also grown more complex because of increasing emphasis on assessing the productivity and effectiveness of agency programs in most
states, although that emphasis apparently declined somewhat in the early 1990s
(Lee, 1997). As noted earlier, assessing productivity and effectiveness often trig-
gers (or makes more explicit) disputes regarding what programs should be
doing and may produce added conflict regarding whether a particular assessment is accurate.

State budgets are constrained by a variety of legal provisions that, with
varying degrees of effectiveness, limit the flexibility of decision makers. As at
the federal level, some state expenditures may be relatively uncontrollable
within the appropriations process. That may occur because state authorization
legislation or a federal mandate requires some expenditures. Also, many state
governments have created special authorities whose operations are not contained within the state budget and are, therefore, relatively immune to the
budget process. Most governors have the authority to veto individual items in
appropriations bills, and some have the power to reduce individual spending
items as well. Many state constitutions contain budgetary provisions of one or
more types: A particular revenue source may be prohibited or limited, some
budgetary decisions may require a public vote, borrowing more than a certain
amount of money may be prohibited, and a balanced budget may be required,
although that provision does not necessarily apply to the entire budget. Some
of these provisions may be undercut by various loopholes—a balanced budget
requirement may apply only to the operating budget and exclude capital projects, such as highways, bridges, and public buildings. Limits on borrowing may
only apply to full faith and credit borrowing and not to nonguaranteed debt.
Overall, studies trying to assess the impact of those various rules have produced
mixed results, but many of the studies find rather weak effects, if any.[7]

In a number of respects the legislatures' role in budgetary adoption is formidable and may have grown stronger since the 1960s.[8] Expanded legislative
staffing has given the typical legislature more expert advice on budgetary issues
and has enabled most legislatures to develop their own budgetary projections
and forecasts rather than relying on the governors' projections. A number of
legislatures increased their formal powers over allocating federal grant funds in
the 1970s. Frequent divided party control between the governorship and legislature, along with growing party polarization in a number of states, has often
made legislators less receptive to gubernatorial leadership on budgetary issues.
Most state legislatures also receive agency budget requests before the governor's
budget is prepared, and almost all states permit agencies to submit their original budget requests to the legislature at some phase in the process, along with
the governor's proposal. Agencies can, therefore, officially indicate disagreement with the governor's proposal, although that can be politically risky at
times. Independently elected state executives may feel little obligation to support the governor's budget request. Multiple, independent executive requests
give the legislature a greater opportunity to make independent decisions. All
things considered, the legislature's role in budgetary adoption is formidable in
most states.

BUDGET ADOPTION AT THE LOCAL LEVEL

Discussing budgetary adoption in local governments is a difficult enterprise in view of the great diversity among local governments in the United States.[9] Some local governments, such as cities and counties, have a wide range of responsibilities. Other local governments, primarily school districts and other special-district governments, are responsible for only one program or, at most, only a few. Some localities serve millions of residents and contain many interest groups and differing points of view. Other localities serve a small population and face fewer variations in public preferences. Local governments in wealthy areas are likely to have a comparatively easy time raising revenues, but local governments in poor areas may be unable to generate enough money to provide generous funding for any program, regardless of the preferences of citizens or officials. Some local governments, such as cities and some counties, are fairly visible to the general public and receive considerable media coverage. Other local governments, especially special districts other than school districts, are practically invisible to many citizens and the mass media. Many local governments, particularly counties and some cities, allow the political parties to formally participate in the government process, but many other local governments, including a great many special districts and a considerable number of cities, are officially nonpartisan, which usually reduces party influence.

In most localities, especially the smaller ones, the adoption phase of budgeting is organizationally and procedurally simpler than at the national or state level. Most local legislatures have only one house and far fewer members than the national or state legislatures. Many local chief executives do not have a veto, and some localities do not have a chief executive. One important exception to the simplicity tendency is that in many localities, a number of budgetary decisions require voter approval.

Many localities use a committee to make a preliminary assessment of the budget proposal. In most localities, that committee will be quite small because the typical local legislature is quite small. Membership on the committee may be limited to members of the legislature, especially in larger cities with large city councils, or the committee may include members of the legislature and some executive branch officials, such as the county treasurer.

Many local legislatures are not ideally suited to dealing with complex budgetary issues. Most local legislatures are part-time institutions whose members have full-time jobs doing something else. They have little time available for detailed exploration of the budget. Turnover on many local legislatures is fairly rapid, and many newcomers will have modest knowledge of budgetary issues. Professional staff support for the legislature is often limited, especially in smaller and poorer jurisdictions. All these considerations enhance the appeal of simplifying devices, such as incrementalism, to help members cope with the budget.

The process of budgetary adoption in many localities is heavily regulated by state laws, which may require a particular budget format, determine the types of revenue sources allowed, limit tax rates and borrowing, and require the provision of particular services. State laws may also require public hearings on the budget and require voter approval for some budgetary decisions, such as raising taxes above a certain level or borrowing more than a particular sum of money. The many state requirements may leave local officials with little flexibility in their budgetary decisions but may also help shield local officials from political conflict at times.

National government mandates also limit local discretion in budgeting. Civil rights policies, environmental regulations, and a host of other federal policies may generate substantial costs for localities. Note, too, that the typical local government is heavily reliant on state and, to a lesser degree, federal grants for financing local programs. Much of that grant money is earmarked for specific programs and cannot officially be spent for anything else, although grant funds may provide more flexibility in the long run than appears possible at first glance (see Chapter 10).

The executive branch's role in budgetary adoption varies considerably from one locality to another. Some chief executives, especially mayors in strong mayor plan cities and elected county executives, have a veto that may be used to block legislative action. Other chief executives, such as weak mayors, city managers, and appointed county executives, do not have veto powers, and some local governments, particularly many small and medium-sized counties, do not have a chief executive of any kind. Executive officials, regardless of their formal powers, are almost always active in advising and trying to influence members of the legislature. Many cities and counties have several independently elected executive officials, each of whom may have quite different preferences regarding the budget.

A major trend in local government budgeting since the early 1900s is the growing diversity of local revenue sources. The property tax, the traditional mainstay of local revenue systems, remains important for many localities, but other revenue sources have become increasingly significant. Many cities and counties and some other local governments now obtain substantial funding from income, payroll, or sales taxes, and many local governments of all types generate considerable revenue from fees and charges for specific services.

A number of localities have also copied the example of governments in earlier eras by requiring or utilizing in-kind contributions. One controversial example of this technique is used when real estate developers seek local government approval for major development projects. As a condition for granting building permits and zoning and land use plan revisions, local officials may require a developer to construct paved streets, sidewalks, streetlights, and other improvements that would otherwise be financed from the local treasury (Gosling, 1997: 188). Developers complain that paying for these improvements greatly increases their financial risk if the properties in the development sell slowly. Defenders of the practice contend that developers (and, indirectly, the residents of a new development) should pay for basic infrastructure, which will benefit them and that the requirements encourage developers to devote more attention to designs that are more economical in terms of street requirements and other infrastructure needs. Many programs make use of volunteer labor or rely on private-sector activities, such as private security guards, to reinforce public programs.

In many localities, officials do not have very much discretion in adopting a budget. State and federal laws and regulations limit local flexibility in many ways. Some local government employees are unionized; collective bargaining agreements may create multiyear financial commitments. Decisions made by previous local officials may have the same effect—for example, borrowing a large sum of money that must be repaid over the next 20 years or constructing a major facility that generates major operations and maintenance costs. Voters may refuse to approve some budgetary options, and local officials often fear that if their taxes are much higher or services much inferior to those of surrounding localities, businesses and wealthier taxpayers will gradually migrate to those other jurisdictions and undermine the local tax base (see Gosling, 1997: 186–188; Nice and Fredericksen, 1995: 226–227).

ACCOUNTING FOR ADOPTION
DECISIONS IN BUDGETING

In recent decades, a great many studies have tried to explain budgetary outcomes. A thorough review of those findings is beyond the scope of this book, but some of the major findings deserve mention. First, economic and social conditions affect many budgetary decisions. Officials in wealthier jurisdictions have an easier time raising revenues and providing generous funding for almost all programs. A larger, more complex, and more interdependent economy and the urban society that accompanies it create a greater need for government activity to manage that complexity and interdependence. Higher levels of wealth and education yield smaller families and a longer life expectancy, with the result that the relative size of the elderly population grows. A larger elderly population in turn increases the need for programs to cover the costs of old age, including health care. Although the theoretical interpretations of the relationships are a matter of some controversy, there is little doubt that social and economic development is a powerful influence on budgets.[10] We will explore the economic dynamics in more detail in Chapter 9.

Many studies also find that budgetary decisions are often shaped by the problem environment. The strength of military rivals and levels of international conflict influence defense spending. The distribution of the population, terrain, and climate shape the cost of transportation programs. A rise in the crime rate creates heavy pressure for more spending on crime control. More children going to school will create upward pressure on education spending. Budgets are not enacted in a vacuum; they are often a reaction to the problems faced by government and society.[11]

Additional evidence reveals that, contrary to common impression, budget decisions often reflect the demands, values, and preferences of large numbers of people. Where more citizens have liberal opinions or support relatively liberal

political parties, more generous funding for education and social programs typically results. Where opinions and party support follow more conservative lines,
more conservative spending patterns emerge. When the public fears that
defense spending is too low, defense spending typically rises. Although many
citizens find the budget process baffling and doubt that public officials pay any
attention at all to citizen opinions, their views do shape budgetary outcomes,
whether directly or through the parties or interest groups.[12]

Budgets are also powerfully influenced by the heavy weight of prior commitments and sunk costs. When decision makers treat many existing programs
as given, to reduce conflict, time pressures, and the information load of decision making, the vast bulk of next year's budget will be quite similar to this
year's budget. When relatively permanent statutes create entitlements, and especially if those laws index program benefits to reflect changes in the cost of living, those legal provisions will shape budgets for years to come. Many spending
programs have powerful political allies; continuation of those programs is generally (though not always) a forgone conclusion. Once long-term projects are
under way, proposals to terminate them will face the complaint that termination will mean that previous expenditures were wasted and that shutting down
the projects will generate shutdown costs as well. Officials who previously supported adoption, expansion, or continuation of current programs are typically
hesitant to cut those programs very much, partly because they believe in the
programs and partly because of fear of adverse political consequences. In a variety of respects, then, future budgetary decisions are powerfully constrained by
decisions of the past. Those previous decisions do not eliminate the possibility
of change but place powerful limits on the scope and pace of change in a great
many cases.[13]

CONCLUDING THOUGHTS

Adopting budgets has not been a very enjoyable enterprise in many jurisdictions in recent years. The heavy weight of previous commitments, mobilization
by more groups with conflicting demands, divided party control and greater
party polarization in national politics and many states, an erratic economy since
the mid-1970s, and citizen resistance to major revenue increases have combined to make budgeting a difficult and frustrating task for many officials. The
increased emphasis on assessing program results in the budget process has also
helped make adoption more controversial. At the national level, the difficulty
of passing legislation has led members of Congress to attach policy proposals
to budget-related bills, such as appropriations bills or legislation dealing with
public borrowing (Meyers, 1997: 28). As a result, conflicts over those policy
proposals, which would traditionally have been handled separately, have
become part of budgetary adoption and increased conflict.

The national government's budgetary conflicts, which have received the
most attention, have led to a number of modifications of the budget process.

Many of the modifications have, in turn, been further modified, sometimes within one or two years, and have sometimes been implemented in surprising ways. For example, a number of critics have complained that "emergency spending," which is exempt from some recent budgetary controls, has been used to fund items that are not, by most standards, emergencies ("Budget Values," 1999). Although budgeting in states and localities has received much less scrutiny, those jurisdictions appear to have budgetary problems that are approximately as serious as the national government's difficulties. Trying to reconcile conflicting demands, high expectations, and a desire for low taxes is not an easy enterprise.

NOTES

1. See Collender (1999: chaps. 1, 5); *Glossary of Terms Used in the Federal Budget Process* (1993); Schick (1995: chaps. 7, 8).

2. For discussions of the early and middle years of the national budget process, see Fenno (1966); Fisher (1975: chaps. 1, 2); Smith and Deering (1990: chap. 2); Stewart (1987, 1989); Wildavsky and Caiden (1997: chaps. 2, 3).

3. For discussions of the 1970s reforms, the events leading up to them, and subsequent events, see Duncombe and Heffron (1983: 421–433); Fisher (1985); Fisher and Joyce (1997); Havemann (1976); Kamlet and Mowry (1985); LeLoup (1988: chap. 6); Schick (1995: chap. 5).

4. See Gilmour (1992); Lee and Johnson (1998: 230–258); Thurber (1992, 1997); Wildavsky and Caiden (1997: chaps. 5, 6).

5. See *An Analysis of the President's Budgetary Proposals for Fiscal Year 2000* (1999); *The Economic and Budget Outlook: Fiscal Years 2000–2009* (1999); *The Economic and Budget Outlook: An Update* (1999); Marmor, Mashaw, and Harvey (1990: chaps. 5, 6); Skidmore (1999).

6. Axelrod (1995: 209–219); Cozzetto, Kweit, and Kweit (1995: 78–97); Duncombe and Heffron (1983: 434–447); Gosling (1997: chap. 5); Lee (1997); Rosenthal (1990: chap. 6; 1998: 306–320); Thompson (1987); Winters (1999).

7. See Mullins and Joyce (1996); Nice (1988, 1991); Winters (1999: 339–344); and the studies they cite.

8. Abney and Lauth (1998); Clarke (1998); Rosenthal (1998: 306–320).

9. Axelrod (1995: 219–220); Bland and Rubin (1997: 84–91); Cozzetto, Kweit, and Kweit (1995: 97–108); Duncombe and Heffron (1983: 447–452); Gosling (1997: chap. 6).

10. Bahl (1969); Dye (1966, 1990); Wilensky (1975).

11. Friedman (1990); Hartley and Russett (1992); Hicks and Swank (1992); Wilensky (1975).

12. Budge and Hofferbert (1990); Fenno (1966: 358–361, 393); Hicks and Swank (1992); Kiewiet and McCubbins (1991: 194–205); Nice (1985); Wright, Erikson, and McIver (1987).

13. Sharkansky (1968b: 14–15, 35–43); White (1994); Wildavsky (1974: 13–16, 216–217; 1992: 7–8).

7

Budget Execution

Modifying the Budget after It Is Adopted

Implementing the Budget: Some Nuts and Bolts

Government-Sponsored Enterprises and Budgetary Implementation

Concluding Thoughts

In 1955 the state senate in Illinois disbanded the state's Committee on
Efficiency and Economy for "reasons of efficiency and economy."

BRYSON

(1980: 13)

Public policy researchers have long known that adopting a policy may mean
little unless the policy is effectively implemented. Policy guidelines on
paper may be ignored in the field or misunderstood. The policy as originally
developed may be deficient in one or more respects, or conditions may change
after a policy is adopted; in either case revisions may be needed. New initiatives may anger some people and face political attack. Government employees,
contractors, and citizens may need time to adjust to new policies and procedures. Assuming that adoption of a policy is the end of the struggle is almost
never a safe assumption.[1]

In the budgetary arena, implementation is a critical phase of the process. As we
will see, the distinction between adoption and implementation is not always
very clear in public budgeting, for budgets may be modified significantly after
they are adopted. In addition, control mechanisms are needed to ensure that
budgetary guidelines are followed and to detect violations of those guidelines
when they occur. As with other aspects of budgeting, the execution phase has
complex political and administrative dynamics.

MODIFYING THE BUDGET
AFTER IT IS ADOPTED

Enactment of the various spending and revenue bills during the adoption phase
of budgeting does not necessarily determine the final form of the budget.
Depending on the jurisdiction, a number of devices may enable officials to
revise the budget after the regular spending and revenue bills are completed.
Although postadoption changes in government budgets are usually not very
large, relative to the overall size of the budget, changes may be large enough to
matter a great deal to individual programs. In some circumstances, larger
changes do occur. Those modifications, large or small, may be adopted for a
number of reasons.[2]

Many modifications during budgetary implementation stem from problems
in forecasting future conditions. If the economy slumps expectedly, revenues
may fall short of projections, and some program costs are likely to rise. Increased
spending or a tax cut may be needed to help stimulate a lagging economy. An
inflationary surge will increase the cost of many programs and may encourage
spending reductions or a tax increase to cool down the economy. The outbreak

of war (or its end) or any other unexpected change in the severity of a problem will substantially alter the funding needed for some programs. Given the lead time required for the development of budgetary proposals and their adoption, even the best forecasting will sometimes miss the mark.

Moreover, budgets are sometimes adopted with patently unrealistic assumptions regarding future conditions or the cost of some enterprise. Advocates of a new program may deliberately understate its likely cost in order to improve the chances for passage. Revenue projections may be manipulated in order to produce lower-than-expected predictions, perhaps to combat spending demands, strengthen the case for a revenue-enhancing proposal, or minimize the danger of a revenue shortfall (see Rogers and Joyce, 1996). Conversely, unrealistically high revenue projections may be used to enhance the appeal of a tax cut proposal, make a costly new project appear more feasible, or create the appearance of a balanced budget. Once reality sets in, if it ever does, officials will need to make adjustments. For example, one explanation for Congress appropriating considerably more money than indicated in its own budget resolutions in 1999 through 2001 is that the budget resolutions, along with the spending caps adopted in 1997, were politically unrealistic (Pianin, 2000).

Budgetary changes may also reflect changes in the political and legal environment. A newly elected president, Congress, governor, or state legislature may not be content to wait until a new fiscal year begins but instead may push through revisions in the budget currently in force in order to reflect different policy preferences. A court ruling may require additional funding for a program or alter the availability of revenues. Changing public sentiments, especially if reflected in a ballot initiative, may change program costs or the availability of revenue without regard for when the new fiscal year begins, as voters in Washington did in the fall of 1999. They voted to slash one of the main revenue sources for transportation programs and, in the process, greatly undercut a new transportation initiative that they had voted to approve a few years earlier.

Decisions by other governments may also force or encourage midyear budgetary revisions at times. A local government may adopt its budget on the basis of the best available estimates regarding the amount of state and federal aid that will be forthcoming, but those estimates may be wrong. A new state or federal mandate may generate unexpected costs, or its repeal may reduce spending pressures. If another level of government fails to deal with a problem, pressures to address that problem may shift to other levels of government. We will examine these and other intergovernmental dynamics of budgeting in more detail in Chapter 10.

Deciding whether and how much to modify a budget after it is adopted presents officials with an awkward dilemma. If they are too reluctant to revise the budget after it has been enacted, they will fail to respond to changing conditions. As a result, money may be spent needlessly, or a critical problem may grow worse. Citizens whose demands are not met will probably become angry. If officials revise the budget too often and too casually during implementation, it will lose its value as a planning guide; if our university's budget may be changed in countless ways after it is enacted, how will we know how many faculty we can afford to hire for the coming year or how many students should receive financial aid? In addition, if many people become aware that the budget can be substantially changed after adoption, political conflict may escalate as groups and officials who are unhappy with the budget as adopted begin trying to rewrite it before the ink is even dry.

Methods for changing budgets during the implementation phase fall roughly into three groups, although in practice they may sometimes overlap a bit. Note, too, that more than one method may be used at the same time, especially when more drastic changes are needed, such as when a major war breaks out.

Increasing Funding

Perhaps the most pleasant type of budgetary change, at least from the standpoint of program beneficiaries and people in the bureaucracy, is increased funding for a program or service. The need for a service, or demand for it, may escalate after the budget is adopted, or the cost of dealing with the problem may be greater than expected. Initial funding may have been unrealistically low in order to improve its chances for adoption or to give elected officials additional leverage over the agency, which must return to them for additional funds before the fiscal year ends. A new administration may want additional funding for programs that were neglected by the previous administration or for new initiatives. Two of the most important methods for making additional funding available are through supplemental appropriations and through emergency or contingency funds.

Supplemental appropriations are the better-known mechanism for providing additional funding.[3] Supplementals are normally passed through the same process that is used for passing regular spending bills. At the national and state levels, that means passage by the legislature and avoiding a veto by the chief executive. In many localities, passage by the relevant legislature (such as the city council) will often be sufficient, although cities with a strong mayor form of government present the risk of a veto as well.

The use of supplemental appropriations at the national level was limited, beginning in the mid–1980s, by concern over the federal budget deficit and by budgetary conflicts between the White House and Congress, conflicts that made passing any spending bills difficult. From 1986 through 1995, net supplementals were usually less than 1 percent of total budgetary authority, although 1991 was an important exception, largely because of the cost of warfare in the Middle East (Rubin, 1997: 233–235).

Supplemental appropriations in many states are made difficult by the part-time status of the legislature. Because supplemental appropriations must be approved by the legislature, supplementals in a number of states may require convening a special session of the legislature if it is not in session when the need for more funds arises. That is likely to upset members who are called away from their regular jobs and to generate additional expenses, for members must usually be paid extra when special sessions are called. However, states with biennial (two-year) budgets offer the opportunity for second-year supplementals when the legislature convenes for its regular session. Early in the 20th century, however, when many state legislatures normally met only every other year and often for quite short sessions, supplementals were quite likely to require a special session of the legislature.

One other difficulty with supplemental appropriations is the matter of promptness. Supplemental bills are subject to all the delays that may afflict any piece of legislation. A rapidly developing crisis may move much more quickly than the legislative process. When speed is essential, emergency or contingency funds may be more appropriate.

Emergency or contingency funds are pools of money made available to the chief executive or an individual agency or department in order to meet unforeseen expenses.[4] The money may be allocated for a fairly specific purpose, such as military research, or a broader purpose, such as foreign aid. In any case, the executive branch has some discretion in deciding what specific projects should receive funding and when. Because the money is already appropriated, it can flow as soon as a need is recognized by the appropriate executive officials.

Emergency and contingency funds are controversial at times. A key sore point is legislators' concern that the funds will be used in a manner that they do not approve, particularly if the executive branch is given more discretion in how the funds may be used and fails to consult with the legislature regarding spending decisions. Giving the executive branch too much flexibility may lead to abuses, but too little flexibility may mean the inability to respond to rapidly changing conditions.

Two other types of financial reserves deserve mention. Most states and some local governments have *rainy day funds,* which are pools of money set aside for recessions or other financial difficulties. These funds are not initially allocated to any programs but are held centrally. If a recession causes a major drop in revenues, officials may dip into the rainy day fund instead of reducing expenditures or raising taxes, although a major recession may exhaust the rainy day fund and require painful medicine anyway (Sobel and Holcombe, 1996).

Some reserve funds may also be held back by the central budget office or at the departmental or agency level. Because running out of money before the end of the fiscal year may anger the chief executive and members of the legislature, holding back some reserves provides a cushion against unexpected expenses. There is, however, a complication. If the agency or department has a significant amount of money left over at the end of the fiscal year, the budget authority for that money may expire. Consequently, the agency loses the funds. Even worse, the chief executive and legislature may conclude that the agency received more money than it really needed (why else would it have money left over at the end of the year?) and cut agency funding for future years. As a result, agency personnel may hurriedly spend the remaining funds shortly before the end of the fiscal year. This last-minute rush of spending may upset officials at times, partly because of concerns that some of the money may be spent hastily and carelessly. That concern is sometimes valid, but agency personnel may also have made careful preparations for the year-end spending, in which case the year-end surge is no cause for concern (*Year-End Spending,* 1998). Officials might have postponed purchasing needed equipment or supplies until near the end of the fiscal year, for example, in order to make certain that adequate funds remained after other financial commitments had been met.

Cutting the Budget

A much less pleasant group of techniques for revising the budget, at least from the standpoints of program beneficiaries and public employees, is used to reduce funding during budget execution.[5] Funding reductions may be needed because of revenue shortfalls, changing political pressures, or increased financial needs of other programs, but funding reductions may also be used to cool down an overheated economy or stem from project delays.

One of the better-known and more controversial methods for reducing spending is the *rescission,* a permanent type of impoundment (see Chapter 6). At the national level, both the president and Congress have the authority to propose rescissions (permanent cuts in spending authority). Under the terms of the Congressional Budget and Impoundment Control Act, proposed rescissions must be approved by both houses of Congress in order to take effect.

Since adoption of the law, Congress has generally rejected most presidential proposals to rescind funding, but presidential efforts and success have varied greatly from year to year. In 1981, President Reagan proposed more than $15 billion in rescissions, and Congress approved more than $10 billion of his proposed cuts. In 1988 he proposed no rescissions at all. From 1974 through 1984, just under half the dollar reductions that presidents proposed for rescission were approved by Congress, but the presidential success rate declined to less than 20 percent from 1985 through 1997. In most years, more dollar savings result from rescissions proposed by Congress than from presidential proposals, although some congressional initiatives are reactions to presidential proposals. Total annual savings from rescissions averaged approximately $5 billion from 1974 through 1997 (not including rescissions of indefinite amounts), a tiny fraction of total federal spending. Savings varied greatly from year to year, ranging from a high of $19.7 billion in fiscal year 1995, a reflection of the Republican takeover of Congress, to a low of $148 million in fiscal year 1976 (Comptroller General, 1998; Havens, 1992). Note, however, that rescinded funding for one year may be restored in some future year or even in the same year by a later supplemental appropriation.

Rescissions may provoke considerable conflict between the White House and Congress if the two branches disagree regarding which rescissions, if any, are needed. Agency personnel and program beneficiaries may also become upset if their programs are targeted for cuts.

Most governors have a somewhat similar authority to reduce spending in one fashion or another, but provisions vary considerably from state to state. Fifteen states give the governor fairly broad authority to reduce spending, at least for executive branch agencies, although this power may be limited to times when a revenue shortfall occurs. Several other states require that cuts by the governor be across the board rather than targeted to specific agencies or programs. A few states require consultation with the legislature when cuts are needed, and several states limit the magnitude of the cuts that a governor may impose. Some states require legislative approval for cuts, and a few states do not appear to have clear legal guidelines regarding the governor's authority. Even if the governor has fairly broad authority to reduce spending, consultation with the legislature or even seeking legislative approval may be politically safer when painful cuts are needed. Traditional practices may also limit the governor's use of formal authority to impose spending cuts. Most states also permit the legislature to adopt spending reductions (*Legislative Authority over the Enacted Budget,* 1992: 36–47).

State and national practices regarding rescissions/spending reductions differ, in part, because Congress is in session virtually all year, whereas many state legislatures are in session for only part of the year. Requiring full legislative approval for spending reductions would, in a number of states, mean calling a special session of the legislature every time a spending cut was needed. Local legislatures normally meet periodically all year long, so obtaining legislative approval for local budgetary reductions does not normally pose scheduling problems.

Another method for cutting spending, sometimes indirectly, involves the use of *administrative controls* to block spending or actions that will produce expenses.[6] These controls, which we will discuss in more detail shortly, vary from one jurisdiction to another and take many forms. For example, a hiring freeze imposed by the state budget office or the city manager will produce savings in salary and fringe benefit outlays. Out-of-state travel may be curtailed, or purchases of new equipment may be prohibited for a time. Agencies may be denied approval to enter into new contracts that would cost money. The imposition of these controls may be based on specific legislation or on discretionary authority granted to the chief executive or other administrative officials. The reductions that result may be relatively permanent or temporary, depending on circumstances.

One virtue of these administrative controls is that they can often be employed quickly, especially if new legislation is not needed. They can often be employed on a selective basis, as well, in order to minimize the hardship and difficulty that would otherwise result. A hiring freeze might permit exceptions when an especially important position is vacant; during a freeze on purchases of new equipment, an agency might be allowed to replace a particularly vital piece of equipment that had failed.

Administrative controls to reduce spending can provoke controversy in a number of cases. If the controls are employed very rigidly, agencies with higher rates of employee turnover or a rapidly expanding workload will be hurt more by a hiring freeze than will agencies with less turnover or a stable workload. Banning purchases of new equipment will create much more difficulty for agencies with old, obsolete equipment than for agencies that have recently modernized. A freeze on new contracts will produce little hardship for an agency that does its own work in-house but considerable hardship for an agency that relies heavily on outside contractors. Conversely, granting exceptions may provoke complaints of preferential treatment from agencies that do not receive any of them.

Administrative controls that are imposed without specific legislative guidance or consultation may also produce complaints that the executive branch is undermining legislative control over the budget. If the legislature approves funding for 150 new highway patrol officers and the governor then imposes a hiring freeze, the legislature's action is thwarted, at least for a time. Legislation to modernize an agency's computer system will be blunted by a ban on purchases of new equipment.

Because administrative controls often receive little publicity, using them to reduce spending may also reduce the budget's value in promoting democratic accountability. People may believe that funding for education or some other program has been increased by 12 percent or that the mayor and city council have agreed to put 25 more police officers on the street, but administrative controls may wipe out some or all of the increases without many people hearing about them.

A number of techniques, including but not limited to administrative controls, are used to delay expenditures at times.[7] At the national level, *deferrals* are used to postpone spending. Under current law, the president can defer spending only to provide for contingencies or because of relatively routine management considerations, such as savings resulting from more efficient program operations or a project falling behind schedule. Presidents cannot defer spending simply because they dislike a particular program (see Schick, 1995: 173, 175). A deferral expires at the end of the fiscal year, but a new deferral may further delay that funding.

Administrative controls can be used to postpone spending in a number of ways. Freezes on hiring, equipment purchases, or other activities may be imposed for a time and then lifted, with agencies then being allowed to fill vacant positions or otherwise compensate for past delays. Legislation may be adopted to do the same things. The national government has periodically adopted "stretch-outs" that implement a project more gradually than originally planned (Wildavsky and Caiden, 1997: 245–249). Legislation providing that the Defense Department will buy 25 fighter planes per year for four years may be revised to allow purchasing 20 fighters per year for five years. The stretch-out reduces the expenditure per year but does not reduce the total cost of the project. In fact, stretch-outs may sometimes lead to higher total costs if altering the procurement schedule raises costs for the contractor.

Processing administrative approvals more slowly can also serve to delay spending. Necessary paperwork can sit on a desk for an extended period, or supplementary information may be demanded. Approval requests may be sent back to the agency because of minor errors, which must be corrected before the approval can be processed. Agencies may be denied permission to begin recruitment of a replacement worker until the position is actually vacant instead of letting a job search begin as soon as a current worker makes plans to retire or resign.

Postponing expenditures can be risky in a number of circumstances. Skimping on maintenance may produce short-run savings but lasting damage to equipment or facilities. Postponing contributions to pension funds may mean a financial crisis later. If a position must be vacant before the search for a replacement can begin, several departures at approximately the same time may leave an agency shorthanded for several months. Delaying purchases from contractors may cause strained relationships and financial hardship for contractors, particularly those that are heavily dependent on government business (*Budget Issues: Capping of Outlays Is Ineffective for Controlling Expenditures,* 1990: 10–11). Agency morale may suffer if promised funding is delayed, and public services may suffer as well.

Reallocating Funds

Budgets may be modified during the implementation phase by reallocating funds from one activity or use to another without changing the total size of the budget. That reallocation may be desirable because of changing needs, new priorities, or cost savings in one area that free up funds that can be suitably used for some other purpose. Two of the main methods for shifting money from one area of the budget to another are reprogramming and transfers between appropriations accounts.

Reprogramming involves moving funds from one use to another within the same appropriations account.[8] Appropriations accounts are legally defined by appropriations bills and can vary over time as well as from one department to another (see *Compendium of Budget Accounts,* 1997). If a department has relatively few large appropriations accounts, reprogramming may produce substantial changes in the budget during the implementation phase. Conversely, if a department has many small appropriations accounts, opportunities for reprogramming will be rather limited.

The rules governing reprogramming vary from one jurisdiction to the next, but it is usually regulated in one fashion or another. For example, the chief executive or a department head may be allowed to reprogram funds, but only with the approval of the central budget office and/or a legislative committee. Less strictly, the official seeking to reprogram funds may be required to give the central budget office or legislative committee advance notice of the planned reallocation or to consult with them; permission may not be needed, but the office or committee will at least have an opportunity to express objections. Those objections may not be legally binding but would be risky to ignore.

Reprogramming may also be subject to a variety of limitations, both formal and informal. A department may not be allowed to reprogram more than a certain percentage of the funds in an appropriations account. Reprogramming for certain purposes, such as starting new programs or hiring additional, permanent personnel, may be prohibited. Overly aggressive use of reprogramming may lead to the legislature revising future appropriations bills to give a department more but smaller appropriations accounts, a response that will greatly reduce future opportunities for reprogramming. Agency personnel may also be concerned that shifting money away from an activity or type of purchase may create the impression that it was too generously funded originally, an impression that may lead to funding cuts for that activity in future years (Lyden and Lindenberg, 1983: 138).

Transfers between appropriations accounts provide additional opportunities for reallocating funds after the budget is adopted.[9] Generally speaking, transfers between accounts are more heavily regulated than is reprogramming, in part because transfers may produce more far-reaching changes in the budget.

Transfers between departments are usually not allowed, although a limited number of states permit interdepartmental transfers. Transfers often require some form of legislative approval; at the state level that may involve the entire legislature or a legislative committee. The central budget office may also have the power to approve or disapprove transfers. Transfers may be subject to other limitations as well. The amount or proportion of funds that can be transferred may be capped, and transfers from some accounts may be prohibited, as may using transfers to start new programs. Transfers from one program to another are sometimes more heavily regulated than are transfers within the same program and may require passage of new legislation in some jurisdictions.

Reprogramming and transfers, at their best, offer flexibility to permit adjusting the budget to reflect changing needs or political preferences. These revisions rarely receive much media coverage, however; extensive use of them may yield a budget that is considerably different than the public believed was adopted. In addition, aggressive use of reprogramming and transfers risks angering members of the legislative branch if they begin to suspect that legislative preferences are being undercut by postadoption changes. That anger may lead to adoption of more restrictions that limit agency flexibility, sometimes to the point that adaptability to changing circumstances is hampered. That, in turn, may produce pressures to give agencies more flexibility again, which may then lead to more complaints regarding agency abuses (Rubin, 1997: 260–269).

IMPLEMENTING THE BUDGET: SOME NUTS AND BOLTS

Even if the budget is not changed during the implementation phase, this part of the budgetary process is critically important. Without adequate control mechanisms, agencies might spend more money than has been appropriated for them or fail to spend money that has been appropriated. Funds might be spent for different purposes than originally approved. Agencies might spend money too quickly, with the result that they run out of funds before the fiscal year ends. Needed funds may be embezzled, as apparently happened recently at a university in Kentucky ("Across the USA," 2000). Officials use a variety of control mechanisms in order to minimize the occurrence of those problems.

Apportionment and Allotment

After the budget has been adopted, the *apportionment* process calls for agencies to submit detailed spending plans that will specify what activities will be conducted, timetables for various actions, and various supporting information, such as evidence of need for some action.[10] The amounts and types of information required vary from one jurisdiction to another and may vary from agency to agency. In some cases this may be simply a more detailed, updated version of materials submitted with the agency's budget request. In budgeting systems that are more top-down oriented, however, much of this material may be new.

These plans will usually be reviewed at the departmental level and then by the central budget office. At either stage, revisions may be requested because of changing conditions, a need for more detail, or concerns that the plans do not adequately correspond to departmental or legislative/chief executive policies. The plans that are reviewed at the departmental level may be more detailed than the plans reviewed by the central budget office.

Some agencies are likely to receive closer scrutiny than others during the reviews of agency plans. Agencies with a history of problems are likely to receive more attention, as are agencies embarking on major new initiatives. The central budget office and political appointees at the departmental level may pay especially close attention to programs that are disliked by the chief executive or that are major initiatives of the chief executive. As with other aspects of budgeting, this phase gives more attention in recent years to goals, productivity, and program effectiveness than was the case with more traditional budgeting, with its emphasis on objects of expenditure.

After the spending plans are approved, the central budget office makes funds available to departments, often on a quarterly or monthly basis. That is done (rather than making an entire year's worth of funds available) for a number of reasons. First, officials in the central budget office may worry that some agencies might spend their money too quickly and then be short of funds for the last several months of the fiscal year. Second, the central budget office usually does not have sufficient funds available to give agencies all their appropriation at the beginning of the fiscal year. Revenues from many sources trickle in all through the year rather than arriving at the beginning of the fiscal year. Third, distributing money on a monthly or quarterly basis gives the budget office some leverage to require updates, progress reports, and other information on agency activities throughout the year. In the event of a revenue shortfall, trimming back funds still held by the central budget office may be marginally easier than trimming funds already distributed to agencies. Finally, when surplus revenues are available, retaining them centrally may permit the jurisdiction to invest them more economically than if surplus funds were dispersed in proportionally small amounts to many different agencies.

The form of apportionments depends in large measure on the form of the appropriations bills. If the appropriations bill follows a lump sum format, funds will often be apportioned in the same way. On the other hand, if the spending bill has detailed line items or pools of money earmarked for specific programs, funds are likely to be apportioned in separate line items or programs (Axelrod, 1995: 223–224).

After funds are apportioned to individual departments, each department in turn *allots* funds to individual agencies. Here, too, allotments often follow the form of the appropriations bills, although exceptions do occur. Units within the bureaucracy may sometimes divide funds within an account for their own record-keeping purposes and/or because one account supports several different programs or activities (see *Forest Service Management,* 1998). Even after funds have been allotted to individual agencies, however, they are not necessarily free to spend the money. A number of other control devices and monitoring systems further regulate budgetary implementation.

Preaudits

Preaudits are a relatively routine process of monitoring agency's financial activities for the purpose of ensuring that pending actions are consistent with the budget. In larger[11] jurisdictions, preaudits are usually conducted primarily by departments to monitor their own operations. In smaller jurisdictions, a central office may conduct preaudits for all departments. Preaudits seek to prevent inappropriate spending before it occurs.

Preaudits, especially by the central budget office, are not necessarily comprehensive in their coverage. They may be targeted to particularly large expenditures and/or programs or agencies with a history of financial difficulty. In addition, a sample of other financial actions, such as purchase orders, may be reviewed periodically in order to check for possible problems. Preaudits conducted internally by a department are more likely to be relatively comprehensive in coverage, but truly complete coverage is difficult to achieve. Less complete coverage increases the risk of some actions slipping through the net, as occurred recently in King County, Washington, which spent $40 million more than was authorized in its budget. This was, however, a small fraction of the total county budget for the year ("Audit Shows King County, overspent by $40 million" 2000).

Preaudits may examine a number of different aspects of financial transactions. Are proper procedures being followed in making a financial decision? Are adequate records being kept? Is the expenditure consistent with budgetary guidelines and legal requirements? Are the proposed actions consistent with current policy goals?

Prior Approvals

As noted earlier, some expenditures, particularly large ones, may also require prior approval by one or more officials. Some approvals are internal, with the head of a department or a departmental office providing permission. Responsibility for other approvals may be placed in the chief executive, the central budget office, or the legislative branch. Major projects may require approvals by several offices or separate approvals for different stages of the project. Not all those approvals may be from budgetary officials; the personnel office may need to approve hiring decisions, and projects with environmental implications may require approval of whatever agency is in charge of assessing the environmental impact of projects.

Monitoring and Updating

Successful implementation of the budget requires ongoing efforts to keep track of revenues and expenditures. Because forecasts are sometimes inaccurate, unforeseen circumstances may alter revenues and/or program needs or costs. Agency personnel may spend more (or less) than the budget provides. Projects may fall behind schedule or proceed ahead of schedule. All these developments may call for modifications of the budget as it is being implemented as well as modifications in budgets for future years. Officials are unlikely to know what to do in these situations unless they have timely and accurate information regarding these developments.

Because of these concerns, jurisdictions compile ongoing records of revenue levels and agency expenditures.[12] These will typically be compiled on a monthly or quarterly basis, although some governments try more frequent updates. In addition, forecasts of future revenues and expenses are also revised regularly. Depending on the jurisdiction, these reports will be circulated to the chief executive, legislators, officials in the central budget office, and agency personnel. In larger jurisdictions this updating is an immense task and has been made considerably easier by the growing use of computers for this as well as other budgetary chores (see Lee, 1997).

This ongoing monitoring enables officials to detect when agencies diverge from authorized spending guidelines or revenues begin to fall short of or exceed expectations. Their awareness of a problem does not guarantee that officials will agree on a suitable response, but timely information increases the likelihood that adjustments can be made in a timely fashion. More frequent updates will permit a quicker response to new developments, but beyond some point, doing updates more and more frequently (daily? hourly?) may require more time and effort than is justified by the added information.

An Anticipated Control: The Postaudit

After agency expenditures have taken place, they are subject to review by departmental personnel, the central budget office, agents of the legislature, and sometimes other personnel as well, including private auditors in some cases. These postaudits may occur on a variety of schedules, from shortly after an expenditure occurs to years later. We will examine auditing in more detail in the next chapter. For present purposes, postaudits are a significant influence on budgetary implementation. The knowledge that the agency's financial operations will be reviewed later is a strong check on financial misconduct, particularly if officials expect the review to be thorough and rigorous.

GOVERNMENT-SPONSORED ENTERPRISES
AND BUDGETARY IMPLEMENTATION

Government-sponsored enterprises (GSEs) are a major complication for budgetary implementation in many governments. GSEs are somewhat autonomous corporate bodies created by government but outside most of the conventional government controls and processes. GSEs typically have their own sources of revenue, although they often receive subsidies from other governments as well. They are usually controlled by a governing board, which may include private citizens as well as government officials, and ownership of the GSE may be partially private. GSEs are often excluded, at least in part, from the budget of the government that created them and are often exempt from many of the controls applied to other government agencies. There are thousands of GSEs in the United States, and their financial activities each year amount to many billions of dollars.[13]

GSEs are created for many reasons. They may provide operational flexibility that conventional agencies lack and may have some insulation from political influences. To the degree that GSEs are off budget, they make the official budget appear smaller and may, therefore, help officials circumvent limits on government revenues, spending, or borrowing. Moving some activities out of the official budget may help reduce its complexity and conflict. GSEs are sometimes used to bridge jurisdictional boundaries, particularly at the local level.

GSEs may complicate budgetary implementation in several ways. The flexibility of their operations may make their actions difficult to predict; unexpected actions may create financial difficulties for other governments, who may find that their project time tables are disrupted. If some agency operations are linked to the activities of GSEs, lengthy negotiations may be needed to allow programs to proceed. GSE projects may create added work for other agencies, and a GSE in financial difficulties may seek financial help from one or more governments and, in the process, draw money away from other agencies. To the degree that GSE operations are exempt from normal government monitoring, efforts to gauge how much money is being taken from the economy and put into the economy by government operations will be impaired.

CONCLUDING THOUGHTS

Budgets can be modified significantly during the implementation phase. Those modifications can permit a faster response to changing circumstances than would be possible were policy makers to wait until a new budget was adopted. The modifications also provoke considerable conflict at times, and the low visibility of most of the modification techniques means that extensive use of them may undercut the budget's value in promoting accountability to the public and sometimes evokes fears that the executive branch is circum-venting legislative control over the budget.

The implementation process involves a great many participants and a con-siderable number of organizations. Although the large number of participants produces some duplication of effort, that duplication can be beneficial at times. One official may overlook a problem that is noticed by another. An official who is dishonest or inept may be caught by another official reviewing his or her activities. When large sums of money are at stake, having multiple watch-dogs is a useful safeguard (see Lynch, 1995: 226–227).

Budgetary implementation, as with other phases of budgeting, has come to place increasing emphasis on policies, programs, and impact on public prob-lems rather than the traditional emphasis on controlling items of expenditure. Concerns regarding those individual items have not disappeared, but their rel-ative importance has declined as more jurisdictions have tried to use the budget as a more explicit instrument of policy guidance and evaluation. This change has meant more monitoring of agency activities and achievements dur-ing the implementation process and more concern for the policy and service impact of budgetary changes (Hendrick and Forrester, 1999).

Budgetary implementation also varies in terms of the extent and depth of scrutiny given to individual agencies and programs. An agency with a history of financial problems or a major new program may be given considerably more scrutiny than an agency with few previous problems and long-established pro-grams. An administrator with a reputation for a solid command of budgetary mat-ters, responsiveness to elected officials and the central budget office, and careful adherence to rules and policies may be given more discretion than an administra-tor whose reputation is less impressive. Note, too, that problems in one or a few agencies may lead to stricter controls on all, sometimes to the point that needed flexibility is lost and triggering complaints that too much time and energy are being consumed by paperwork, inspections, and red tape generally. That situation will eventually lead to calls for loosening the controls again, which may set the stage for further problems (Axelrod, 1995: 232–234; Rubin, 1997: 260–275).

NOTES

1. For general works on policy implementation, see Edwards (1980); Mazmanian and Sabatier (1983); Nakamura and Smallwood (1980); O'Toole (1999); Pressman and Wildavsky (1979). For overviews of budgetary implementation, see Axelrod (1995: chap. 9); Bland and Rubin (1997: 145–154); Hale and Douglas (1977); Hendrick and Forrester (1999);
Lee and Johnson (1998: chap. 10); Rubin (1997: chaps. 7, 8).

2. Fisher (1975: 76); Gosling (1997: 206); Rubin (1997: 223–227).

3. Lyden and Lindenbert (1983: 141); Rubin (1997: 231–238); Schick (1995: 130–131, 166).

4. Bland and Rubin (1997: 54–55, 152–154); Fisher (1975: 66–71); Sobel and Holcombe (1996).

5. Fisher (1975: chaps. 7, 8; 1997: 204–207); Gosling (1997: 208–212); *Legislative Authority over the Enacted Budget* (1992: 35–47); Schick (1995: 173–175).

6. Axelrod (1995: 235–236).

7. Axelrod (1995: 229); Schick (1995: 173–175); Wildavsky and Caiden (1997: 245).

8. Axelrod (1995: 235); Fisher (1975: chap. 4).

9. Fisher (1975: chap. 5); *Legislative Authority over the Enacted Budget* (1992: 25–35); LeLoup (1988: 231–232).

10. Hendrick and Forrester (1999: 570–571); Reed and Swain (1997: 172–174); Steiss (1989: 153–154).

11. Axelrod (1995: 237–239); Gosling (1997: 216–217).

12. Axelrod (1995: 227–228); Hay (1980: 122–124); Lynch (1995: 227–228).

13. *Government Sponsored Enterprises* (1990).

8

8

Financial Management

Capital Budgeting

Techniques of Capital Budgeting

Problematic Aspects of Capital Budgeting

Auditing and Accounting

Debt Administration

Cash Management

Some General Guidelines for Money Management

Concluding Thoughts

Always live within your income, even if you have to borrow money to do so.

JOSH BILLINGS, AMERICAN HUMORIST

(Quoted In Goldberg, 1994: 151)

Although financial management is not one of the most visible aspects of public budgeting, at least most of the time, sound management of financial resources is a critically important part of budgeting. Moreover, financial management is sometimes woefully misunderstood by many people, a crucial problem if budgeting is to provide accountability to the public.

In this chapter, we will explore the major facets of financial administration, broadly conceived. We will examine capital budgeting, auditing and accounting, debt administration, and cash management. If these critical budgetary tasks are not performed well, a budgetary process that appears to perform well in all other respects is likely to encounter great difficulties.

CAPITAL BUDGETING

Virtually all governments must occasionally make decisions regarding major projects that will be very expensive and that are expected to last and to produce benefits for a considerable number of years. Depending on the level of government, those projects might include highways, airports, dams, office buildings, schools, hospitals, and/or major defense installations. These types of decisions are involved in capital budgeting, and many observers believe that it presents special complications for decision makers.[1]

One important complication presented by capital budgeting, especially in smaller and poorer jurisdictions, is due to the fact that capital projects are typically very expensive. As a result, many jurisdictions will be unable to undertake very many of them at the same time. Some process will be needed to decide which projects should be first priority this year, which projects can wait for one or more years, and which projects should be postponed into the distant future or rejected entirely.

Note that this problem is not entirely unique to capital budgeting. Budgeting virtually always involves the need to set priorities among possible activities and projects, for there is virtually never enough money to do everything that everyone wants.

Because capital projects are expected to produce significant benefits for an extended period—in some cases, 30 years or longer—other distinctive dynamics come into play. Accurate forecasting over an extended time period is crucial if officials are to make sensible decisions regarding capital projects, and forecasting is typically more difficult as we try to cover longer time spans. Faulty forecasting may mean major expenditures for a project that is not actually needed or is more extensive than needed, or officials may fail to create a facility that is adequate to meet future needs. A new highway bridge or free-way built in an area of expected traffic growth may be a waste of money if the expected growth fails to materialize. The failure to expand the city water purification system may mean water shortages and the lost opportunity to attract new manufacturing industries if later population growth exceeds the system's capacity.

The difficulty of making accurate, long-term forecasts in capital budgeting is further complicated by the possibility that the capital project may affect future conditions that officials are trying to forecast in order to assess the need for the project. Improvements in the freeway system may encourage more people to drive and more businesses to locate near the freeway. A new hydroelectric dam may attract new industries that use large amounts of electricity. Assessing future reactions to the different environment is often a tricky business; how many people would use a mass transit system where none currently exists? Would a new, more attractive city hall make downtown merchants more willing to keep their businesses downtown?

The high cost of capital projects, coupled with the fact that they produce benefits over many years, enhances the appeal of financing them by borrowing and paying back the loan over a period of many years, in part to enable (and/or require) the people who benefit from a facility to help pay for it. If city officials save money from city government revenues for 20 years in order to raise enough money to construct a major bridge, many people who helped pay for the bridge will die or move away before the bridge is finished; they will have paid but received no benefit. By contrast, if city officials borrow the money to build the bridge and then pay off the loan after the bridge is built, the taxpayers who are paying off the loan can also enjoy use of the bridge. An even closer link between benefits and costs can be made if the project produces much of the revenue for repaying the loan, as in the case of a toll bridge.

According to some observers, capital budgeting is also distinctive because capital projects, although durable, will eventually wear out or become obsolete. A highway eventually develops cracks and potholes; the climate control system of a school gradually ages and requires more and more costly maintenance. Beyond some point, the cost of maintaining aging structures and facilities may exceed the cost of new ones, and neglected maintenance today can mean higher costs tomorrow. A state-of-the-art computer becomes an antique in a few years; a bridge, airport, sewage treatment plant, or school may eventually be too small to handle the workload. Consequently, budgeters need to consider *depreciation,* the declining value of facilities, in assessing program needs and in making future decisions. Unfortunately, that consideration is often neglected in public budgeting.

Estimating depreciation is a tricky business for a number of reasons. Officials may not know the effective operating life of a capital asset in advance; a new freeway expected to last for 40 years may begin falling apart after 20 years. Major population growth may render a bridge that is structurally sound totally inadequate for handling rush hour traffic. Higher pollution standards may make a sewage treatment plant obsolete much sooner than expected. Renovations

**Table 8.1 Useful Operating Life
and Depreciation of Capital Investments**

USEFUL OPERATING LIFE	ANNUAL DEPRECIATION OF AN ASSET WORTH $100 MILLION
5 years	$20 million
10 years	$10 million
20 years	$5 million
30 years	$3.3 million

NOTE: Depreciation estimate does not take into account inflation or possibility that the capital asset might have some resale value when fully depreciated.

and modifications may extend the life of a facility far beyond original expectations. If officials misjudge the operating life of a facility, their estimates of depreciation may be highly inaccurate (see Table 8.1). In addition, inflation may increase the value of a facility and so increase the amount of depreciation that occurs each year. A facility worth $100 million and lasting 10 years will lose approximately one-tenth of its value per year—about $10 million. However, if inflation increases the value of the facility to $200 million over time, it will lose $20 million in value per year—a key concern if officials want to gauge replacement costs in the depreciation process. Note, too, that a depreciated asset may sometimes have resale value. A fire engine that is obsolete for fighting fires in high-rise buildings may still be perfectly adequate for a smaller community with no tall buildings. The failure to consider depreciation may mean that a program is quietly accumulating financial needs that catch everyone off guard when obsolete facilities or equipment need to be replaced.

Special consideration of capital projects may also be necessary because those projects may affect the operation of other programs and may influence future development of the society. A new local government office building will probably house personnel working in a variety of agencies. If the building is poorly designed, people in those agencies may be less able to do their jobs. A new mainframe computer system or computer network may serve a number of different offices; flaws in the system may hamper the performance of several agencies. More broadly, improvements in infrastructure, such as the transportation system, water and sanitation systems, and power supply may make an area more attractive to new businesses and stimulate economic growth (see Dye, 1990: 170–171) and more generally affect the quality of life. Inadequacies in those systems may have the opposite effect. Better freeways may encourage more people to drive and encourage movement to the suburbs. The condition of schools may affect an area's ability to attract and retain mobile residents.

Capital budgeting, at its best, may help produce better budgetary decisions in several ways. First, capital budgeting may help link the cost of a program and its benefits. This linkage helps reduce the risk of starting projects that are not worthwhile and may promote fairness of a sort by having people who benefit from a project help pay for it. Capital budgeting may also provide a more realistic perspective on project costs. For example, a facility costing $10 million may seem terribly expensive, but if it will produce benefits for 30 or 50 years, the cost may seem less appalling. Conversely, a facility that will cost $10 million to build but will also cost a great deal to maintain in usable condition over the next 40 years may seem less appealing than it did at first glance.

Especially in smaller jurisdictions, capital budgeting can also help reduce the risk of major peaks and valleys in government costs and, therefore, tax rates. By scheduling projects in sequence rather than in large bunches and by financing them over a number of years, capital budgeting reduces the risk that officials will be forced to adopt major tax increases, an action that risks angering the public. Finally, careful use of capital budgeting techniques can reduce the danger of costly mistakes that could damage the operation of any number of public programs and harm the economy and overall quality of life as well.

TECHNIQUES OF CAPITAL BUDGETING

Capital budgeting can be carried out in a number of different ways, but several components exist in many capital budgeting systems.[2] First, officials need to develop a preliminary long-term capital improvement plan. Second, they need careful financial analysis to guide the capital budgeting decisions. Third, officials must try to reconcile project costs, the availability of financial resources, and the priorities attached to individual projects.

The Capital Improvement Plan

Developing a capital improvement plan begins with an assessment of the locality's (or state's or nation's) long-term needs. How much population growth is expected in the next 20 years? Are new laws likely to require the county to make public facilities more accessible to people in wheelchairs? Will enough oil be available to fuel all the cars and trucks? How many school-age children will be living in the area in the future? What new programs would we like to begin? A great many future conditions may affect the workload of public facilities, and officials need a thorough canvass of the major developments.

In addition, officials need an assessment of the current condition of public facilities. This assessment will typically include a description of each facility's physical condition and also its adequacy for meeting current needs and capacity for handling additional demands.

The forecast of future conditions and the inventory of current facilities will then be used to develop a preliminary list of potential projects that appear needed for replacing decaying facilities and for replacing or upgrading facilities that are in sound condition but are or will be inadequate for future needs. Under all but the most favorable conditions, a glance at the list will reveal that it involves greater costs than the jurisdiction can afford in a brief time frame. Officials must, therefore, make some tentative decisions regarding which projects should come first, which should come somewhat later, and which should be postponed for a considerable period.

Decisions regarding the ordering of projects are usually based, in large measure, on urgency of need. A water treatment plant that is already operating at maximum capacity and unable to meet peak demand, a bridge that is structurally unsound, or a school with asbestos in the ceiling tile will normally call for prompt action. Facilities that are currently adequate but expected to fall short in one respect or another within a few years will appear less urgent but go next in line. Facilities that are likely to be adequate for a number of years go to the end of the line (although this must be reassessed periodically as conditions and projections of future conditions change).

Some complications may arise as officials try to decide which projects should be begun first. In some cases, completing one project may make another project easier; if we build the road to a new subdivision first, then moving in equipment to build sewer mains will be easier. In other cases, working on one project may damage another facility or slow work on another project in the same vicinity. If a community repaves a street and then breaks up portions of the new pavement to lay new water lines or telecommunications cable, the life expectancy of the new pavement may be shortened considerably.

Officials may also believe that their jurisdiction can finance only a certain amount of new capital spending each year. If they are unwilling or unable to finance more than $100 million annually in new capital projects, then they cannot normally begin three new projects, each costing $80 million per year, in the same year.

Financial Analysis

After officials have completed this preliminary assessment, the next stage of capital budgeting is detailed financial analysis of the various projects and the broader financial status of the government unit. Officials will need updated forecasts of future revenues, expenses, and interest rates (a critical concern for projects financed by borrowing) and an assessment of special revenue sources that might help to finance any of the proposed projects. A new bridge might be financed by toll charges if the jurisdiction is allowed to charge them and if they are politically acceptable. Some universities have updated their computer systems with the help of donations from computer companies. Officials will also need to assess their jurisdiction's current amount of debt and whether some of it is likely to be retired soon. When financial conditions are difficult— slow revenue growth, heavy ongoing expenses, and substantial existing debt— capital projects are often vulnerable to being postponed.

After the overall financial situation has been assessed, analysts must develop detailed analyses of the individual projects, including the cost of each project, its projected operating life, and the number of years recommended for financing the project. These estimates, coupled with projected interest rates, will provide a basis for calculating the total cost of the project (including interest costs) and the annual cost of each project. An office building costing a total of $10 million, including interest, and financed over 10 years will cost $1 million per year.

Analysts and officials must also develop an estimate of what the jurisdiction is likely to be able to afford to spend on capital projects each year, taking into account predicted revenues, interest rates, and the cost of ongoing programs. Note that if officials can generate additional revenues or trim the cost of ongoing projects, more money will be freed up for capital projects. Note, too, that faulty forecasts may mean that a jurisdiction embarks on more capital projects that it can readily afford or needlessly postpones some projects.

Analysts and officials may also explore alternatives to major capital projects in some cases. An effective water conservation program may extend the operating life of city water plant. Overcrowding in a county office building may be relieved by renting some additional office space from a private company or another unit of government instead of building a new building. Encouraging greater use of carpooling and public transportation may reduce traffic congestion without building a major new freeway. Alternatives that require cooperation from many citizens may encounter difficulty, however, if that cooperation fails to materilize.

Reconciliation

The third major phase of capital budgeting is reconciliation of the preliminary capital improvement plan and the analyses of costs and financial concerns. Many considerations are involved at this phase: safety concerns, legal requirements, promoting economic development, and minimizing disruptions of other programs and activities. A community with heavy summer tourist traffic will often try to avoid major street repaving projects during the peak of the tourist season if weather permits doing the work at other times. Political considerations of several types may also be at work: Projects serving vocal, well-organized groups may be given a higher priority than projects serving less active and less influential groups. Officials may also try to distribute improvements across the state or locality to minimize the danger of complaints of preferential treatment from neglected areas.

A critical part of this reconciliation process is recognition of the related costs generated by a new capital project. A new facility will often generate a variety of costs: maintenance, staffing, utilities, and equipment. Failure to consider those related costs can mean fiscal difficulties.

The capital improvement plan is never finished; it needs to be updated on a regular basis to reflect changing needs, priorities, and conditions. Unexpectedly rapid revenue growth may open the door for projects that had been postponed. A new engineering report revealing structural problems in a major bridge will make renovation or replacement of that structure a higher priority. An election may bring in new officials with different concerns and interests.

PROBLEMATIC ASPECTS
OF CAPITAL BUDGETING

According to critics, capital budgeting can create or aggravate several problems in public budgeting.[3] The tasks of developing a capital improvement plan, with its accompanying analysis, and regularly updating the plan involve a significant amount of work and can generate additional budgetary conflict. Given the cost and importance of capital projects, however, the additional work and conflict may be worthwhile. Even so, officials in poorer jurisdictions may be hard-pressed to generate the financial resources needed to support rigorous analyses needed for the process. The added complexity introduced by capital budgeting may make public budgeting even more confusing for the average citizen.

In a related vein, capital budgeting may create additional opportunities for budgetary manipulation and gimmickry. Officials may try to shift some non-capital expenditures into the capital budget in order to conceal the use of borrowing or minimize the apparent size of the operating budget. During New York City's financial problems of the 1970s, city officials used the capital budget (among other techniques) to hide the city's financial problems for a time. The U.S. General Accounting Office suggests that capital assets fall into two groups: physical assets, which are publicly owned, expected to last and produce benefits for more than two years, and cost more than $25,000, and financial assets, such as loans and bonds (*Budget Issues: Capital Budgeting for the Federal Government,* 1988: 17–19). Even these guidelines are not entirely clear. If a major piece of equipment is a capital expenditure, what about the accessories or other smaller equipment that might enhance its capabilities?

Some critics also believe that capital budgeting, especially if coupled with revenue sources earmarked for capital projects, encourages a bias in favor of "bricks and mortar" projects, such as buildings, highways, and dams, at the expense of benefits for people—although this bias, if it exists, may not be due entirely to capital budgeting. Public officials may like to be able to show the public something tangible that has been created with their tax dollars. Officials also have a high degree of confidence that a capital project will remain where it is. By contrast, if we spend money educating children or upgrading the skills of county employees, they may leave, and other jurisdictions will reap the benefits. Traditionally, public projects were often used to reward political supporters; contractors who supported the governor's reelection campaign would receive contracts to build roads, buildings, and bridges.

Dealing with the capital budget and the operating budget separately may hamper efforts to deal with public programs in a comprehensive way and, consequently, produce incoherent decisions, especially if capital projects are funded from a separate pool of money. In the late 1990s, a major university spent a considerable sum of money on a new library building; at the same time, the operating budget for the library was repeatedly cut, a process that led to staffing reductions, cutbacks in purchases of books and journals, and an inability to replace items that were lost, stolen, or worn out. The risk of inconsistency between operating and capital budget decisions may be reduced by grouping related operating and capital budget items together in the budget. Nevertheless, if operating and capital items are financed differently, officials may still treat the different items inconsistently.

Decision makers may also encounter difficulty in capital budgeting because of the need to simultaneously consider total costs and annual costs of projects. If officials overemphasize total costs and neglect annual costs, they may face problems with unexpectedly high costs in some years. The result may be a tax increase and angry voters. If officials overemphasize annual costs and neglect total costs, they may fall prey to the camel's nose and begin more projects than the jurisdiction can ultimately afford.

Overall, if capital budgeting is done poorly, officials may fail to approve needed projects and approve projects that must later be postponed or canceled; according to one study of the U.S. Department of Defense, a large majority of capital projects were either canceled or postponed over a two-year period. In some cases, changes reflected changing needs or priorities, but other changes seemed to stem from inadequate planning and faulty analysis (*Defense Budget: Capital Asset Projects Undergo Significant Change between Approval and Execution,* 1994). At its best, capital budgeting can help officials focus on projects that will meet vital needs and weed out projects that are of marginal value. Some reformers have called for creating a capital budget for the federal government, and several initiatives during the 1990s have encouraged use of at least some capital budgeting techniques in federal agencies (see *Executive Guide: Leading Practices in Capital Decision-Making,* 1998). Many states employ some form of capital budgeting, although practices vary from state to state (*Budget Issues: Capital Budgeting Practices in the States,* 1986).

AUDITING AND ACCOUNTING

A budget is an agreement among the various participants in the budgetary process. Without adequate safeguards, that agreement might be violated without some of the participants knowing about it. Auditing and accounting systems are used, in part, to ensure that the agreement is followed. *Accounting* refers to recording, classifying, and reporting financial transactions. *Auditing* involves reviewing records, actions, and proposed actions in order to assess agency operations (see Coe, 1989: 6, 218; Mikesell, 1995: 554, 556). As with other aspects of budgeting, the scope of auditing and accounting has increased greatly over the years. Auditing and accounting systems perform a number of tasks.[4]

Uses of Auditing and Accounting

At their most basic level, auditing and accounting compile and assess information about the financial activities of government. That information can alert officials when agency spending is outrunning budgetary targets, when projects fall behind schedule, when program guidelines are not being followed, or whether resources allocated to one activity are being diverted to some other activity without proper approval. Careful accounting or auditing can alert officials to the presence of idle, surplus resources that could be better employed in some other way.

Accounting and auditing systems, especially in recent years, may also help guide future budgetary decisions. Analysts may try to assess how much was accomplished by a program, whether a plan was followed, or whether some strategy or guideline was realistic in the first place. Patterns of errors may indicate a need for clearer guidelines, better training, or stronger financial controls. Reviews that discover inadequate agency record keeping may trigger efforts to improve documentation of agency financial activities.

Auditing and accounting systems can be used to monitor revenue and expenditure flows for a variety of purposes. Seasonal variations in sales tax revenues or welfare caseloads may change as the economy changes. Revision of the tax code or the regulations governing a major program may produce unexpected changes in revenues or program outlays. Providing early warning of those developments can permit adjustments and prevent extensive harm. Older forecasting models may lose their accuracy as conditions change; auditing and accounting systems can alert analysts and officials that new developments need to be considered.

Potential Problems

By monitoring and analyzing revenues and expenditures on an ongoing basis, problems can be detected early. This in turn may enable officials to begin corrective action early and prevent avoidable damage, although awareness of a problem does not necessarily mean that officials will be able to agree on a workable solution. The problems that may be detected take many forms.

One moderately common problem is inadequate record keeping. Agency records may not be fully clear regarding when money was spent or received, whether specific procedures were followed, or why particular courses of action were chosen rather than other options. Faulty record keeping stems from a number of causes, from a lack of time to document actions fully and losses of information (files inadvertently discarded, computer files accidently erased, or information misfiled) to deliberate efforts at concealment and inadequate guidance regarding what information needs to be recorded.

Reviews may also reveal that agencies failed to report on their activities in a timely fashion. Late reports may reflect carelessness or lack of adequate staffing, poor communication regarding deadlines, and/or the use of delaying tactics by agency personnel who may feel that reporting information late will give them more freedom to act without being sidetracked.

Audits may show that an agency did not follow proper procedures for some activities. If an agency is required to obtain prior approval before beginning major new projects, auditors will want to check whether that approval was actually obtained prior to the beginning of the project. If transfers between appropriations accounts need approval of the central budget office and/or a legislative committee, was that approval actually received?

Accounting and auditing reviewers will be on the alert for evidence of violation of budgetary guidelines. Was spending for a specific program within the limits set by the budget? Minor deviations below the limit will not normally be cause for alarm, but exceeding the limits or falling far below them will normally require an explanation, at least. Were earmarked revenues spent for appropriate purposes? If money was given with regulatory restrictions (e.g., that it could not be used to support segregated schools), were the regulations obeyed?

Some of the more spectacular but rare problems that may emerge from reviews include "ghosting" (paying an employee who never comes to work), bid rigging (if a government contract must go through a competitive bidding process, bid rigging seeks to prevent fair competition and, therefore, inflates the cost of the project), and diversion of public resources. Diversion can take many forms, from outright theft of government property to borrowing government property for private use. In the 1970s, a township official in Michigan loaned himself thousands of dollars (interest free) of township money to finance the purchase of a boat.

Reviews of agency records may also reveal problems with contract enforcement. Because governments buy many goods and services from private companies and from other governments, there are always dangers that the contractor may fail to meet the terms of the agreement. The products or work may be of substandard quality, or a contractor may fall far behind schedule. Unless contracts are carefully written and firmly enforced, government agencies may not receive full value for the public's dollars.

Some Changing Emphases

In the past several decades, the scope of accounting and auditing has expanded dramatically. As noted earlier, the most visible aspect of that expansion is the growing emphasis on assessing productivity, effectiveness, and accomplishments in addition to the more traditional concerns regarding compliance with budgetary guidelines and limitations. This change reflects the changing emphasis in budgetary formats from object-of-expenditure budgets to performance and program budgeting.

Accounting and auditing have also come to place more emphasis on early detection of problems and anticipation of problems rather than waiting until after considerable damage has already been done. The widespread use of computers in accounting and auditing has helped speed up the processing of information and made quicker detection of problems much easier.

A third important development is the growing emphasis on linking information on financial transactions, program operations, personnel, and all other aspects of agency operations into an integrated system in order to promote coordination of decisions and provide more comprehensive information to decision makers. As in the case of other reforms designed to inject more analysis into public budgeting, however, it is possible to generate more massive volumes of information than officials can comprehend. Note, too, that compiling and analyzing immense amounts of information is not cost free; people must devote considerable time and effort to the task. That may leave less time and effort for getting work done. Some information may also be politically sensitive, especially if it indicates performance problems or calls attention to activities that are controversial.

DEBT ADMINISTRATION

Many governments borrow money.[5] They borrow money when revenues fall short of expenditures, to finance capital projects, to refinance old debts that cannot be fully retired with available revenues, and to cover short-term lags between costs and the arrival of revenues. This last consideration is especially common at the local level, where property tax payments often arrive only once or twice per year but expenses continue all year long.

The National Government

For most of American history, the national government borrowed money primarily for the purposes of financing wars and coping with major recessions. Some borrowing also resulted from earmarking of federal revenues. If one agency is supported by earmarked revenues has more money than is needed for current operations, officials will normally want to invest that money in a secure manner in order to earn interest or dividends. At the same time, other agencies may find themselves short of funds. The solution: Agencies with surplus funds invest them in federal government securities, such as Treasury bills and bonds, which are very safe investments. The funds invested are then available to finance other programs.

Almost all federal debt, and all of the U.S. Treasury's debt instruments, are *full faith and credit,* which means that the federal government is legally required to redeem them at full value when they mature. This requirement makes them a very safe investment but also makes interest costs one of the relatively uncontrollable items in the federal budget. As federal budget deficits and the debt ballooned in the 1980s and early 1990s, interest costs grew to be one of the largest expenditure items in the federal budget.

State and Local Government Debt

Although the rapid growth of federal borrowing received considerable notice in the 1980s and early 1990s, state and local government borrowing has also risen considerably since the early 1970s. Contrary to the national government's use of full-faith-and-credit debt, most state and local government debt is *nonguaranteed.* That is, it has no legal claim on the issuing government's general revenues. Instead, the bonds are to be paid from the revenues from a specific

source, such as the motor fuel tax. If the revenues from that source are not sufficient to pay off the bonds, the investors may lose some of their money.

Nonguaranteed bonds must normally pay a higher interest rate than full-
faith-and-credit bonds because of the greater risk that investors may not be
paid. Nevertheless, nonguaranteed bonds are often exempt from legal limits on
state and local governments borrowing and so are appealing to state and local
officials.

The great number of local governments in the United States, coupled with
great variation in the financial resources available from one locality to another
and a history of occasional defaults on locally issued bonds, makes potential
investors interested in expert guidance regarding the riskiness of local bonds.
Two companies, Moody's and Standard and Poor's, provide ratings of municipal bond issues in order to give investors that guidance. The ratings are based
on a number of criteria, including the type of debt instrument (e.g., full faith
and credit or nonguaranteed), the financial condition of the government issuing the bonds, the debt history of that government, the condition of the local
economy, and the purposes for which the bonds are being issued ("Municipal
Finance Criteria," 1996; "The Fundamentals of Revenue Bond Analysis,"
1996). If a bond is rated as a riskier investment, the locality issuing the bond
must usually offer a higher rate of interest in order to sell the bonds. That will,
in turn, increase the cost of the projects financed by the bonds.

Local officials who fear the prospect of a riskier bond rating, with its attendant higher interest costs, may be able to avert that danger by seeking third-
party backing for the bond issue. One possible option is to seek a state credit
guarantee, which provides the guarantee of state backing for some or all of the
financial losses of investors if the local government is unable to pay off the
bonds when they mature. State guarantees come in a number of forms, but
they often require the locality to comply with a variety of state regulations and
may not cover all types of losses. Alternatively, a local government may buy
municipal bond insurance from a private firm to cover possible defaults. The
cost of the insurance is based generally on the value of the bonds at maturity
and the riskiness of the bond issue.

The interest paid on state and local bonds was traditionally treated as
exempt from federal income taxes, a feature that made those bonds attractive
to investors in higher income tax brackets. The tax exemption enabled states
and localities to pay lower interest rates on their bonds and still attract
investors. Beginning in the 1930s, state and local governments began issuing
bonds to finance private activities. Those bonds, sometimes called *industrial
development bonds,* come in several forms, but essentially the state or locality
issues the bonds and then uses the funds raised to help a private company
finance a new factory, office building, or some other facility.

Critics complained that the industrial development bonds were fundamentally unfair; some companies would have to finance construction in the private
market and pay prevailing private interest rates, but other companies would
receive, in effect, discounted credit. One provision of the 1986 Tax Reform Act
restricted the use of tax-exempt state or local bonds for private purposes.

Essentially, the law provides that if more than 5 to 10 percent of a bond issue is for private purposes, interest income from those bonds is not exempt from federal income taxes. There are some exceptions, including for construction of moderately priced housing and for infrastructure, including airports and water systems. Interest on bonds issued for public purposes remains exempt from federal income taxes.

Although the advice "Live within your income" is generally sound, borrowing is a sensible strategy for coping with temporary emergencies, such as a war or major depressions, and for financing capital investments that will produce benefits for a number of years. However, because borrowing sometimes appears to be a painless way of financing projects, at least in the short run, officials (and private individuals) must always be careful to avoid taking on too much debt. Accumulated interest costs can present serious problems in the event of a revenue slump or unexpected cost increases for major programs.

CASH MANAGEMENT

In recent years, cash management has been a subject of increasing interest in public budgeting, although some of the public discussion of cash management has been somewhat misleading. Governments may have cash on hand for a number of reasons, from running an overall budget surplus to having some revenues earmarked for specific programs that do not need all the revenue being generated at present. In addition, a project may fall behind schedule, leaving funds for its completion sitting idle.

A simple rule for cash management is that funds on hand should, when possible, be invested to produce some form of return (interest or dividends). Especially in an era when large sums of money may be in pension funds and other trust funds, significant revenues may be generated from prudent investment of funds on hand. That means fewer dollars must be taken from taxpayers. Recent complaints of "raiding" the Social Security trust funds are largely complaints regarding this practice; surplus Social Security funds are invested in U.S. government securities, which the federal government is legally obligated to repay with interest.

As with other aspects of budgeting, however, cash management involves a number of conflicting goals. Officials will normally want a secure investment—one with very low risk of financial loss. Officials also want the funds to be available when needed, including for unexpected developments. Like any other investor, officials want to receive a high rate of return on the invested funds. Finally, some investment options may be available only for large pools of money; combining modest amounts from a number of agencies or even a number of different governments may open the door to investment opportunities that offer greater returns.

Unfortunately, secure investments are likely to offer a relatively modest rate of return. Investments with a higher average yield are likely to present a greater risk of volatility and financial loss. Some investments can offer a greater return if the funds are left invested for an extended period and if the investor is flexible regarding when the money must be available—to wait out a slump in the stock market, for instance. That option may not be available in the event of an unexpected emergency.

Funds on hand may be divided into three pools, although some governments may use only one or two. First, some money is normally kept available for immediate use, typically in cash and in checking accounts. These funds are available for immediate use but generally earn little or no interest. Placing too much money in this pool will mean a loss of interest income, but placing too little money in this pool may mean an inability to pay bills on time or financial penalties when money is pulled from other pools.

Other funds that are not needed immediately but may be needed fairly soon are placed in short-term investments, which come in many forms but allow access to the invested funds in a relatively short time period without risk of financial penalty. Officials will normally avoid investments with a risk of volatility for funds that are likely to be needed soon; a major drop in the stock market means a serious financial loss for a jurisdiction if its stocks must be sold before the market rebounds.

Money that will not be needed for an extended period may be allocated for long-term investments. Pension funds to support pensions for public employees who will not be eligible for a pension for a considerable number of years, for example, or funds being accumulated for a major capital project 10 years from now may be committed to long-term investments that offer a higher rate of return (with the attendant risk of greater volatility). Officials can afford to wait out market fluctuations as long as they pay close attention to when the funds will be needed and shift the funds out of the more volatile investments as the time when the funds will be needed grows closer.[6]

The investment of funds on hand is normally not one of the more visible or exciting aspects of public budgeting, but occasionally investments become a major public issue. One of the most spectacular instances of that phenenomenon in recent years was the case of Orange County, California, in the 1990s.[7] Orange County ran in investment pool that included its own funds and funds belonging to a number of other local governments. Traditionally, most officials have been very cautious in investing public funds and avoid risky investments. However, pressures to fund public services without tax increases led officials in a number of jurisdictions to try riskier investments that offered the possibility of higher rates of return.

Orange County's treasurer managed an investment pool of approximately $7.5 billion by the early 1990s. He generated an impressive rate of return by investing much of the money in relatively volatile investments, particularly repurchase agreements (a contract selling securities and then repurchasing them at a particular date and price) and derivatives (a common type is a commitment to buy some asset, such as foreign currency or marketable bonds, at a fixed price on some future date). If he correctly anticipated which way the market would move, the investment pool would reap a significant profit.

When the market failed to move as expected, however, the pool dropped in value. Some local governments began withdrawing their money from the pool, and the investment houses that had worked with Orange County became alarmed. The state of California declined to bail out the county, and the investment pool was liquidated with a loss of $1.7 billion. Ironically, four separate audits of the investment pool shortly before the problems erupted found no serious cause for alarm. Several other state and local governments (as well as a number of private investors) also suffered substantial financial losses from risky investments in the 1990s. These problems suggest that governments should probably avoid the more volatile investment options.

SOME GENERAL GUIDELINES
FOR MONEY MANAGEMENT

Experts on money management offer a number of general guidelines for public officials.[8] The guidelines are generally simple in practice, but they sometimes raise awkward political problems.

One of the most fundamental principles is to make certain that money owed to the government is paid on time. This in turn requires that agencies make certain that people know how much they owe and when it is due. In addition, government agencies must enforce payment requirements, including pursuing people who fail to pay what they owe. That can, however, be a sensitive matter, as the public image of the Internal Revenue Service reveals. Many property tax assessors have learned that being involved in determining what people owe the government is a good way to make enemies.

Less controversial is the principle that money received should be deposited promptly, especially if anything more than a very small amount of money is involved. Traditionally, many government agencies were sometimes slow to deposit incoming funds in a bank account; partly to save labor, agency personnel would wait until a number of transactions could be completed in one trip. By quickly depositing money in an account that generates interest, significant added income may be generated over the course of a year. The national government and many states now rely heavily on electronic fund transfers, especially for larger sums of money, in order to get the money from the payer to a government account as quickly as possible.

A related guideline is to pay the government's bills precisely on time rather than paying early or late. Paying late annoys people and may generate financial penalties. Paying early means a loss of interest income that the funds would produce if left invested for another week or 10 days. While the loss of interest income from a single payment amount may be small, the combined loss on many transactions can be substantial. Here, too, electronic fund transfers can be helpful in ensuring that bills are paid in a timely fashion.

Personnel who handle funds must also take care to comply with relevant government regulations regarding money management. Those regulations cover many topics, including record-keeping requirements, rules regarding which people are allowed to perform which transactions, and restrictions on what types of investments are allowed. Especially for local governments that rely heavily on state and federal aid, officials may need to follow several sets of regulations at the same time.

Good money management requires thorough, accurate records and multiple information sources that are relatively independent of one another. If one person records the arrival of funds, a different person should record deposits. If one person makes investment decisions, another person should review his or her actions on a regular basis. Any inconsistencies will then alert officials to a potential problem. In a related vein, cash transactions should be avoided for all but very minor transactions; checks, credit cards, and electronic fund transfers generate a paper trail that can be more easily checked.

Another important guideline, noted earlier, is to pool funds on hand for investing rather than having a separate investment program for each agency and/or funding source. Larger amounts of money are often eligible for more attractive investment options, and a single large investment fund may generate lower brokerage costs than many small funds invested separately. As some local government officials learned from the Orange County experience, however, relying on others to manage investments may sometimes produce disappointing results.

CONCLUDING THOUGHTS

Financial management involves a number of crucial concerns that usually attract little attention from the general public but that may affect the financial health of a national, state, or local government in many important ways. Because of the public's lack of interest in public financial management, the many other demands on officials' time, and the fact that many officials find financial management to be uninteresting and confusing, even public officials are prone to neglecting financial management concerns at times. Improvements in financial management that seem sensible in the abstract may, nonetheless, entail risks that discourage making the improvements.

A sound capital budgeting system can, at best, lead to better-informed decisions regarding major, durable projects, such as buildings and airports. Even the best capital budgeting system cannot, however, do very much about a lack of financial resources for funding needed projects or powerful interest groups that oppose projects that would benefit the general public or demand projects that provide limited public benefit.

Sound accounting and auditing systems can help detect deviations from the approved budget, alert officials to changing conditions, and provide a better basis for evaluating program performance, among other benefits. At the same time, some information may foster political conflict or criticisms regarding agency performance, and the cost of generating and analyzing more and more information may sometimes exceed the benefits gained from that information.

Careful debt administration and cash management can enable governments to reduce the cost of public programs, link the benefits of projects to the costs of providing them, and generate revenues from funds on hand. Mistakes in these areas can mean unnecessary financial losses, but efforts to improve debt administration and cash management can also produce conflict, for even sensible borrowing may generate criticism, and efforts to make people pay money that they owe the government are likely to make those people angry.

NOTES

1. For discussions of various aspects of capital budgeting, see Aronson and Schwartz (1996); Bland and Clarke (1999); *Budget Issues: The Role of Depreciation in Budgeting for Certain Federal Investments* (1995); Chapman (1996); Mikesell (1995: chap. 6); Reed and Swain (1997: chap. 13); Vogt (1996).

2. See Bland and Clarke (1999: 658–667); Reed and Swain (1997: 238–243); Mikesell (1995: 220–253).

3. See *Budget Issues: Capital Budgeting for the Federal Government* (1988: 29–37); *Budget Issues: Restructuring the Capital Component* (1989: app. III).

4. See Chan (1999); Coe (1989: chaps. 2, 8); *High Risk Series: An Update* (1999: 82–114); Holder (1996); Rabin, Hildreth, and Miller (1996: chaps. 44–53); Reed and Swain (1997: chap. 17); Steiss (1989: chaps. 2, 3).

5. See *Budget Issues: Overview of State and Federal Debt* (1988); Coe (1989: chap. 6); *Federal Debt: Answers to Frequently Asked Questions* (1996); Leonard (1996); Mikesell (1995: chap. 14); Rabin, Hildreth, and Miller (1996: chaps. 32–39); Reed and Swain (1997: chap. 14); Steiss (1989: chap. 9).

6. Coe (1989: chap. 5); *Debt Collection: Improved Reporting Needed on Billions of Dollars in Delinquent Debt and Agency Collection Performance* (1997); Khan (1996); Mikesell (1995: chap. 15); *Prompt Payment: State Laws Are Similar to the Federal Act but Less Comprehensive* (1989); Reed and Swain (1997: chaps. 11, 12); Schwartz (1996); Steiss (1989: chaps. 4, 5).

7. Fromson (1995); Jorion (1995).

8. Hildreth (1991: 162–167); Lynch (1995: 225–227); Reed and Swain (1997: 205–217); Steiss (1989: 83–89).

9

The Economy
and the Budget

How the Economy Affects Government Budgets

Public Budgeting's Impact on the Economy

Perspectives on the Role of Government in Shaping the Economy

Tools for Stabilizing the Economy

Promoting Economic Growth

Concluding Thoughts

> When more and more people
> are thrown out of work, unemployment results.
>
> ATTRIBUTED TO CALVIN COOLIDGE
> (Quoted In Baker, 1990:41)

The relationship between the economy and the budget is complex and, in some respects, controversial. Part of the complexity results because the economy and the budget affect each other, and trying to sort out the relationships when there are many government programs and many facets to the economy is a formidable task. In addition, government budgets and the economy frequently change, sometimes in ways that are not understood for some time. Many aspects of the relationship are also ideologically charged as well; personal beliefs color many assessments of budgetary-economic dynamics. We will begin with an exploration of the impact of the economy on the budget and then turn to the more controversial issue of the impact of the budget on the economy.

HOW THE ECONOMY AFFECTS GOVERNMENT BUDGETS

At some risk of oversimplifying, we can divide economic effects on the budget into two broad categories: short term and long term. Both categories affect public budgeting substantially, but each raises some distinctive issues for participants in the budgetary process.

Short-Term Economic Forces

Economies are subject to short-term fluctuations,[1] which are often discussed in the context of the business cycle. An economic boom begins: New companies are formed, and old companies expand. More workers are hired, and many workers are asked to work longer hours as businesses struggle to keep pace with orders. More goods are manufactured and sold, and incomes and profits rise. Overall, the economy expands. Eventually, however, the economy may begin to cool off. Some companies saturate the market with their products, and then new purchases begin to decline. Investors may become anxious about future sales and begin pulling their money out of some firms. The leaders of creative firms may become more cautious or overconfident and lose their competitive energy. Companies cut back on investing in new equipment, lay off workers, and try to trim pay and benefits. Workers cut back on purchasing, and the entire economy declines.

Recessions The business cycle affects public budgets in a number of ways. First, a recession, or economic slump, will generally cause government revenues

ary outcomes. A rich nation, state, or locality will usually have higher levels of government revenue and higher levels of spending for a wide range of programs than will a poor nation, state, or locality. A society based on subsistence agriculture will have lower levels of government revenues and spending than will a society with a complex, modern economy. Why these relationships exist is a point of some controversy, but the patterns are commonly found.

As noted in Chapter 2, one explanation for the relationship between economic development and budgetary outcomes is Wagner's Law, which holds that a wealthier, more modern economy creates a greater need for government activity of many kinds. A modern economy needs better-educated workers than does an economy based on subsistence agriculture. A modern economy requires a modern transportation system and a modern communication system. A more complex economy produces more disputes among the various actors in the economy—between consumers and producers, between firms competing with one another, between wholesalers and retailers, and so forth. Resolving those disputes will often require government action. Greater mobility and urbanization weaken the social control mechanisms that regulate behavior and create demand for government action to control misconduct.

Wealthier societies may also have higher levels of government revenues and spending because they can more easily afford them. In a very poor society, taking resources away from the public may push people into starvation. In a wealthy society, by contrast, paying taxes may cause a family to cut back on consumption of any number of things, but the necessities of life will usually remain affordable—although a wealthy society may still have poor residents, and some taxes may still bear heavily on the poor.

Some analysts argue that wealthier people may sometimes have a greater preference for government programs, especially programs that may benefit them. Members of a wealthier, better-educated family may support educational programs because they appreciate the value of a good education or environmental protection programs because they value a clean environment. In the United States at least, this tendency does not apply to welfare programs, for wealthier Americans tend to be be less supportive of welfare than are poorer people (Erikson, Luttbeg, and Tedin 1991: 169–170).

A wealthier and more modern economy may also foster higher levels of revenues and spending because economic activity is better documented and easier to detect. In a traditional, agricultural society, many economic interactions may be done by bartering rather than paying with a check or credit card. Detecting those barter transactions for tax purposes is often extremely difficult. In more modern economies, many economic transactions involve checks, credit cards, or electronic fund transfers and involve large organizations (such as banks) that keep records of the transactions. Detecting those transactions for tax purposes is, therefore, easier, although some individuals will still try to conceal their economic activities, at least in part to avoid paying taxes.

The economy may also affect the politics of budgeting in significant ways. In an economy dominated by one or a few major industries, those industries will probably have a great deal of influence in the budgetary process, largely because there may be no groups powerful enough to oppose them. In that case, there will usually be little political conflict in developing and adopting a budget. As the economy grows more diverse and complex, with many different types of businesses, their differing interests are likely to increase the amount of conflict in the budgetary process. Firms needing highly educated workers will lobby for more funding for education, but other businesses employing less skilled workers may oppose paying higher taxes for something that does not help them. A business that ships large quantities of merchandise may advocate major improvements in the transportation system, but service firms that do much of their work by telephone, mail, and electronic mail may have little enthusiasm for costly transportation improvements. Not all budgetary conflict is economically rooted, but a more complex economy is likely to produce more economic conflict. Individual industries may be less influential politically than in economies dominated by a single major industry, but coping with the budgetary conflicts produced by a complex economy may be difficult.

A cautionary note: The distinction between long- and short-term economic developments is not always clear-cut. A city's economy may be declining because of a national or regional recession, or the decline may reflect a lasting change arising from the exhaustion of nonrenewable resources, such as coal or silver, or a secular decline in major local industries. A state's economy may be growing because the growth phase of the business cycle is in full swing or because relatively durable changes in the state economy have created new bases of wealth. If officials adopt short-term remedies to cope with an economic decline that is likely to last for many years, they will still have painful decisions to make in future years. Conversely, if officials launch costly new programs in the belief that greater prosperity will endure for many years and later learn it was only a temporary economic boom, followed by a slump, some of those programs may prove too costly to continue. Here, too, accurate forecasting can reduce the danger of future unpleasantness and permit a more timely response. Knowing what future conditions are likely to be does not, however, guarantee that officials will be able to agree on a course of action or have the courage to make needed changes that may anger politically active, organized interests.

PUBLIC BUDGETING'S IMPACT
ON THE ECONOMY

The more controversial aspect of the budget-economy relationship is the effects that the budget may have on the economy. Much of controversy centers on the questions of what role government should play in a society and, relatedly, what type of a society is desirable. A useful way to approach this bundle of issues is by distinguishing among three different roles that government may play in shaping the economy and the society in general: allocation, distribution, and stabilization.[3]

The Allocation Function

The *allocation function* of government emphasizes providing goods, services, and facilities that the private sector may not provide adequately. That function will usually focus primarily on public rather than private goods. A public good is one that, if provided, becomes readily available to people, regardless of whether they helped to pay for it. If the air is made cleaner, that clean air is available to everyone in the area. Private businesses are usually reluctant to provide public goods because many of the beneficiaries will not pay for them voluntarily—unless the number of beneficiaries is relatively small. Unless government steps in, the public good will be poorly provided, if at all.

Governments also become involved in providing *merit goods,* which are goods that society decides should be provided to people without regard to their ability to pay for them. In most Western democracies (but not the United States), access to health care is considered a merit good. As a result, government programs provide access to medical care to all people—although wealthier people may have health care options that are not available to poorer people. Deciding what goods should be treated as merit goods and deciding how much of them should be provided can generate considerable controversy, as President Clinton discovered when he proposed broadening access to health care in 1994.

Correcting for *externalities* (sometimes called spillover effects) is another aspect of the allocation function. In market transactions, externalities are effects on people who are not directly involved in an economic transaction. If a manufacturing plant pollutes the environment, the pollution affects people in the area, even though many of them may not buy the company's products or own stock in the company. If some families have their children vaccinated against common childhood diseases, other children are made somewhat safer because the vaccinated children are less likely to spread those diseases.

Because externalities affect people who are not directly involved in a market transaction, the market may not make very efficient decisions regarding those externalities. If the people who buy a manufacturer's products are not affected by the pollution the company generates, more pollution may result than if the customers also endured the pollution. A beneficial externality, such as children being made safer because other children are vaccinated, may be underproduced by the market because people may be reluctant to pay for a benefit that flows to other people (who do not pay for it).

Deciding what constitutes an externality and whether it is serious enough to warrant government intervention are often controversial. Efforts to control pollution often pit advocates of a cleaner environment against people who are troubled by the costs of pollution control. Requiring vaccinations may provoke complaints from people who, for a variety of reasons, do not want to be vaccinated. Programs to encourage oil conservation may anger people whose lifestyles require large amounts of petroleum to power their recreational vehicles and commute long distances in vehicles that get poor gas mileage.

Government involvement in the allocation function can take a number of forms. Public officials may create a public agency to provide a service that the private sector will not provide or may provide subsidies to private organizations to alter their behavior. Laws and regulations may be used in an effort to compel people to produce fewer harmful externalities or more beneficial ones. In the case of complex externalities, more than one method is often used.

The Distribution Function

The *distribution function* is concerned with the distribution of income and wealth in a society (in much of the political science literature, policies involved with this function are labeled "redistribution"). Budgetary decisions involving this function are often controversial. Advocates of government action to reshape the distribution of income and wealth often contend that the private sector's decisions are sometimes biased. Some people inherit great wealth that they have done nothing to earn; a large business, if unrestrained by competitors, may use its economic power to pressure small firms or individual customers. If wealth is very unevenly distributed, the market will have little incentive to respond to the needs or preferences of people who have little or no money. Some critics object to the prospect of people who can afford virtually any luxury while other people lack basic necessities of life. Great inequality may also foster resentment, political tension, and even antisocial behavior as wealthy people try to preserve their higher status and poorer people lose confidence in the fairness of the system and their chances of improving their lot in life.

Critics of government action to alter the distribution of wealth and income contend that those efforts are likely to reduce economic growth and efficiency. If people who work hard and are productive find that much of their reward is taxed away from them and given to others who do not work hard or perform effectively, the desire to be productive may decline. Moreover, how do we decide what constitutes a proper distribution of wealth? Raising the issue of altering the distribution of income may provoke considerable conflict. In addition, wealthy people who fear the loss of their wealth may decide to move away instead. Because of this possibility, which is most likely at the local level (for relocating to another city or county is easier than moving to another country), local government officials are usually reluctant to consider proposals to redistribute wealth from the rich to the poor.

The Stabilization Function

The *stabilization function* involves trying to keep the economy performing smoothly, with high levels of employment, low inflation, and significant economic growth. At a minimum, performing this function requires that officials be aware that budgetary decisions may affect the economy's performance and, consequently, try to avoid causing unintentional harm. Somewhat more controversial is the view that the economy, left to itself, may not always perform very well and that government action may be needed to combat excessive unemployment, high inflation, or slow economic growth. Governments may employ a variety of approaches to managing the economy, and not all those approaches necessarily involve the budget, but deliberate efforts to manage the economy usually have budgetary implications. We will explore a number of economic management strategies later in this chapter.

As with other aspects of budgeting, the three major budget functions involved in shaping the economy may conflict with one another at times. Controversies regarding the fairness of a tax proposal (a distribution issue) may hamper revenue raising and, as a result, leave too little money to provide needed public goods or correct for externalities (the allocation function). Pressures to cut spending to curb inflation may also leave too little money for needed public goods; conversely, spending more money to stimulate economic growth or combat unemployment may produce too much spending on public goods. Shifting the distribution of wealth from richer to poorer people may discourage work and investment and, therefore, stifle economic growth. Conversely, incentives to promote economic growth may sometimes yield complaints that the wealthiest people receive an unfairly large share of the benefits. Some of these conflicts are tied to differing views regarding the proper relationship between government and the economy. Several major viewpoints deserve mention.

PERSPECTIVES ON THE ROLE OF GOVERNMENT IN SHAPING THE ECONOMY

Citizens, officials, and scholars have long argued about the role that governments should play in influencing the economy.[4] Two of the older perspectives, laissez-faire and mercantilism, call, respectively, for a very limited government role and a very extensive government role. Two of the more recent perspectives, Keynesian economics and supply-side economics, call for government to help stabilize the economy (the Keynesian view) and for eliminating government obstacles to economic growth and development (the supply-side view). Elected officials generally recognize that, regardless of their own views regarding government management of the economy, a poorly performing economy will often produce unhappy voters.

Laissez-Faire

The *laissez-faire* perspective is that government should play only a quite limited role in shaping the operation of the economy. Adherents of this view contend that the private sector is more efficient, creative, and productive than government and should be left alone to the maximum degree possible (with some differences of opinion on what is the maximum degree possible). Because the market functions by agreement and consent rather than compulsion, people have more flexibility and freedom with market decision making. In addition, the marketplace in a large, complex society disperses the workload of decision making across millions of decision-making arenas—businesses, families, individual consumers and business managers, and so forth. That dispersal makes coping with the enormous number of decisions much easier than would be the case if a limited number of governments had to make all those decisions.

In addition, the incentives of the market reward efficiency, productivity, and responsiveness. Inefficient workers and businesses are punished (and so given an incentive to change), and efficient actors will be rewarded with higher incomes and higher profits. Government, by contrast, tends to be a monopoly, with less incentive to be efficient or responsive.

Some advocates of the laissez-faire perspective also emphasize that the market places greater value on individual people, who are free to pursue opportunities wherever they occur. A worker can move to another city or state if better opportunities exist there. A business owner can shift production to another country if the result will be lower production costs or higher quality. In the long run, this flexibility will produce a better life for enormous numbers of people.

Bear in mind that most adherents of laissez-faire thinking support some government involvement in the economy. Governments will need to enforce contracts and prevent the unauthorized use of other people's work (by enforcing patents and copyrights). Government will also be needed to maintain order and protect property, as well as provide public goods, such as national defense. Because of government's many shortcomings, governments should balance their budgets, so that the pain and political risks associated with taxes will discourage frivolous or unnecessary spending.

Critics of the laissez-faire perspective charge that, in many respects, private-sector transactions are often not as voluntary as they appear. If a worker is fired from his or her job, in what sense is that voluntary from the worker's standpoint? If jobs are scarce and a worker has a mortgage to pay and receives health insurance from work, how free is that worker to resign rather than endure an abusive boss? Recall that during the era when laissez-faire thinking was most influential, workers were free to work with dangerous machinery, and small children were free to work long hours in factories; the alternative might be going hungry.

Critics also complain that people may find the complexities of private-sector decision making just as overwhelming as public officials find public budgeting. Trying to determine what would be a good investment opportunity, a suitable home-owner's insurance policy, or a reliable car can be a frustrating exercise in many cases, especially if companies mislead consumers regarding the quality of products or their true costs. Certainly the emergence of the consumer movement since the 1960s, amid numerous complaints about defective and/or dangerous products and warranties and insurance policies filled with baffling language, suggests that not everyone is entirely satisfied with private-sector actions.

Some critics of the laissez-faire viewpoint contend that its emphases on individualism and on material wealth may be socially harmful if carried too far.

If people become overly preoccupied with winning benefits for themselves and cease to care about what happens to other people, the social fabric of a community may begin to unravel. If wealth is more important than anything else, why not steal it or sell products that may be harmful to people if the products generate immense profits?

Mercantilism

Mercantilism (sometimes called economic nationalism when national governments are involved) presents a very different perspective on the government's role in shaping the economy. Mercantilists believe that government has a positive duty to preserve and promote economic prosperity, even at the expense of governments and people in other parts of the world (or, in the case of state or local governments, people in other states or localities). In this view, a government should adopt policies to encourage expansion of the economy and prevent other governments from gaining a competitive advantage. The methods that might be used vary considerably.

During the Industrial Revolution, England gained a major advantage over other countries in the field of textile production with the invention of several machines that greatly reduced the cost of making cloth fabrics. The English government passed laws banning the export of the machines or their designs in order to prevent other countries from enhancing their competitive positions. Many governments through the ages have used military force to help provide access to vital raw materials. Governments have provided financial assistance to businesses in hopes of helping them to expand, and government programs have supported research that has led to new products and new industries in fields ranging from computers and aviation to farming.

Mercantilists often assume that the supply of economic activity and wealth is relatively fixed and that one country (or state or locality) can enhance its share only by taking some away from other jurisdictions. Officials must, therefore, be constantly alert for opportunities to expand their country's share of the wealth and for threats that other countries may be trying to do the same thing. Officials who succeed in fostering economic growth will gain the goodwill of many citizens and have a much easier time raising revenue.

Critics of mercantilism charge that, over time, the total supply of wealth is not fixed but can grow dramatically. If other countries become wealthier, they may buy more products from our country and enhance our prosperity, too. Policies designed to promote the economic advantage of a single country (or state or locality) may actually encourage inefficiency and slow economic progress by slowing the spread of new technologies and encouraging businesses to depend on government assistance rather than doing a better job to become more prosperous.

Critics of mercantilist policies in recent years have also complained that, in many cases, the policies do not appear to work very reliably. Officials may spend considerable sums on economic development programs that accomplish very little. We will return to that issue later in this chapter. There have also been complaints that economic development programs sometimes provide benefits to wealthy people without producing much benefit for the rest of the public.

Keynesian Economics

This perspective, which is named for British economist John Keynes, primarily focuses on the role of government in the stabilization function. Keynes contended that the market economy, left to its own devices, might remain at high levels of unemployment or inflation for extended periods. Even if the economy might eventually correct itself, the correction might take years to reach a satisfactory level of unemployment or price stability. However, government could counteract those problems, primarily by modifying levels of demand for goods and services. That could be done in a number of ways, some of which involved budgetary decisions.

The Great Depression stimulated a great deal of interest in Keynes's ideas, which have become considerably influential in budgeting circles. However, Keynesian economics raises a number of complex issues. First, what is the optimum level of unemployment and inflation—especially if efforts to combat unemployment may, beyond some point, make inflation worse and vice versa? Addressing those issues in a direct way makes budgeting more controversial. Second, some critics contend that Keynes's ideas, which included running budget deficits to stimulate a sluggish economy, weakened the traditional belief in balanced budgets and, consequently, contributed to the budget deficit problems found in many countries beginning in the 1970s. Keynesian ideas did not seem to offer much help to officials struggling with the economic problems of the 1970s, with a combination of high inflation and high unemployment.

Two other problems that are linked to the Keynesian perspective are practical in nature. First, if managing the economy calls for prompt changes in the budget in order to respond to changing economic conditions, how readily can public budgets actually be revised? As noted earlier (see Chapter 6), the national government has had considerable difficulty in making prompt budgetary decisions since the late 1960s. Many state legislatures are part-time institutions; major budgetary changes may require a special session of the legislature. Cutting back spending to cool off an overheated economy may anger people whose programs are trimmed. Boosting spending (or cutting taxes) to stimulate a sluggish economy may create expectations for future services (or tax rates) that cannot be maintained for long.

The other practical problem involves levels of government and stabilization policy. State and local governments are probably not very effective in stabilizing the economy, in part because getting all or nearly all of them to act in concert is usually very difficult. In addition, if individual states and localities act to help stabilize the economy, the effects will spread out across other parts of the country (an externality), with the result that jurisdictions that do nothing to help will still reap some benefits from the actions of other jurisdictions. The effects of those individual actions, however, diluted across an entire country, will probably be too small to be effective. The growing importance of the global economy creates a similar problem for national governments in the modern era. As a result, we have seen the increasing use of economic summits involving officials from a number of countries in the hope that concerted action by a number of national governments will be more effective than a single country acting alone. Gaining agreement among the various governments has not always been easy, however.

Supply-Side Economics

Supply-side economics offers a fourth major perspective on the government's role in managing the economy. A number of President Reagan's economic advisers favored the supply-side perspective, which has much in common with the laissez-faire perspective. Supporters of supply-side economics charged that Keynesian economics placed too much emphasis on demand and too little on supply, especially factors that may discourage economic growth and productivity. Good economic policy must try to minimize those factors and, in the process, encourage economic growth.

Supply-side analysts contended that excessively high taxes were likely to reduce economic growth. People will have less incentive to work hard if much of what they earn is taken away in taxes. Heavy business taxes will reduce the profits that are needed to reward productivity and finance investment in new equipment. Beyond some point, increasing tax rates may slow the economy so much that government revenues actually go down. Cutting tax rates could, in some cases, stimulate enough economic growth to produce higher total government revenues.

Supply-side analysts also charged that government regulations often discouraged economic growth. Regulations that stifle business competition protect inefficient firms, and regulations of many types may slow the development of new products and new technologies. The cost of complying with regulations pulls money away from investments in new equipment and the development of new products as well. Cutting back or eliminating many regulations would help to encourage faster economic growth.

Unlike most laissez-faire economists, many of the supply-siders placed little emphasis on balancing the budget, at least in the short run. They contended that tax reductions and deregulation would stimulate enough economic growth to produce a high level of revenues and, therefore, a balanced budget (eventually).

Critics of supply-side economics complained that although tax rate reductions might, in cases, produce so much economic growth that higher revenues would result, the theory was somewhat vague on precisely when that effect would occur. Under some conditions, tax rate reductions would produce lower revenues. Unfortunately for officials, distinguishing between those different circumstances was difficult.

National officials experimented with supply-side policies during the 1980s, with tax rate cuts and deregulation. The tax cuts did not, however, produce the revenues that had been forecast, and large budget deficits followed. An extended economic expansion began in the early 1980s, a development consistent with the supply-siders' expectations, but supporters of the Keynesian perspective noted that the large budget deficits might have helped fuel the expansion.

TOOLS FOR STABILIZING THE ECONOMY

Governments commonly rely on two main approaches to stabilizing the economy.[5] Monetary policy does not generally involve the budget process in a direct way but has important implications for the budget. Fiscal policy, contrast, is directly tied to the budget.

Monetary Policy

Monetary policy involves control over the money supply and the availability of credit. Expanding the money supply and lowering interest rates will encourage economic expansion by making it easier for consumers to finance credit purchases and easier for businesses to finance investments in new equipment and facilities. In the United States, primary responsibility for making monetary policy lies with the Federal Reserve Board (the Fed), an arm of the national government. The Fed, whose members are appointed by the president for long, overlapping terms, can influence the supply of money and credit in a number of ways.

In *open market operations,* the Fed buys and sells U.S. government securities. If it buys large amounts of U.S. bonds and Treasury bills from investors, more money is pumped into the economy, and investors who have sold their U.S. government securities to the Fed may reinvest the proceeds in the private sector, which will tend to lower interest rates and make credit easier to obtain. If the Fed sells large amounts of U.S. securities, that will pull money out of the economy and push up interest rates as private investment options must compete more vigorously for potential investors' funds.

The Fed can also shape monetary policy by revising the *discount rate,* the rate that the Fed charges banks that need to borrow money from it. Raising the discount rate will tend to push up the interest rates that the banks charge borrowers and may also reduce the amount of credit available if some banks reduce their amount of borrowing from the Fed because of the higher discount rate. Conversely, lowering the discount rate will tend to reduce the interest rates that banks charge borrowers and make credit easier for borrowers to obtain.

The Fed also sets monetary policy by setting *reserve requirements,* the financial reserves that commercial banks must have on hand in order to conduct a given volume of business. Raising the reserve requirement reduces the amount of money that banks can legally lend; lowering the requirement makes more money available for loans.

Especially since the late 1960s, monetary policy has been an attractive approach to managing the economy, in part because the Fed has often been able to make decisions more quickly than the president and Congress. In addition, because the members of the Fed do not have to answer to the voters, the Fed has sometimes been more willing to administer painful (but possibly necessary) economic medicine than have the president and Congress.

Critics of the Fed worry, however, about the accountability of a board whose members are not elected by the public and whose decisions are often made secretly. If citizens do not agree with the actions of the Fed, they have little ability to punish its members—although the President and Congress have noticeable influence over the Fed.

Some critics also contend that monetary policy may not always be an effective way to manage the economy. In a very severe recession, confidence in the economy may fall so low that many consumers and business executives do not want to borrow money, even at extremely low interest rates. A person without a job will probably not want to borrow money, regardless of the availability of credit, to buy a house or car. A business executive whose products are piling up in warehouses will usually not want to borrow large sums to modernize company factories.

High interest rates, which will tend to slow down the economy and curb inflation, also present difficulties. High interest rates will inflict considerable harm on economic sectors dependent on borrowing, such as home purchases financed by mortgages. A company that cannot afford to finance the purchase of new equipment may be driven out of business by competitors who had the good luck to modernize before the credit market tightened. Financial institutions that made many long-term loans at low interest rates may be put into financial difficulty by higher interest rates (which they must pay to attract and retain investments) if they cannot revise the interest rates they are charging through, for example, the use of adjustable rate mortgages.

Although monetary policy can be determined outside the budget process, as is done in the United States, monetary policy can significantly affect the budget. Any government that borrows money (and many do) will have to pay higher interest rates along with the rest of society when the credit market is tight. For governments with large debts, the rise in interest rates may generate large costs. In addition, the economic effects of monetary policies will influence government revenues as the economy expands or contracts and influence demand for unemployment compensation, public assistance, and other programs designed to help people in financial difficulty.

Fiscal Policy

Fiscal policy, which is more directly linked to budgeting, involves trying to influence the economy by altering revenue and/or expenditure levels and, consequently, the level of spending relative to the level of revenues. Increasing spending, reducing revenues, or running budget deficits will yield more money and purchasing power in the economy and, as a result, stimulate economic expansion. Increasing revenues, reducing spending, or running a budget surplus will take money out of the economy and cool it down. These changes can be made in a number of ways.

Automatic Stabilizers *Automatic stabilizers* are policies designed, in part, to help stabilize the economy without the adoption of new public policies. For example, a progressive income tax may serve as an automatic stabilizer because rising incomes will push people into higher tax brackets. As a result, more money will be taken out of the economy, a development that will cool it down somewhat. In a slumping economy, people will fall into lower tax brackets; their taxes will fall faster than their incomes and, consequently, cushion the recession.

Income support programs, such as unemployment compensation, welfare, and Social Security, also serve as automatic stabilizers. People who lose their jobs may qualify for assistance that enables them to continue spending (although not at the level they could manage when employed) and pump money into the economy. Welfare reforms adopted in 1996 reduced the stabilization value of Temporary Assistance to Needy Families (formerly Aid to Families with Dependent Children) in some respects. Placing a cap on federal welfare aid to the states presents the risk that states might be overwhelmed in a major recession, although pressure to raise the cap would eventually develop. Limiting the length of time that people can receive assistance presents the risk that people might be cut from the rolls while a major recession is still in progress (recall that the Great Depression lasted for roughly a decade).

A great virtue of automatic stabilizers is that they can begin to work without the passage of new legislation. For any government, such as the American national government, that has difficulty in making budgetary decisions promptly, that is a significant strength. However, automatic stabilizers may also be problematic in some respects.

First, automatic stabilizers can produce large, unexpected changes in the budget when the economy does not perform as expected. Revenues may fall below expectations, and program costs may exceed projections in a recession. If some of the spending programs are entitlements, budget uncontrollability will increase as those programs grow.

Automatic stabilizers also tend to be reactive; that is, they do not begin to operate very powerfully until people have lost their jobs or until incomes have already begun rising or falling. Preventive remedies, which begin to work before the problem develops, might produce less pain and suffering, assuming that problems can be forecast accurately in advance.

Moreover, there appear to be large gaps in the social safety net. Many people who lose their jobs do not qualify for unemployment compensation, and many needy people do not qualify for Medicaid. People who do qualify for assistance may not apply for it because they do not know they are eligible, because they are embarrassed by their economic difficulties, or because they believe they can manage without assistance. Assistance may be denied because of minor technical errors, prejudice, or any number of other reasons. Assistance that needy people do not receive will not help to stabilize the economy.

Discretionary Fiscal Policy   *Discretionary fiscal policy* is the main fiscal policy alternative to automatic stabilizers. Discretionary fiscal policy often requires enactment of legislation, although some discretionary actions may be controlled by the chief executive, within limits, without adoption of new legislation. Tax rate reductions may help stimulate the economy, or a tax increase may help cool the economy. Increased government spending can encourage economic expansion, and spending cuts may have the opposite effect.

With accurate forecasting, discretionary fiscal policy can help prevent major economic disturbances rather than waiting until unemployment or inflation soars to painful levels. In addition, discretionary fiscal policy can sometimes yield improved economic stability and improvements in the allocation function at the same time. During the Great Depression, public works programs gave jobs to the unemployed but also built many needed public facilities, such as sidewalks, bridges, and roads.

Discretionary fiscal policy is subject to a number of difficulties, however. If economic forecasts are inaccurate, a government may fail to adopt needed fiscal policy changes or adopt remedies that are not actually needed. Less dramatic forecasting errors may produce corrective actions that are stronger or weaker than needed.

If budgetary decisions cannot be adopted in a timely fashion, discretionary fiscal policy presents the risks of acting too late to prevent major economic fluctuations and of applying remedies that might have been helpful months earlier but that might be unnecessary or even harmful by the time they are adopted. If the economy slides into a recession and officials adopt measures to stimulate the economy months later when a recovery is already under way, the result may be a round of inflation.

Discretionary fiscal policy also adds more conflict to the budgetary process. Officials may not agree with one another or with the public regarding what constitutes a suitable level of unemployment, inflation, or economic growth. Conflicts may also erupt regarding when corrective action is needed and over how much corrective action is needed. If tax increases or spending cuts are needed to cool off an overheated economy, people whose taxes might increase or whose programs face cuts will often object. Some critics object to the entire idea of government trying to manage the economy. In the modern era, however, elected officials who ignore major economic problems are likely to be voted out of office.

PROMOTING ECONOMIC GROWTH

Encouraging economic growth is a significant concern for many public officials at all levels of government.[6] Although state and local governments are not usually able to stabilize the national economy very effectively, they have become increasingly active in trying to boost their individual economies in recent decades. Not all these programs involve budgeting in a direct way, but all of them have budgetary implications.

Public Relations

Public relations activities are one aspect of economic development initiatives. States and localities employ advertising, brochures and magazines, toll-free telephone numbers, and Web sites, among other methods, to attract tourists and businesses. These activities are relatively inexpensive and rarely controversial.

Credit Assistance

Credit assistance, such as low-interest loans, may be used to help a new business get started, attract a new business, or help an existing business expand or survive economic difficulty. Credit assistance is sometimes controversial, in part because helping one company but not another may raise complaints of unfairness. In addition, local merchants may feel resentful if their tax dollars are used to attract a major competitor who, in turn, pulls business away from the local merchants.

Tax Reductions

Tax reductions are also used to attract new businesses, encourage expansion of existing firms and, on occasion, to prevent an existing company from leaving. Tax reductions may be adopted formally; for example, a city may sign a written agreement that includes a provision that a new factory will pay no property taxes for 10 years. Less formally, a local government may unofficially assess a large business' property at below its actual value. Like credit assistance, tax reductions may raise complaints of unfairness, especially if the practice appears to favor large firms at the expense of small ones or business properties at the expense of home owners.

Infrastructure Improvements

Infrastructure improvements are another important method for promoting economic development. A better transportation system may enhance a location's appeal to many business managers, who will usually be concerned about the ease of shipping supplies and orders. Expanding the city water plant may help attract a manufacturer whose production processes require large volumes of water. A new sports arena may be needed to keep a major league team from leaving or to bring in a team from elsewhere. Major infrastructure improvements can be very costly, and a major investment in a facility that benefits primarily a limited number of people may provoke major criticism. Proposals to provide public funds for sports facilities have generated controversy in a number of cities, in part because of doubts that the average citizen benefits very much from those projects. If improvements produce more broadly distributed benefits, such as a major upgrading of a metropolitan area's freeway system, criticism is likely to be less severe.

Foreign Trade Missions

State and local governments have also been increasingly active in recent decades in trying to stimulate foreign trade and investment. Those efforts have included all the preceding techniques and added visits by state and local officials to other countries to promote sales of local products abroad, build goodwill, and encourage foreign companies to build facilities in the officials' home states or localities.

How well do these programs perform? Efforts to assess their impact have produce mixed results. Some economic development programs appear to work some of the time, but the same programs may have no impact in another time period. Part of the difficulty in assessing the impact of these programs stems from the difficulty of gauging what a particular state or locality's economy would have done in the absence of the program. If the managers of a company choose a location first and then convince state or local officials in the area to provide credit assistance or a tax reduction, adoption of the policy will appear to lead to a new company coming to the area; in reality the policy may not have mattered. Development programs that appear to work are often copied by other jurisdictions, with the result that the effect, if any, is quickly muted. Even if a policy succeeds in attracting a new firm or keeping an old one afloat, the effect may not last. The company may later relocate anyway, especially if fundamental business considerations, such as access to customers, make another location more attractive.

CONCLUDING THOUGHTS

The economy affects public budgeting in many ways. Recessions generally produce lower revenues, higher demand on income-support programs, and budget deficits, unless corrective action is taken. Economic growth brings higher revenues and a chance for budget surpluses. Inflation brings higher revenues (at least in raw dollars) and higher costs for any programs. A wealthy economy will tend to produce higher revenues and spending than will a poor economy.

Budgets can also affect the economy by providing goods and services (the allocation function), altering the distribution of income and wealth (the distribution function), and promoting economic stability and growth (the stabilization function). The ideal amount of government influence over the economy is a matter of considerable controversy, with adherents of the laissez-faire and supply-side perspectives preferring a relatively limited government role and supporters of the mercantilist and Keynesian perspectives calling for a more activist government role.

National governments may try to promote economic stability through monetary policy, which affects the cost and availability of credit, and through fiscal policy, which adjusts revenues and/or spending to promote economic growth or price stability. Fiscal policy may rely on automatic stabilizers, which can help stabilize the economy without passage of new legislation, or on discretionary policies, which usually require enacting new legislation.

Many state and local governments in the United States are actively involved in trying to promote economic growth. Those activities include many tactics, from public relations programs and credit assistance to tax reductions, infrastructure improvements, and foreign trade missions. Although those efforts are sometimes controversial, as are many government actions to influence the economy, officials often believe that prosperity will mean happier voters than will a poor economy.

NOTES

1. See Bahl (1984: chap. 4); Clingermayer and Wood (1995); Gold (1995: 370–377); Lowery (1985); Schick (1995: 38, 102–103, 193); Winters (1999: 306–308); Wolkoff (1999).
2. Bahl (1969); Campbell and Sacks (1967); Dye (1966; 1990: 52–56); Wilensky (1975).
3. Fisher (1988: 20–44); Musgrave and Musgrave (1980: chaps. 1, 3–5).
4. For discussions of this issue, including some perspectives not included here, see Bronfenbrenner, Sichel, and Gardner (1990: chaps. 10, 17); Kettl (1992: 17–25); Stapleford and Figuro (1983: 566–577).
5. Bronfenbrenner, Sichel, and Gardner (1990: chaps. 11–14); Cohen (2000: chaps. 8, 9); Gosling (2000: chap. 2); Musgrave and Musgrave (1980: chaps. 27–31); Ooms, Boster, and Fleegler (1999).
6. See Banovetz, Dolan, and Swain (1994: chap. 5); Fisher (1988: chap. 21); Green, Fleischmann, and Kong (1996); Saiz and Clarke (1999); Swindell and Rosentraub (1998); and the studies they cite.

10

10

JMG

Intergovernmental Aspects of Public Budgeting

Why Have Multiple Governments?

Problems with Budgeting with Multiple Governments

Intergovernmental Grants

Other Financial Relationships among Levels of Government

Horizontal Dynamics in Fiscal Federalism

Mandates

Concluding Thoughts

Now ride off in all directions.

Film Director MICHAEL CURTIZ, TO GARY COOPER

(QUOTED IN IN FOSS 1997: 23)

An important feature of public budgeting in almost all countries is the existence of multiple governments within the same country. Public budgetary decisions in the United States, for example, are made by the national government, 50 state governments, and over 87,000 local governments, including cities, counties, and special districts. When those governments have some degree of autonomy from one another, have differing responsibilities, and are subject to different political pressures and incentives, budgetary dynamics may be very different from one decision-making arena to another. Moreover, the budgetary decisions of one government may be affected in various ways by other governments. This chapter will explore a number of those dynamics.

WHY HAVE MULTIPLE GOVERNMENTS?

Although a country could, in theory, have only one government, that approach does not appear to be very practical for nations unless they are very small. Countries of any size typically have a national government and numerous local governments, and many have an intermediate level, such as states or provinces as well. Having a number of governments within a country can produce several beneficial effects for the budget process, although some difficulties may result as well.[1]

One benefit of having multiple governments is that they can adapt to differing needs or preferences from one part of the country to another. If people in one area are particularly fond of driving, they can budget more generously for highways. If people in another area particularly dislike property taxes, they can rely on other revenue sources instead (if they are free to choose which revenue sources they use, which is not always the case). This benefit is most likely to result if budgetary decisions reflect public desires or needs, of course, a circumstance that may not always occur.

Budgeting by multiple governments can also help officials cope with the complexity of public budgeting and the conflict it generates. Local officials in the United States do not need to make many decisions regarding budgeting for defense programs; that responsibility lies primarily with the national government. National officials do not need to struggle very much with budgeting for fire protection; that burden falls mainly on local officials. By dividing responsibilities to some degree, officials at each level reduce the range of issues that they must consider.

Budgeting by multiple governments may help political systems cope with conflict in a number of ways. As noted previously, if different governments adopt different policies, people can seek out the state or community that most closely matches their preferences rather than fighting with other people where they live. People who are disappointed by the budgetary decisions of one government may take their case to another government, which may sometimes be more responsive. If responsibilities are shared among governments, a defeat in one arena may be softened by modifications in another arena. For example, when the national government required states to adopt a 55-mile-per-hour speed limit as a condition of receiving federal highway aid, people who wanted to drive faster were apparently able to convince officials in a number of states and localities to tolerate violations of the law on a considerable scale.

Budgeting by multiple governments may also help provide a better link between the benefits provided by a program and the cost of providing it. If a new local park will be used primarily by the residents of one community, financing that park at the local level will cause the people who use the park to pay for it. If a new highway will largely benefit people in one state, budgeting for that highway at the state level will cause the beneficiaries to also bear the cost. In this way, wasteful and unnecessary spending will be discouraged, for citizens are not likely to approve of taxes to pay for benefits that they do not value very highly. In a related vein, if a program provides some localized benefits but also some national benefits, as in the case of improved Amtrak service that helps provide mobility for one state but is also used by some people from other states, sharing of financial responsibility may lead to more sensible decisions than if one level of government acted alone and paid too little attention to the effects felt at the other level.

Having a number of governments may also provide competition that will encourage efficiency and responsiveness to the public. If people in one community learn that a neighboring community has comparable services but lower taxes, they are likely to contact their officials and ask why. If citizens find that their local officials do not respond to their needs, those citizens may move to another locality where officials are more responsive. People can compare what they are receiving from their state or local governments with what is offered elsewhere and, one way or another, seek improvements. This process will operate most effectively if people have accurate information regarding the activities of state or local governments; unfortunately, many people are not very well informed about government finances at any level. This process also works best if people are free to move from one place to another, a requirement that is not always met.

Having large numbers of governments can stimulate the development and testing of new approaches for dealing with policy problems. A proposal that is ignored by one community may be adopted in another community. If the proposal is successful, it may then be copied by other communities or even by other levels of government. Officials who face a serious problem often borrow ideas from other governments, a process that has become easier with the proliferation of associations of state and local officials who often share information on new policy remedies (Walker, 1969).

One other benefit of having numerous governments is that when a problem is too large for a small unit of government to handle alone, a larger jurisdiction can provide assistance of one form or another. A small community may not be able to establish its own crime laboratory but might make use of the state police's crime lab. A state that could not economically have its own school of veterinary medicine might establish a cooperative relationship with another state and share the costs instead. For any program or facility offering economies of scale (i.e., the cost of providing a unit of service is lower when the service is provided on a larger scale), taxpayers may save money if larger governments become involved.

In a related vein, the existence of many state or local governments reduces some of the political and administrative burden carried by the national government. National officials do not need to devote enormous attention to the condition of each city park or school; the bulk of that burden falls on local governments.

PROBLEMS WITH BUDGETING
WITH MULTIPLE GOVERNMENTS

Pessimists like to say that every silver lining has a cloud. Although some aspects of budgetary decision making may be improved by have numerous governments, they may also create a number of difficulties.[2] Citizens may be confused or overwhelmed by the numerous governments and their even more numerous budgetary decisions. If I am unhappy with a public service or program, which officials are responsible? Does the fault lie with the national government, my state government, the city or county where I live, a special district government, or some other state or locality? Could more than one government be responsible? How can I tell? One person may be affected by the budgetary decisions of dozens of governments. Keeping track of what each of those governments is doing and which people are making the decisions is a difficult task.

Budgeting in the context of large number of governments may also lead to problems with externalities or spillover effects, which are effects felt in one jurisdiction because of a decision made in another jurisdiction. If a community dumps raw sewage into a river, that action will affect other communities downstream. If a state spends large sums to support a major university, many of whose graduates move to other states, those other states reap a benefit. Taxpayers are often reluctant to pay for a benefit that flows to nonresidents or to solve a problem felt largely by nonresidents, and those nonresidents may be reluctant to pay to solve a problem (such as pollution) being caused by some other community.

Budgeting by large numbers of governments can create serious coordination problems across governments. A crackdown on crime in one community may cause criminals to shift their activities to another community. Changes in federal aid may complicate state and local budgeting, and changes in state aid may complicate local budgeting. Completion of a major transportation project crossing several communities may be delayed if one or two communities pare back funding for the project because of other demands. Even greater difficulties may result if some communities refuse to participate in the project at all. Officials in one state or locality may try to encourage a major company to leave its current location; the state or locality where the company currently operates will suffer a loss of tax revenue if the effort succeeds.

If levels of wealth vary from one jurisdiction to another (a common phenomenon), problems of inequality will follow. A wealthy community will be able to provide generous funding for schools, libraries, and everything else with modest tax rates. A poor community may levy higher tax rates and still have much less revenue to support public services. As a result, some children may receive a better education than others; some motorists will drive on better-maintained roads than do other motorists. Some poor people will receive more generous welfare benefits than do others because of where they live. These differences do not necessarily reflect differing preferences regarding public services but rather reflect differing abilities to raise revenue. In addition, wealthy localities may use zoning, land use controls, and a host of other mechanisms to exclude poorer people who could not contribute a great deal to the local tax base. As a result, not everyone is able to shop around for the public services they desire. Local governments and, to a lesser degree, state governments will be inclined to give preferential treatment to wealthy people and businesses that can contribute a great deal to the tax base.

INTERGOVERNMENTAL GRANTS

As noted in Chapter 2, one of the most striking developments in public budgeting in the United States is the heavy reliance of state and especially local governments on grants-in-aid from higher levels of government. Although the numbers vary from year to year, state governments in recent years have received roughly one-fifth of their total revenues in grants, primarily from the national government, and localities have received about one-third of their revenues from grants, primarily from state governments (see *Statistical Abstract,* 1999: 311). This reliance is largely a 20th-century development; states and localities raised the vast bulk of their revenues themselves in 1900. Grants can be used for a variety of different purposes and may have a number of different effects.[3]

Grants are sometimes used to correct for externalities. A higher level of government can raise revenues from all the people who are affected by or contributing to a problem and target the revenues to the governments that can resolve the problem. In the real world this can be done only approximately, for a general program may cover some areas where the externalities do not occur but that demand a share of the program benefits as a price for supporting the program.

Grants can also help equalize financial resources and the need for a program or the cost of providing it. A higher level of government can raise more revenues in wealthier areas and redistribute that revenue to poorer areas. Added funding can be given to areas with greater needs, such as a larger proportion of their population in school, or where a program is more costly to provide, such as highway building in mountainous terrain. This can sometimes provoke controversy, for people in wealthier areas may oppose having their tax dollars spent to benefit people in other parts of the state or nation. Conflicts may also erupt over how to measure needs; should aid to education be based on the number of pupils, or should added funding go to schools having more students with learning disabilities, more problems with school violence, or older buildings in need of repair? Seemingly minor differences in the definition of needs may mean large differences in the distribution of money, a consideration that may produce complex political maneuvering over grant provisions (Dilger, 1983).

Grants can enable higher levels of governments to provide a more uniform standard of service when that seems desirable, in contrast to the greater variations in services that can result when decisions are made locally. When transportation officials wanted to establish a national system of interstate highways with consistent guidelines for clearances, sharpness of curves, and so forth, national grants helped provide that consistency. Grants may give recipient governments the financial ability to offer a program that they could not afford on their own and may also give them an incentive to do something that their officials might not choose to do if they had to bear the full cost themselves. Disputes may arise, however, regarding just how much uniformity or consistency is truly needed in a program; one person's consistency is another person's inflexibility.

Grant programs can also help encourage greater creativity and innovation in policy making. If a locality tries something new, the citizens and officials in that locality run the risk that the new program will not work well and the risk that people in other jurisdictions will benefit from what is learned from that locality's efforts without paying anything or sharing the risks of experimentation. Those risks may discourage innovation in many communities. If, however, higher levels of government are willing to help pay for the development and testing of new policies, the sharing of risks may make officials in lower levels of government more willing to try something new from time to time. Encouraging innovation probably requires a type of grant that does not provide money for continuing to do what has been done for many years but that may encourage recipient governments to repackage old programs to appear new and different—the "old wine in new bottles" tactic.

Grant programs can enable lower levels of government to remain involved in programs that they cannot afford to finance on their own. Rising public expectations, modern technologies, and a host of other factors have increased the cost of education, health care, and other public services. Many state and local officials find that they cannot fund many major programs without outside assistance. When that situation occurs, grants-in-aid offer an alternative to transferring the program entirely to a higher level of government. Sharing of responsibilities helps diffuse the political heat generated by controversial programs, such as welfare, and can provide a compromise between the uniformity of a program operated entirely by a higher level of government and the flexibility and variability of a program operated entirely by a lower level of government. Sharing of responsibilities can also produce confusion, however, regarding accountability: who deserves blame for failures or credit for successes when many officials and governments are involved?

Grants can be used to redistribute wealth. With some exceptions, local governments generally have little ability to redistribute wealth from richer to poorer people. Local officials often fear that trying to help the needy will cause the out-migration of wealthier people and businesses to other localities that do not try to redistribute wealth. Those other localities will often use a variety of methods to exclude poor people. A higher level of government, however, can raise revenue from wealthy individuals and businesses and redistribute that revenue to poorer people. Bear in mind that some of those people and businesses may decide to relocate to another country, but that is a much more drastic step than simply moving from one city to another in the same state or country.

In a related vein, grants can shift the burden of financing programs across different income groups. The federal tax system draws a larger proportion of its revenues from wealthier people than does the typical state or local tax system (bearing in mind that revenue systems vary considerably from one state or locality to another). Financing a program with some federal grant money will, therefore, place a somewhat larger share of the program's costs on wealthier taxpayers than would be the case for the same program financed entirely with local revenues.

Types of Intergovernmental Grants

Intergovernmental grants come in a number of varieties,[4] and deciding what form a particular grant should take sometimes provokes considerable conflict. When we add that conflict to disputes regarding whether a grant is needed at all, disputes over levels of funding, and arguments over what sort of rules and regulations, if any, should accompany the money, the total amount of controversy can be substantial.

One basic issue in grant design involves the question of flexibility: Should recipient governments be able to spend the grant funds for virtually any purpose, or should the grant be targeted to some specific program? Revenue sharing (also called a general grant or general fiscal assistance) provides funds that can be spent for almost any purpose; a limited number of uses, such as promoting discrimination, may be prohibited. Block grants provide funding that can be spent only in some broad functional area, such as transportation. Within that area, recipients have flexibility to support roads and highways, mass transit, bike paths, or other activities. Categorical grants give recipients the least flexibility; categorical funds can be used only for a rather narrowly defined purpose, such as drug rehabilitation.

Because categorical grants target funds to a specific program or portion of a program, correcting for externalities or promoting uniformity in a particular program can best be done using categorical grants. Giving recipients more flexibility might result in the funds being spent on something unrelated to the externality problem or the program for which uniformity is desired. However, critics of categorical grants complain that they may provide funding for some programs that may not need assistance in some states or localities that have other pressing needs for which no categorical funding is available. The inflexibility of the categorical grant does not allow those governments to shift the money to where they have greater needs, at least officially (see the following discussion of fungibility). Grants allowing more discretion at the recipient level permit greater adaptation to recipient needs and preferences but leave officials at the granting level with less influence over how the money is spent. That may help explain why a large majority of federal grant funding is usually distributed in categorical grants (*Characteristics of Federal Grant-in-Aid Programs to State and Local Governments,* 1995: iii, 3).

A second issue in grant design concerns whether a grant should include a matching requirement. Matching grants require recipient governments to help finance the program receiving grant support. A 50/50 match requires the recipient government to contribute one dollar for each dollar of grant funding. Other matching ratios have also been tried, and some programs vary the match from one jurisdiction to another. Some federal social welfare programs, for example, have allowed a larger federal share in poorer states. Advocates of matching rules contend that they discourage wasteful spending, for officials at the recipient level may be more vigilant if they have to raise some of the money for a program themselves. Matching rules are also appropriate for programs that provide some localized benefits and some benefits that occur more broadly; in those situations, the matching rule guarantees that both the higher and the lower levels of government contribute some funds to the program. In addition, matching requirements mean that the program will receive more funding than just what the grant provides.

Matching rules can present problems, however. If some recipient governments are too poor to provide the necessary matching contribution or if providing that contribution is too controversial, some potential recipients will not participate in the program. In addition, poorer recipient governments may only be able to generate the necessary matching funds by taking money away from other programs that are just as deserving but do not qualify for matching funds. For these reasons, quite a few grants do not have matching provisions.

Another cluster of issues in grant design involves the distribution of funds. A formula grant allocates funding on the basis of a decision rule that is written into the legislation creating the grant. A very simple formula might allocate state highway aid to counties according to the number of miles of state highway in each county. A more complex formula might provide additional funding where roads are in poor condition, where there are dangerous intersections, or where traffic is especially heavy, among other possible considerations. Conflicts often erupt regarding grant formulas. One common symptom of those conflicts is policy makers who are carrying computer printouts depicting how much money each recipient government will receive under each of the various formulas. Decision makers who are skillful in crafting formulas may reap great benefits for the people they represent (Dilger 1983).

Project grants use a very different method for allocating grant funds. The granting level of government creates a pool of money and invites applications from potential recipient governments (and, in some cases, private organizations). Applicants develop a proposal that documents the need for the funds and describes a project that would be financed with the grant money. An agency at the granting level reviews the applications and awards funds to those projects that appear most deserving.

Project grants may be particularly suitable when officials at the granting level of government want to encourage innovations at the recipient level; funds can be targeted to states or localities that are trying something new rather than continuing long-established programs. Project grants may also be attractive when the amount of money involved is relatively small. Members of Congress may not want to devote weeks of complex negotiations to developing a formula to distribute $50 million nationwide, but a grant distributing $10 billion might be worth the trouble required to develop a formula. Critics of project grants, however, complain that they give an unfair advantage to states or localities that have people who are skilled in *grantsmanship,* the ability to determine what funds are available and write a grant application that will gain approval. A project proposal, together with its supporting documents, may include hundreds or even thousands of pages of material, sometimes prepared on short notice. Officials in small local governments often complain that they cannot compete with larger jurisdictions, many of which hire professional grant application writers (Hale and Palley, 1981: 80–81). The result can be money flowing to states or localities that submit impressive project proposals rather than to where the funds are most needed. Legislators may also be uncomfortable about giving an agency too much control over the allocation of funds. In part because of those concerns, some project grants include a distribution formula that limits the granting agency's discretion (e.g., by placing limits on how much money each state or locality may receive; see *Characteristics of Federal Grant-in-Aid Programs to State and Local Governments,* 1995: 14, 31), or members of the legislature may give the agency control over some of the funds but also earmark some money for designated projects.

Officials designing a grant program must also decide whether it will be open-ended or closed-ended. An open-ended grant has no official, global limit on the amount of money available. An open-ended grant to help the unemployed would, therefore, provide additional money to a state or locality if more people became unemployed. That flexibility can be attractive if future conditions are difficult to predict or if officials value a speedy response to a problem (in preference to waiting for a new bill providing more funds to make its way through the legislative process). That same flexibility can create problems if recipient governments try to milk the program for more and more money or if officials at the granting level become alarmed at their inability to estimate or control program costs from one year to the next (see Derthick, 1975).

A closed-ended grant includes a formal cap on the amount of money available. Officials worried about runaway costs may prefer having a firm ceiling on spending, although that ceiling may mean delays in responding to rapidly changing conditions. Ceilings may also be difficult to maintain in the face of heavy pressure to expand a program. The national government's decision to place a ceiling on federal funding for Temporary Assistance to Needy Families, for example, risks slowing the program's ability to assist needy families in a major recession.

These various aspects of grant design can be combined in a number of different ways, depending on the needs and priorities of decision makers. Of critical concern to budgeters is some mechanism for controlling program costs—a matching requirement, a narrow range of eligible activities (a categorical grant), a formula that specifies how much funding each recipient will receive, strict scrutiny of project grant applications, an overall ceiling on grant funding, and/or thorough audits to check on recipients' use of grant funds. Thrifty budgeters will often want more than one mechanism. At the same time, however, too many controls may antagonize officials at the recipient level and may prevent funds from reaching governments and people who truly need them.

The Impact of Grants

One of the most controversial aspects of intergovernmental grants is their impact. With hundreds of billions of dollars flowing from one government to another each year in the United States, the question of impact is important. With hundreds of grant programs and thousands of governments, answering the question of impact is not easy.[5]

One of the most obvious types of grant impact is on the spending decisions of recipient governments. Studies examining this type of impact generally find that grant funds lead to higher spending by recipients but that the effect is usually less than the amount of the grant, other things being equal (*Federal Grants*, 1996). This finding suggests that some of the grant money may be replacing funds that recipient governments planned to spend from their own revenues.

Grants stimulate spending, in part, by giving recipient governments revenues that they would not have been able to raise on their own. In addition, a grant for a specific program enables recipient governments to fund that program at a lower price (in terms of the revenues they must raise on their own). A project that seems too expensive if the county must raise all the revenues itself may seem more appealing if a state or federal grant will pay half the cost. That consideration may help explain why agencies are more likely to press for spending increases when they receive a larger proportion of their funding from grants (Hedge, 1983).

The grant system has also increased the complexity of public budgeting at all levels. Officials at the national and state levels must make decisions regarding hundreds of grant programs that distribute funds to thousands of recipient organizations, both public and private. Those decisions, in turn, require assessment of the needs and capabilities of those many potential recipients, a process that often involves considerable conflict. Should a grant be given only to local governments, or should nonprofit organizations be allowed to participate? How should funds be distributed? Should a federal grant be given directly to local governments or channeled through state governments? Because a great deal of money is at stake, potential recipients engage in lobbying efforts to influence decisions regarding grant programs (see Beer, 1976; Derthick, 1975).

The grant system complicates budgetary decision making at the recipient level in a number of ways. Because budgetary timetables vary from one government to another and are not always followed, recipient governments must often make budgetary decisions on the basis of predictions of how much money will be available for various purposes. If those predictions are incorrect or if the money is not available as soon as expected, painful changes in recipients' budget may be needed. In a similar fashion, if midyear changes in grant funding occur, recipient budgets may require changes, too. Over the longer term, services and facilities funded by a grant program may create an expectation that they should be continued. If grant funding is later reduced, recipient governments may face the difficult choices of raising more revenues on their own or cutting back on support for those services or facilities. All these possibilities encourage recipient governments to lobby granting levels of government and to monitor the budgetary decisions of those levels of government.

The intergovernmental grant system also adds complexity because of the rules and regulations that often accompany grants, reports that must be filed regarding grant use, the application process for project grants, and the variety of deadlines. Smaller local governments especially find that coping with the numerous rules, regulations, reporting requirements, and application procedures is difficult. There have been a number of efforts to simplify the grant system over the years, but new programs and provisions seem to bring new complexity over time.

Bear in mind that a great many factors contribute to the complexity of public budgeting in the modern era. Even were the grant system to disappear tomorrow or be converted into a single revenue sharing grant, public budgeting would be a very complicated task in view of the many programs, interest groups, social needs, officials, agencies, and units of government involved in public budgeting in the United States. The complexity of the American and global economies and their many links to public budgeting add further complications.

The grant system may also contribute to centralization of power, although this conclusion is often based on the assumption that the alternative to having the grant would be funding the program entirely at the lower level of government, an assumption that may not be entirely reliable. Advocates of the centralization hypothesis contend that the financial resources provided by the higher level of government, coupled with the rules and regulations that often accompany the money, give higher levels of government great influence over recipient governments.

Although grants undoubtedly do give some influence to the granting level of government, a number of factors limit the centralizing effects of many grants. First, recipient government officials often influence the adoption of grant programs and may be able to obtain modifications in provisions that they dislike. In addition, enforcement of grant program requirements varies considerably; some guidelines may be vigorously enforced, but others may be subject to negotiation or even ignored (Ingram, 1977). Recipient governments may decline to participate in grants that are not sufficiently attractive. This is especially likely for grant programs involving relatively limited amounts of money.

One other important limitation on the centralizing effects of grants is the phenomenon known as *fungibility*. Fungibility is the use of grant funds to free up money that the recipient government planned to spend anyway; that freed-up money can then be spent for some other purpose. For example, state officials plan to spend $250 million for school construction in the coming year. A new federal grant gives the state $100 million for school construction. State officials put the grant into the funds for school buildings but take out $100 million of their own money and reallocate it to recreation and environmental protection. The education grant, therefore, leads to higher spending for other purposes instead. Although designers of grant programs sometimes try to prevent fungibility, their efforts do not appear to be very successful over the long term, in part because of the difficulty in gauging what a government would have spent in the absence of the grant 5 or 10 years from now. In addition, some grant programs do not have very substantial safeguards to prevent fungibility (Break, 1980: 132–133; *Federal Grants,* 1996).

Officials at the recipient level sometimes complain that the frequent use of categorical grants (which provide a large majority of federal grant funds) produces excessive inflexibility. A city might need improvements in its water system and have a perfectly adequate police budget, but if grant funding is available for law enforcement but not water systems, what are city officials to do? Aside from fungibility, those officials have little choice but to spend the grant money on law enforcement or else refuse the funds. That lack of flexibility may also enhance the political autonomy of agencies that receive large amounts of grant funding; if federal highway aid must be spent for highways and nothing else, administrators in the state highway agency know that the governor and legislature will have to let them have the money or else return it to the federal treasury (Brudney and Hebert, 1987).

Complaints regarding inflexibility should probably be taken with a grain or two of salt. When state or local officials are confronted by angry people who want to know why their favorite programs have not been funded more generously, blaming inflexible grant programs is a convenient way to shift blame elsewhere. This is an example of the "I'd love to help you but . . ." technique (Wildavsky, 1974: 80–81), in which the official tries to create the impression of being sympathetic but constrained by outside forces. Having flexibility carries the risk of attracting more blame and anger from disappointed people. This may help explain why the nation's governors once voted against a resolution calling for giving the states more flexibility in spending federal highway aid

(Berkley and Fox, 1978: 241–242). Years later, when the states were given more flexibility in spending their federal highway aid, most states made little or no use of that opportunity (*Department of Transportation: Flexible Funding*, 1997). Could it be that state officials did not want to anger the many interest groups that support highway programs?

OTHER FINANCIAL RELATIONSHIPS AMONG LEVELS OF GOVERNMENT

Although grant programs are probably the most visible aspect of financial relationships among levels of government, there are other important financial relationships, some of them indirect. One important variety is the use of tax credits, exemptions, and deductions that a taxpayer may use to reduce his or her tax liability to one level of government.[6] For example, the federal income tax allows taxpayers to deduct state and local property taxes on their homes from their taxable income. In effect, this provides a federal subsidy for people who pay relatively heavy property taxes, if they itemize their deductions. In turn, this makes the property tax a little less painful and makes local revenue raising a little easier (local governments are the major users of property taxation in the United States).

Another important tax deduction is interest on bonds issued by other levels of government. For many years, interest earned from state and local government bonds was exempt from federal income taxes. In effect, this enabled states and localities to borrow money more cheaply, for the interest paid on their bonds was tax exempt. Critics complained, however, that some state and local bonds were being used to finance essentially private activities, such as industrial parks and sports facilities. Critics also complained that some states and localities were issuing tax-exempt bonds and then investing the money they raised from the bonds in securities paying a higher interest rate, a practice known as arbitrage. These complaints led to reforms in 1986. The Tax Reform Act restricted the issuance of state and local bonds for essentially private purposes and also required that most arbitrage profits be rebated to the federal government. Deductions of interest paid on bonds issued to support public projects, such as schools or public hospitals, survived (Leonard, 1996: 321–325).

Another important vertical relationship at the state-local level is found in a collection of state programs to provide property tax relief at the local level. The property tax is consistently one of the most unpopular taxes in the United States, in part because it is believed to be especially burdensome to poorer people (although this is a point of dispute). The property tax does not register changes in income unless a family moves, a quality that seems unfair if the family breadwinner becomes unemployed. In addition, the property tax must be paid in one or two painful chunks in many jurisdictions, in contrast to sales taxes, which are paid in many transactions over the course of the year. Finally, during periods of rapidly rising property values, a family's property tax burden may increase much faster than the family's income (Nice, 1987).

Property tax relief programs come in many forms (*Significant Features of Fiscal Federalism,* vol. 1, 1995: 130–143). Some programs provide relief to home owners only, but other programs include renters. Some programs restrict relief to certain types of people, such as the elderly or disabled. From the standpoint of local revenues, a critical distinction is whether the program offers a property tax exemption, which simply reduces the taxpayer's property tax liability (and so reduces local revenues), a ceiling on property tax rates (which has the same effect), or a circuit-breaker program, which provides a state-financed refund to people whose property tax bill exceeds a state-defined reasonable amount. Circuit breakers provide an indirect state subsidy of local property tax systems by, in effect, paying part of the property tax bills of people whose property taxes are high relative to their incomes (Peterson, 1976: 102). In states where the circuit-breaker programs are restricted to certain categories of people, however, raising local property taxes high enough to activate circuit-breaker coverage may anger taxpayers who are not covered by the program.

Another important bundle of issues in relationships among different levels of government includes tax coordination, tax separation, and political spillovers from one level of government's budgetary decisions to another level's decisions. Vertical tax coordination is a concern when two or more levels of government are trying to raise revenues from the same people. There is a risk that some people may be treated unfairly or subjected to unnecessary inconvenience by the multiple revenue decisions of the different levels of government (Break, 1980: chap. 2). To take an extreme example, if several levels of government all adopted income taxes, in the absence of coordination, they might conceivably tax away all a taxpayer's income.

Some reformers recommend tax separation as a way to foster tax coordination. Tax separation involves each level of government using different revenue sources, such a local property tax, state sales tax, and national income tax. The great flaw in this strategy is that using different types of taxes at different levels of government does not ensure that the individual taxpayer will be treated any more fairly than would be the case if several levels used the same type of tax. Politically, however, tax separation may have some value to budgeters, for if several levels of government all use the same tax, taxpayers may be a little more sensitive to overall tax levels. Drawing on a number of differing revenue sources may soften the discomfort produced by revenue raising. The same possibility may also hold for individual levels of government: Drawing on a variety of revenue sources may lessen the pain created by the overall revenue system. Impressionistic evidence in support of this proposition may be seen in the tendency for the most unpopular taxes in America to be the federal income tax and local property taxes. State tax systems, which draw revenues from a wider range of sources than do local or national revenue systems, do not seem to annoy people as much (see *Changing Public Attitudes on Government and Taxes,* annual).

Tax coordination can also be encouraged by the use of tax deductions and tax credits. As noted earlier, governments may sometimes provide tax deductions or credits to taxpayers on the basis of the taxes that they pay to other levels of government. An important justification for this practice in the case of income taxes is that they are supposed to reflect, at least in part, the taxpayer's ability to pay. Income that must be paid in taxes to other levels of government reduces the taxpayer's ability to pay. However, some analysts have noted that the tax savings from federal income tax deductions benefit primarily wealthier taxpayers because they are more likely to itemize their deductions and because a given deduction produces a greater tax savings for people in higher income tax brackets (which means people with higher incomes). Some conservatives have also complained that these tax credits and deductions encourage government growth by softening the pain of state and local taxes. This latter concern led the Reagan administration to propose abolishing federal income tax deductions for state and local taxes paid. The proposal produced considerable opposition from many state and local officials and a fair number of taxpayers. After the dust settled, deductions for state and local income and property taxes survived, but the deduction for sales taxes (which had long raised questions because people cannot readily establish what they have actually paid in sales taxes over the course of a year) was abolished (Gramlich, 1990: 163–169; Nice and Fredericksen, 1995: 78).

Tax coordination can also take other forms. Officials at different levels may levy the same tax and, in order to simplify administration and the work of the taxpayers, may define the tax base in the same way or with only minor differences. A number of states define taxable income very similarly to the federal definition. Taxpayers in those states find that filing their state and federal income tax returns is a simpler job than it is in states where the definitions of the two levels are quite different. A number of states have both a state sales tax and local sales taxes (though not necessarily in all localities). Here, too, the tax is easier to administer if the tax base is the same at both levels.

Administration and compliance can be made even simpler with centralized tax administration. If two or more levels of government levy the same type of tax on the same tax base, the higher level of government can do all the administrative work and tax collection, an arrangement that will reduce administrative costs and make life easier for taxpayers, who must only file one form and pay one bill instead of two (or more). Some states and localities use this system for administering state and local sales taxes. However, centralized administration does not offer much flexibility; each level is usually required to have the same tax base, although with computerized equipment, this is probably less true than was the case 20 years ago. Centralized administration also works more smoothly when there is trust and regular consultation between officials at the different levels involved.

One other important aspect of budgetary relationships among levels of government involves the spilling over of unmet demands from one government to another. If one level of government fails to satisfy public demands, those dissatisfied people are likely to take their case to another policy-making arena where they have hopes of a more positive reception (Schattschneider, 1960). One reason for the adoption of a number of national environmental programs in the 1970s was the lack of effective state or local action in many parts of the country (Jones, 1976: 404–406). Conversely, if one level of government does an especially good job in satisfying public demands for a particular program, that may lead to less budgetary pressure on other levels of government. However, more complex interactions may occur. Increased funding by one level of government may energize supporters of the program and cause them to step up the pressure that they place on other governments. Opponents of those groups may also step up their efforts in hopes of undercutting their victories. The result may be increased political pressures on the budgetary processes of many different governments in the country.

HORIZONTAL DYNAMICS
IN FISCAL FEDERALISM

A number of important aspects of fiscal federalism involve relationships among governments at the same level. Although those relationships have not received as much attention as the vertical relationships, the horizontal dynamics have considerable relevance to public budgeting.

Tax competition is one of the most important and controversial horizontal dynamics in fiscal federalism.[7] Tax competition occurs when officials in a state or locality make revenue decisions on the basis of what they anticipate or fear that officials in other states or localities are going to do or on the basis of what those officials have already done. If officials in one state offer a major tax break to a large corporation in hopes of attracting it to their state, officials in other states may start a bidding war with tax breaks of their own. Similar competition can erupt at the local level. Early in the 20th century, a few state governments tried to lure wealthy senior citizens from other states by banning inheritance taxes and income taxes, a move that caused considerable anxiety in a number of state capitals.

Tax competition can produce a number of problems. Either the revenue lost because of the adoption of tax breaks for numerous companies must be replaced by raising taxes on other people or businesses or funding for some programs must be cut. Tax reductions appear to be particularly targeted to large businesses, a tendency that generates complaints from smaller firms and from ordinary citizens, who do not have the economic clout to pressure states or localities into giving them similar treatment. People may begin to doubt the fairness of revenue systems if large, profitable companies pay little or no taxes. Moreover, if officials are not careful, they may grant more in concessions than the company contributes to the state or local economy. Reform of revenue systems may be discouraged if state or local officials fear that changes may set off a new round of bidding that may require costly new concessions to various companies.

Another important horizontal component of fiscal federalism involves service contracting, which is especially common at the local level. A city government might pay another city or county or a private company to provide a service instead of creating a new city department to provide the service. Service contracts may be especially appealing to small local governments, many of which cannot afford their own jail, sewage treatment plant, or other costly facilities. Through service contracts, several localities can share a landfill, police communication system, or team of highly trained personnel and, in the process, save money. In a similar manner, the national government, a state, or a locality may purchase a service from a private company rather than providing the service through a government agency. According to two recent assessments, at least half of all cities and counties in the United States are now involved in service contracts, and more than half of all state and local governments contract out at least some social services (Hamilton and Wells, 1990: 155; *Social Service Privatization,* 1997: 2).

Service contracts have a number of potential benefits, including cost savings, providing access to expertise that the government does not have, and higher service quality. Using a private contractor may provide greater flexibility in program operations, and if one contractor proves unsatisfactory, the next contract may be awarded to a different firm (Savas, 1982).

However, service contracts can also present a number of risks. If officials are not careful in drafting, awarding, and enforcing the contract, they may encounter inflated costs, poor services, and even outright fraud. The benefits of contracting out services appear to be greater when there is more competition among possible contractors; when highly specialized skills or equipment are needed, or in rural areas where large sums of money are often not at stake, there may be little competition. If state or local officials cannot readily monitor what the contractor is doing, assessing whether services are adequately provided will be difficult. There may also be further confusion regarding who is responsible for results: the officials who awarded the contract, the contractor, or both. In addition, long-term relationships with major contractors may create powerful pressures to maintain or increase program funding (Kettl, 1993; *Social Service Privatization,* 1997).

MANDATES

One of the more controversial features of intergovernmental relations in recent years is the mandate, which is a legal requirement imposed by a higher level of government on a lower level of government. Mandates come in many forms. Some mandates are attached to grant funding; recipients must comply (or at least appear to comply) with those mandates in order to receive the money. Other, more controversial mandates are simply legal commands, whether in legislation, administrative regulations, or court rulings, that the lower level of government is required to obey. A mandate may require provision of a service or adoption of a particular policy, may prohibit some action, or may require the use of a specific process or procedure in the operation of a program.[8]

Mandates are controversial, in part because they may pressure state or local officials to do something that they do not wish to do or that will anger state or local voters or interest groups. Mandates that do not come with funding may strain state or local budgets, and state and local officials may resent having to raise funds to carry out policies that are forced on them. In addition, those unfunded mandates allow officials at one level of government to adopt a policy without taking the responsibility for providing the funds for it, a separation that may lead to inadequate attention to cost considerations. Many states impose mandates that require localities to use specific budgetary procedures (and forbid others), restrict local choices regarding revenue sources and borrowing, and in general limit local budgetary discretion. Those constraints may limit local officials' ability to cope with local needs.

Mandates can be beneficial in providing a degree of uniformity, when that is needed, and in fostering coordination across different levels of government and across different governments at the same level. Mandates can also offer a degree of political protection for officials who may agree with the mandate but can fend off critics with the explanation that the action is required by the mandate (another variant of the "I'd love to help you but . . ." tactic).

Controversies over mandates have produced a number of efforts to limit or regulate mandate use at the national and state level. In 1995 the national government adopted the Unfunded Mandates Reform Act, which requires that for any federal law imposing a cost of $50 million or more on state and local governments, Congress must either provide the money or hold a separate vote to waive the requirement. Federal agencies must develop processes to consult with affected states, localities, and tribal governments that might be affected by mandates, and agencies must consider alternative proposals and select the one that is least costly, most cost-effective, or least burdensome (Davidson and Oleszek, 1998: 357–358; *Unfunded Mandates,* 1998: 1–2). Almost all states require analysis of the estimated costs, if any, that proposed legislation would impose on local governments (*Book of the States,* 1998: 103–104), and some have adopted other restrictions on the use of mandates.

Efforts to stop or limit the use of mandates recurrently run into a basic problem: Whenever additional revenues are difficult to raise (a common situation in recent years), the temptation to support initiatives by shifting some of the costs to lower levels of government is very difficult to resist. Procedural devices to stop or limit mandate use are constantly at risk of being bypassed, circumvented, or watered down (see Hosansky, 1995; *Unfunded Mandates,* 1998).

CONCLUDING THOUGHTS

Public budgeting in the United States and in many other countries is affected in many ways by the numerous governments within each country. Higher levels of government in many countries provide financial assistance to lower levels. Those intergovernmental grants come in many forms, and the money is often accompanied by rules and regulations.

Budgetary interactions among governments take many other forms as well. Different levels of government may try to coordinate their revenue systems to encourage fairness and to simplify administration and compliance. State and local governments compete with one another for industry and investment, but cooperative arrangements between levels of government or among governments at the same level are also common. Budgetary decisions made by one government may affect the political pressures placed on other governments; unmet demands in one government often mean more demands placed on other governments.

Mandates are one of the more controversial aspects of intergovernmental relations in recent years. Officials in lower levels of government especially complain about unfunded mandates, which may generate major budgetary headaches for them. A number of efforts to limit the use of unfunded mandates have yielded mixed results, in part because unfunded mandates are often attractive to officials at higher levels of government when revenues are tight.

NOTES

1. Dye (1990: chaps. 1, 8); Fisher (1988: 82–91); Furniss (1974); Musgrave and Musgrave (1980: 514–524); Nice and Fredericksen (1995: 15–20).

2. Downs (1973); Musgrave and Musgrave (1980: 527–531); Nice and Fredericksen (1995: 20–23, 202–205).

3. Break (1980: 76–87); Musgrave and Musgrave (1980: 524–532); Oates (1996: 62–66).

4. *Balancing Flexibility and Accountability* (1998); *Characteristics of Federal Grant in Aid Programs to State and Local Governments* (1995); Fisher (1988: 347–350); *Grant Programs* (1998); Musgrave and Musgrave (1980: 532–538, 558–559).

5. Break (1980: 95–99); Fisher (1988: 350–362); *Intergovernmental Relations* (1992); Musgrave and Musgrave (1980: 532–538).

6. Gramlich (1990: 163–170); Nice and Fredericksen (1995: 71–75).

7. *Financing State Government in the 1990s* (1993: 29–32, 69–71); Maxwell and Aronson (1977: 128–131); Nice and Fredericksen (1995: 129–130, 134–135).

8. Beam and Conlan (1993); Hosansky (1995); Posner (1998); Rubin (1998: chaps. 7, 8); *Unfunded Mandates* (1998).

11

ꙮ

The Frustration
of Budget Reform

The Budget Reform Cycle

The Item Veto

Balanced Budget Laws

Gramm-Rudman-Hollings

The Appropriations Committees as a Budget Reform

Budget Reforms and Budget Reality: A Mismatch

Budget Reform as a Case of Institutional Nonlearning

Concluding Thoughts

Every man is a reformer until reform tramps on his toes.

EDGAR WATSON HOWE

(Quoted In Baker, 1990: 188)

In recent years many observers have expressed concern about public budget-ing in the United States, and much of that concern involves the federal budget. Critics have decried the recurring budget deficits, the use of budget-ary gimmicks to create apparent compliance with budgetary guidelines, the use of inconsistent terminology to camouflage spending cuts and increases, and the frequent failures to meet budgetary deadlines, with the accompanying problem of last-minute budget packages, some of them very large and understood by few people. Those concerns were heightened during the winter of 1995–96, when budgetary wrangling further delayed the passage of budget bills that were already months behind schedule. As a result, a lack of money triggered several shutdowns of federal agencies.[1]

Reformers have called for a variety of changes in the federal budget process, including a balanced budget amendment to the Constitution, an item veto for the president, a biennial budget, and a capital budget. Expressions of alarm have come from many sources, including the academic community, journalists, the public, and participants in the budget process. Although budget reforms spring from a variety of motives, some reforms are clearly advocated in order to change budget outcomes. When people are unhappy with government's financial deci-sions, calls for budget reform often follow (Rubin, 1997: 80–81, 96–99).

Critics of state and local government budgeting in the United States have also expressed concerns regarding a number of problems. Complaints regarding the unequal funding of education from one school district to another have led to lawsuits in a number of states. Competition among states and localities for busi-ness investment and wealthier residents hampers revenue raising and leads to budgetary decisions that, according to critics, give preferential treatment to wealthy interests. Loopholes in state and local revenue systems hamper revenue raising, but the cost of many programs continues to rise. Excluding social insur-ance funds (such as those for pension programs), state and local governments spent more money for current services than they raised in revenues for most years between 1961 and 1990. In short, contrary to what a number of public officials said during the 1980s and early 1990s, states and localities were run-ning budget deficits.[2] Budgetary problems are not unique to the United States, either: Many countries have struggled with budget problems of one form or another over the years (*Deficit Reduction*, 1994; Wildavsky, 1986).

Unhappiness about government budgeting is not a new phenomenon in American politics, however. Complaining about government finances is a venerable American tradition, dating back to before the Declaration of Independence. During the colonial era, Americans complained about taxes and tariffs imposed without their consent and the manipulation of salaries to control judges. There were also recurrent budgetary conflicts between the lower houses of the colonial legislatures (the lower houses usually being elected by the voters) and colonial governors, who generally were controlled by the British government (*Declaration of Independence*, 1991; Simmons, 1976: 62–310).

From time to time complaints regarding government budgeting have crystallized into a feeling that there must be a better way. If that feeling lasts long enough, some sort of budget reform is likely to follow. Governments at all levels in the United States have been tinkering with their budget processes in many different ways for more than 150 years. New legislative committees have been created; chief executives have become increasingly involved. All sorts of procedural and substantive guidelines have been adopted and revised.

Although systematic evidence is not available, American citizens and officials are apparently not much happier with the condition of government finances today than they were 150 years ago (bearing in mind that many people are not very well informed regarding government finances). From 1958 through 1980, the percentage of Americans who believed "that the people in government waste a lot of money we pay in taxes" rose from 45 to 80 percent, then declined somewhat to 64 percent by 1988 (Asher, 1992: 20). That is hardly a positive evaluation. If, after 150 years of reform efforts of many types, we are not much more content with government budgeting than we were at the start, perhaps the time has come to reassess the potential of budget reforms as a remedy for our financial concerns. We also need to assess why budget reforms ostensibly designed to change budgetary outcomes continue to receive serious attention as budget remedies despite the lackluster record of those types of reforms.

THE BUDGET REFORM CYCLE

The history of budget reforms designed to change budget outcomes appears, broadly speaking, to follow a three-phase cycle. First, disappointment with some feature of government's finances (too much spending on X, too little spending on Y, taxes on Z are too high) crystallizes to a point that demand for improvement is voiced. Second, some type of budgetary reform is adopted. Third, people are disappointed with the results or are disappointed generally, which eventually starts the process all over again. Understanding the nature of this process is crucial in assessing the likely value of budget reforms.

The reasons for the virtual certainty of disappointment at the third phase of the budget reform cycle are rooted partly in the reasons for disappointment in the first stage and partly in the performance of the budget reforms. At the outset, budgeting is to some degree an inherently disappointing activity. One of the most basic reasons why governments (or businesses or families) budget is that we typically want more than we can afford.[3] Although Americans profess considerable cynicism regarding politicians, the public also demands a great deal in the way of public services. At the same time, Americans have high expectations regarding their personal lifestyles—homes, cars, televisions, home appliances, vacations, and so forth. Those expectations are reinforced by advertisements and many aspects of popular culture that emphasize the link between happiness and owning various commodities. Consequently, budgeting inevitably results in unmet demands (because we want more than we can afford). No budget reform can solve that problem.

Budgeting is also inherently disappointing because governments (like all other organizations) budget for a number of different purposes (see Axelrod, 1988: 7–16; Schick, 1990: 1; Wildavsky, 1992: 425–427), and sometimes those purposes are not compatible. For example, budgets need to offer a guide to the future, not only for long-term projects, like highways, but also to enable people to plan their personal futures. A worker who expects to retire in 10 years needs some degree of certainty regarding Social Security benefits; parents who hope to send their children to the state university in eight years need to know how much to save for tuition and other expenses. Business owners who are trying to decide where to locate a new factory or warehouse need some predictability regarding the condition of the transportation system, the availability of law enforcement, and the condition of other public facilities in future years.

The use of budgets as a guide to the future usually calls for considerable stability and predictability in the budget, for frequent, large changes make planning difficult. However, that stability conflicts with another budgetary task: adapting to changing conditions. When conditions change substantially, as when a recession hits or a war begins, officials may stick to long-term plans and commitments or may alter the budget to deal with the new environment, but they can rarely do both. Large budgetary revisions designed to respond to changing conditions mean unexpected changes for large numbers of people and disrupted plans (for a discussion of this conflict regarding entitlement programs, see Wildavsky, 1992: chaps. 7, 8).

Budgeters also confront the incompatibility between the need to set priorities in the budget and the need to keep conflict at a manageable level. A number of the common features of traditional budgeting, such as treating an agency's budget base as a given, allocating increases on the basis of fair shares, and treating budgetary decisions as if they were nonprogrammatic (Wildavsky, 1974) were, in part, devices for keeping conflict at a manageable level, but those devices hamper efforts at setting priorities explicitly and especially hamper efforts to change priorities (although incrementalism does not preclude changing priorities; see White, 1994: 118–119). Confronting policy issues more explicitly in the budget process and reconsidering agency budget bases may lead to more effective priority setting and easier changing of priorities (if agreement is eventually reached) but may escalate conflict to the point that budgeters have great difficulty in making or adhering to budgetary decisions (on recent problems regarding conflict in the national budget, see Wildavsky and Caiden, 1997: chaps. 4, 5, and pp. 309–335). No budget reform can fully reconcile the diverse tasks of budgeting.

Budgeting is also inherently disappointing whenever people disagree with one another regarding how large the budget should be, how funds should be allotted among programs, or what guidelines should accompany the funds. In a context of diverse preferences and a large number of programs, a considerable number of people are virtually certain to be disappointed in the final budget. No budget reform can solve that problem.

At the outset, then, all budget reforms face the problem that a number of the sources of dissatisfaction with government budgeting are in the nature of the task and cannot be reformed away. Subsequent disappointment with any reform is, therefore, highly likely. The track records of a number of budget reforms offer another reason for disappointment: The reforms often fail to produce much impact on budgetary outcomes, especially over the long haul. A few examples illustrate that phenomenon.

THE ITEM VETO

A number of budget reformers, along with a number of presidents, have called for giving the president an item veto on expenditure items in appropriations bills to help control federal spending and reduce the federal budget deficit. Supporters of this proposal contend that the item veto would enable the president to overcome congressional generosity and bring the budget under more effective control (see Abney and Lauth, 1985: 372; Ross and Schwengel, 1982). Part of the case for the item veto is usually some reference to the states' experience with it, but advocates generally do not discuss what the track record actually is.

Studies of the impact of the item veto at the state level generally conclude that most governors with item veto powers rarely use them and that the item veto has no detectable effect on spending once other influences are taken into account. This is particularly noteworthy because some governors have item veto powers that are considerably more powerful than are most versions that have been proposed for the president. Some governors can use the item veto to delete substantive language in spending bills as well delete spending items, and some governors' item veto powers include the power to reduce spending items somewhat without eliminating them entirely. The latter power, if available, gives the governor much more flexibility. No governor is likely to completely eliminate construction funds for highway building or salaries for state university employees, but some governors might occasionally want to trim an important item by 2 percent or some other modest amount. Even the strongest item veto powers, however, have virtually no effect on state spending.[4]

The item veto's feeble record at the state level reflects a number of factors. Governors often want to support programs financially, and even if the inclination to cast an item veto is present, the political costs may be very high. Citizens, interest groups, and/or members of the legislature may react angrily to cuts in their favorite programs. State legislatures may craft spending bills to protect individual items (e.g., by combining a vulnerable item with an item valued by the governor), and many expenditures are required by law. The item veto may even encourage spending in some instances; a governor might threaten to kill or cut some items favored by the legislature unless projects favored by the governor receive adequate funding, too.

Evidence from the national level gives further grounds for skepticism regarding the item veto's probable impact. A study by the General Accounting Office tried to estimate that impact by assuming that appropriations that exceeded the Office of Management and Budget's Statements of Administration Policy (SAPs) would be item vetoed. Using this procedure, they concluded that an item veto would have reduced the deficit by less than 7 percent from 1984 through 1989 (*Line Item Veto,* 1992: 1–2). This estimate is probably too generous, for it assumes that the SAPs are true statements of the president's position rather than including a bargaining component. By the 1980s, presidential positions on budgetary issues often resembled an "opening bid" rather than a clear guide to the final outcome desired by the president (Schick, 1990: 162–163). If we estimate the extent of likely item veto use based on rescissions proposed by the president, the likely impact appears much smaller: For fiscal years 1984–89, proposed rescissions from the administration averaged $3.1 billion annually, less than one-third of the projected savings based on SAPs (*Line Item Veto,* 1992: 15). This may provide an overly cautious estimate of likely savings in light of the norm that rescissions should not be too overtly used as policy instruments, though presidents are not likely to propose major rescissions in programs they support. At any rate, neither estimate suggests substantial savings.

The item veto's impact nationally would be limited by the large proportion of the federal budget that is mandated by law, the fact that every president wants to spend money on many programs, the political support that protects many programs, and the congressional practice of aggregating numerous items in spending bills, with detailed breakdowns included in committee reports rather than legislation (Fisher, 1993: 201; Wildavsky, 1992: 451–458). Relatively few items would actually be suitable candidates for item vetoes, then.

Even the fundamental assumption of presidential thrift and congressional generosity (an assumption made by many item veto advocates) is dubious: Since 1974, most of the savings produced by budget rescissions stem from proposals originating in Congress, not the White House. Even with conservative Republican presidents in office, Congress proposed greater dollar savings through rescissions than did the White House in all but one year from 1984 through 1990 (Havens, 1992: 3, 7). Nor has Congress called for dramatically higher spending than the president when we compare the presidential budget proposals and congressional budget resolutions (Schick, 1995: 60). Taken together, the state and national evidence clearly indicate that the item veto has done little to reshape state budgets and has little promise for substantial national impact.

In 1996, Congress granted the president enhanced rescission authority, with that authority to become effective in January 1997. The law gave the president a power that was somewhat more flexible than the item veto. Under the law, within five working days after signing an appropriations bill, the president could send Congress a list of items to be canceled. The items could be in the appropriations bill or in the accompanying committee reports. The cuts would take effect unless Congress passed a disapproval bill within 30 days; the disapproval bill was subject to presidential veto, which could only be overridden by a two-thirds vote of both houses of Congress. The enhanced rescission authority was to expire in 2002 unless renewed by Congress (Oppenheimer, 1997: 381–384).

By applying to committee reports as well as appropriations bills, the enhanced rescission authority was more powerful than the usual item veto proposal. However, it was still useless against legally uncontrollable spending items, and few presidents would have been inclined to use it on programs that they favored or that had powerful clientele support. Note, too, that with the volume of information contained in a major appropriations bill and its accompanying committee reports, five working days is not a very long time in which to prepare a list of proposed cuts. Nor was it clear at the outset that enhanced rescission authority would be found constitutional (on the latter point, see Oppenheimer, 1997: 384). That concern was confirmed when the Supreme Court declared the enhanced rescission authority unconstitutional in 1998 (Nelson, 1999: 247–252).

BALANCED BUDGET LAWS

Critics of the recurring federal budget deficits have repeatedly called for amending the Constitution to require a balanced federal budget. Part of the case for the balanced budget amendment is the belief that the structures and incentives of the current budget process encourage program expansion but resistance to revenue increases and, therefore, produce chronic budget deficits (see Break, 1980: 256–266). The current system, therefore, could not correct the problem without major changes in the budget process, including a prohibition on deficits. As with the item veto, the reformers have emphasized, in a general way, that balanced budget requirements have a track record at the state level. Here, too, there is typically little or no discussion of that track record in the public debates.

Research on state balanced budget laws and debt limits (many states have both) generally finds that they may affect how debt financing is carried out but do not affect how heavily governments rely on debt financing. Through a host of devices, state officials find that those legal requirements and restrictions can be readily circumvented when the desire to borrow is present.[5] Among the techniques used to circumvent the requirements are creation of off-budget enterprises (which do the needed borrowing but whose activities do not count in determining whether the state government's budget is balanced), use of nonguaranteed debt (which is not backed by the full faith and credit of the government borrowing the money and is now a large majority of all state-local debt), and shifting debt-producing tasks to local or quasi-local governments.[6] Given that Congress and the White House already have ample experience with similar devices (Schick, 1980: 42, 79; Wildavsky, 1980: chap. 6), a balanced budget amendment is hardly likely to fare better nationally than at the state level. Federal budgeters also managed to balance the budget by 1998 without a balanced budget amendment (*The Economic and Budget Outlook: Fiscal Years 2000–2009*, 1999: 15), and budgetary debates quickly shifted to questions of how best to spend the large surpluses that were projected to emerge in the ensuing decade.

GRAMM-RUDMAN-HOLLINGS

In response to growing anxiety over the mushrooming budget deficits beginning in the early 1980s, Congress enacted the Balanced Budget and Emergency Deficit Control Act of 1985, more commonly known as Gramm-Rudman-Hollings I. The law created a set of deficit limits designed to gradually reduce the federal deficit to zero by 1991. In addition, the law established an automatic mechanism to reduce the deficit if the limits were exceeded; proponents hoped the mechanism's painful implications would goad the White House and Congress into serious action on the deficit.[7]

The initial effect of the law was, instead, to encourage the use of unrealistic assumptions and budgetary gimmicks to produce the appearance of compliance. Apparent spending was reduced by unidentified savings to be determined later. One-time sales of government property were used to generate revenue, a practice that obviously could not continue indefinitely. Once those devices were no longer sufficient, the deficit limits were changed. The law did not lead to stronger presidential proposals for deficit reduction, contrary to some expectations, and new budget timetables were not followed consistently. The law ran afoul of, among other things, disagreements over how to reduce the deficit, a lack of support for painful actions needed to reduce the deficit, and the delaying tactics that the law encouraged to protect programs from targeted cuts. No real progress in reducing the deficit resulted.[8]

THE APPROPRIATIONS COMMITTEES
AS A BUDGET REFORM

As noted in Chapter 6, Congress created the appropriations committees in the 1860s and gave them responsibility for all the appropriations bills. Their creation was rooted in a number of concerns, including the growing volume and complexity of the federal government's finances, but one clear concern was a desire (in some circles) to limit spending (Fenno, 1966: 8–9, 504). Reformers apparently hoped that committees that focused entirely on spending and made up of tightfisted members would be able to do a better job weeding out wasteful or unnecessary government expenditures. When the appropriations committees proved too enthusiastic in pursuing that goal, Congress proceeded in the 1870s and 1880s to take jurisdiction over a number of spending bills away from the appropriations committees. More generous program funding resulted, both for appropriations bills that were taken away from the appropriations committees and for bills retained by the committees (Fenno, 1966: 43–44; Stewart, 1987: 587–600).

In later years, after the appropriations committees largely regained control over all spending bills, frictions over spending levels resumed. Over the years, members of Congress developed a variety of techniques for providing program funding that the appropriations committees could not control. As discussed in Chapter 6, loan guarantees, contract authority, borrowing authority, entitlements, and other devices created financial obligations that the federal government was legally required to meet. Several considerations fostered the use of those devices, including the desire to shield programs from the uncertainty of future budget decisions, whether they are made in the White House or Congress, but one motive clearly has been ensuring that the appropriations committees' efforts to guard the Treasury (when the inclination is present) do not hamper the flow of funds to various programs (Fenno, 1966: 46–47, 518–520; Gottron, 1982: 48–51). By the 1970s, most federal spending was beyond the effective control of the appropriations committees.

The experience of the appropriations committees strongly suggests that changing budgetary procedures and structures is not a dependable way to shape budgetary outcomes. Instead, changing structures and procedures appear to reflect outside pressures that shape both budgetary structures and budgetary outcomes; when the structures appear incompatible with the outcomes supported by the broader environment, the structures will probably be changed or bypassed (Stewart, 1987: 600; White and Wildavsky, 1991: 283).

BUDGET REFORMS AND BUDGET REALITY: A MISMATCH

Scholars have been studying budgetary outcomes for many years, and their research shows that those outcomes are driven by very large and very powerful forces. The lackluster track record of budget reforms designed to change budget outcomes is partly an outgrowth of the imbalance of power between the reforms and the major influences on budgets.

Researchers have found that long-term social and economic developments strongly influence many budgetary decisions. Officials in wealthier jurisdictions have an easier time raising revenues. A larger, more complex, and more interdependent economy, and the urban society that accompanies it, create a greater need for government activity to manage that complexity and interdependence. Higher levels of wealth and education yield smaller families and a longer life expectancy, with the result that the relative size of the elderly population grows. A larger elderly population, in turn, increases the need for programs to cover the costs of old age, including health care. Although the theoretical interpretations of the relationships are a matter of some controversy, there is little doubt that social and economic development is a powerful influence on budgets.[9]

Many studies also find that budgetary decisions are often shaped by the problem environment. The strength of military rivals and levels of international conflict influence defense spending. The distribution of the population, terrain, and climate shape the cost of transportation programs. A rise in the crime rate creates heavy pressure for more spending on crime control. Budgets are not enacted in a vacuum; they are often a reaction to the problems faced by government and society.[10]

Additional evidence reveals that, contrary to common impression, budget decisions often reflect the demands, values, and preferences of large numbers of people. Where more citizens have liberal opinions or support relatively liberal political parties, more generous funding for education and social programs typically results. Where opinions and party support follow more conservative lines, more conservative spending patterns emerge. When the public fears that defense spending is too low, defense spending typically rises. Although many citizens find the budget process baffling and doubt that public officials pay any attention at all to citizen opinions, their views do shape budgetary outcomes, whether directly or through the parties.[11]

Budgets are also powerfully influenced by the heavy weight of prior commitments and sunk costs. When decision makers treat many existing programs as given, to reduce conflict, time pressures, and the information load of decision making, the vast bulk of next year's budget will be a function of this year's budget. When relatively permanent statutes create entitlements, and especially if those laws index program benefits to reflect changes in the cost of living, those legal provisions will shape budgets for years to come. Many spending programs have powerful political allies; continuation of those programs is generally (though not always) a forgone conclusion. Once long-term projects are under way, proposals to terminate them will face the complaint that termination will mean that previous expenditures were wasted and that shutting down the projects will generate shutdown costs as well. Officials who previously supported adoption, expansion, or continuation of current programs are typically hesitant to cut those programs very much, partly because they believe in the programs and partly because of fear of adverse political consequences. In a variety of respects, then, future budgetary decisions are powerfully constrained by decisions of the past. Those previous decisions do not eliminate the possibility of change but place powerful limits on the scope and pace of change in a great many cases.[12]

When we consider that budgets are driven by very large and powerful forces—the size and complexity of the economy and society, the serious problems facing the society, the demands and beliefs of large numbers of people, and the immense weight of established budgetary commitments—trying to blunt the effects of those forces by something as small and weak as budget reform is likely to be an exercise in futility (see Schick, 1981: 327). In the ensuing mismatch, the budget reform is very likely to be overwhelmed, for no budget reform is likely to make a poor community into a rich one, alter the nature of the problems facing society, or change what the public wants from government. Budget reforms are similarly unlikely to eliminate prior commitments in government, particularly when those commitments are established in law, have powerful political support, or reflect the magnitude of various problems, such as the size of the school-age population or the ruggedness of terrain; the experiences of program budgeting and zero-based budgeting are particularly instructive in that regard (see Chapter 4).

BUDGET REFORM AS A CASE
OF INSTITUTIONAL NONLEARNING

Despite the relatively lackluster record of budget reforms, they continue to attract the attention and support of people who are unhappy with the budget situation. One possible (and plausible) explanation for that phenomenon is the well-known tendency for people in the political arena to pay relatively little attention to academic analyses unless they support the preferences of the political actors. Other forces may also be at work, however.

The Wright Brothers Phenomenon

The fact that some enterprise has repeatedly failed in the past does not preclude the possibility of success at some future date. History provides many examples of unsuccessful efforts (powered flight, surgery, and home videocassette recorders, among others) that were eventually followed by success of one sort or another. Some advocates of budget reform may be proceeding with an awareness that previous reforms have generally had little impact but with the belief that the next effort could be the breakthrough that yields success. Unfortunately, this explanation is not consistent with some of the public statements of some budget reform advocates who at least imply and sometimes claim outright that the reforms have a track record of previous success.

Reform as a Delaying Tactic

When officials face a particularly painful decision, one that is likely to anger many people no matter how it is decided, a common coping mechanism is stalling for time (Edwards and Sharkansky, 1978: 107–109). By delaying, officials hope that the problem will go away, that the public will lose interest in it, or that the officials will have left office, leaving a future group of policy makers to struggle with the painful problem. Numerous delaying tactics are available when officials want to stall for time: appointing a commission to study the problem, adopting a timetable for eventually solving the problem but without specifying precisely how that will be done, and proceeding against the problem at the slowest possible pace.

One other delaying tactic is to take the position that a problem cannot be addressed unless some other step is taken first. This technique requires, of course, choosing a prerequisite that will take a great deal of time to complete or that cannot be completed at all, especially if the failure to complete it can be blamed on someone else. For example, the president or a member of Congress proclaims that serious action on the deficit requires enactment of a balanced budget amendment or an item veto for the president. Whether the prerequisite step would actually help resolve the problem is not particularly relevant in this case. The key point is that a lack of progress on the prerequisite step may provide political cover for the official using the tactic.

Reform as a Symbolic "Remedy"

When leaders confront a problem that they do not know how to solve or do not want to solve, cannot agree on a course of action, or fear that genuine remedies for a problem will produce unacceptable political costs, they may decide to offer a symbolic response that will create the appearance of action without actually doing anything about the problem. Symbolic responses come in many varieties, from giving a speech about the problem or visiting the site of the problem to creating a powerless agency or proposing or adopting a reform that will do little or nothing except to reassure people that their officials are aware of the problem and trying to produce a remedy. If the tactic works, the officials involved will be protected against complaints that they are ignoring a serious need, and public anxieties will decline to a more comfortable level (Edelman, 1988: 24, 59).

At best, symbolic responses may help officials buy time while they search for an effective remedy or while a gradual remedy attacks the problem bit by bit. At worst, symbolic responses may deceive the public into believing that a problem is being addressed while no actual progress is occurring or likely to occur.

CONCLUDING THOUGHTS

After roughly 150 years of budget reforms, we probably should face up to the prospect that budget reforms are unlikely to produce major changes in budget outcomes. Some of our frustrations with budgeting are inherent in the nature of the task, and the forces that drive budgets are much too large and powerful to be stemmed by new budget processes or formats. A new budgeting system cannot make a society simpler or more prosperous; a new budget format will not change what people want from government or the problems that society faces.

This suggests that the solutions to budgetary discontents (to the degree that solutions are possible) are more likely to be found through political organization and mobilization and changing public expectations regarding government rather than through budget reforms. Other plausible strategies may include finding or developing ways to provide services at lower costs or emphasizing less visible revenue sources. Some of the recent interest in privatization, for example, is based on the belief that greater use of private mechanisms for service delivery and/or greater competition between public agencies and private firms for delivery of public services will provide more services per dollar.[13] Public officials may also try to expand the economy in order to produce more revenues and to reduce the need for some programs, such as unemployment compensation (see Chapter 9). None of these strategies for resolving budgetary difficulties is particularly easy to employ, but we now have enough evidence on the results of various budget reforms to indicate that they offer very little hope of reshaping budgetary outcomes in any substantial way.

Bear in mind that not all budget reformers are trying to change budgetary outcomes in general. Reformers may be trying to improve the quality of budgetary decisions (very much a judgment call in many situations) without a particular intent to reduce the overall size of the budget or the allocation of funding across different programs, for example. The reformers may hope to direct greater attention to budgetary matters, such as evidence of program impact, that have received inadequate attention in the past (Grizzle, 1986). Other reformers may be trying to reduce the risk of fraud or provide officials with better information (e.g., improved revenue forecasting), regardless of whether noticeable changes in the broad contours of the budget result. These reformers may be less likely to be disappointed in the results of their efforts than are reformers who hope to produce dramatically different budgetary decisions through reforms.

NOTES

1. Kettl (1992: 1–3, 13–14, 93–94); Maraniss and Weiskopf (1996: 146–205); Schick (1990: 1–5).
2. For discussions of state and local budgetary problems, see Aronson and Hilley (1986); *Financing State Government in the 1990s* (1993); Gold (1995: chaps. 1–3); *Intergovernmental Relations* (1992).
3. A basic principle of economics is that valued things are scarce. See Bronfenbrenner, Sichel, and Gardner (1990: 2 and chap. 4).
4. Abney and Lauth (1985); *Fiscal Discipline in the Federal System* (1987: 42–43); Nice (1988).
5. Aronson and Hilley (1986: 176); Heins (1963); Kiewiet and Szakaly (1992); Nice (1991); one study disagreed but omitted a relevant control variable. See *Fiscal Discipline in the Federal System* (1987: 39–42).
6. Aronson and Hilley (1986: 176); Bennett and DiLorenzo (1983: 34–46); Heins (1963: 19–20).
7. Gosling (1992: 88–92); Schick (1990: 4–5); Vogler (1993: 257–258).

8. Kettl (1992); Reischauer (1990: 225–228); Rubin (1997: 202–203); Schick (1990: 204–205); Thurber (1992: 264–266); White and Wildavsky (1991: 516); Wildavsky (1992: 260–263).

9. Bahl (1969); Dye (1966, 1990); Wilensky (1975).

10. Friedman (1990); Hartley and Russett (1992); Hicks and Swank (1992); Wilensky (1975).

11. Budge and Hofferbert (1990); Fenno (1966: 358–361, 393); Hartley and Russett (1992); Hicks and Swank (1992); Kiewiet and McCubbins (1991: 194–205); Nice (1985); Wright, Erikson, and McIver (1987).

12. Sharkansky (1968: 14–15, 35–43); White (1994); Wildavsky (1974: 13–16, 216–217; 1992: 7–8).

13. The literature on privatization is large and growing rapidly. See Donahue (1989); Kettl (1988); Savas (1982); the Symposium section of *Policy Studies Journal* (1996: 627–675).

References

Abney, Glenn, and Thomas Lauth. 1985.
"The Item Veto and Expenditure
Restraint." *Public Administration Review*
45:372–377.

——— 1998. "The End of Executive
Dominance in State Appropriations."
Public Administration Review 58:388–394.

"Across the USA." 2000. *USA Today,*
February 25, p. 12A.

Allison, Graham. 1980. *Public and Private
Management: Are They Fundamentally
Alike in All Unimportant Respects?*
Proceedings for the Public
Management Research Conference,
November 19–20, 1979. Washington,
DC: Office of Personnel
Management, pp. 27–38.

American Almanac. 1996. Austin, TX:
Hoover's.

*An Analysis of the President's Budgetary
Proposals for Fiscal Year 2000.* 1999.
Washington, DC: Congressional
Budget Office.

Anderson, James. 1994. *Public Policymaking,*
2nd ed. Boston: Houghton Mifflin.

Aronson, J. Richard, and John Hilley.
1986. *Financing State and Local
Governments,* 4th ed. Washington, DC:
Brookings.

Aronson, J. Richard, and Eli Schwartz.
1996. "Capital Budgeting." In
J. Richard Aronson and Eli Schwartz,
eds., *Management Policies in Local
Government.* Washington, DC:
International City/County
Management Association,
pp. 433–456.

Asher, Herbert. 1992. *Presidential Elections
and American Politics,* 5th ed. Pacific
Grove, CA: Brooks/Cole.

"Audit Shows King County Overspent by
$40 Million." 2000. *Daily Evergreen,*
Pullman, WA, January 12, p. 3.

Axelrod, Donald. 1988. *Budgeting for
Modern Government.* New York:
St. Martin's.

———. 1995. *Budgeting for Modern
Government,* 2nd ed. New York:
St. Martin's.

Bahl, Roy. 1969. *Metropolitan City Expenditures.* Lexington, KY: University of Kentucky.

Baker, Daniel, ed. 1990. *Political Quotations.* Detroit, MI: Gale Research.

Balancing Flexibility and Accountability. 1998. Washington, DC: General Accounting Office.

Banovetz, James, Drew Dolan, and John Swain. 1994. *Managing Small Cities and Counties.* Washington, DC: International City/County Management Association.

Beam, David, and Timothy Conlan. 1993. "The Growth of Intergovernmental Mandates in an Era of Deregulation and Decentralization." In Lawrence O'Toole, ed., *American Intergovernmental Relations,* 2nd ed. Washington, DC: Congressional Quarterly Press, pp. 322–336.

Beer, Samuel. 1976. "The Adoption of Revenue Sharing: A Case Study in Public Sector Politics." *Public Policy* 24:127–196.

Behn, Robert. 1980. "How to Terminate a Public Policy: A Dozen Hints for the Would-Be Terminator." In Charles Levine, ed., *Managing Fiscal Stress.* Chatham, NJ: Chatham House, pp. 327–342.

Bennett, James, and Thomas DiLorenzo. 1983. *Underground Government.* Washington, DC: CATO.

Berkley, George, and Douglas Fox. 1978. *80,000 Governments.* Boston: Allyn and Bacon.

Berry, John. 2000. "No Quick Fix Needed." *Washington Post National Weekly Edition,* November 6, pp. 17–18.

Berry, William, and David Lowery. 1987. "Explaining the Size of the Public Sector: Responsive and Excessive Government Interpretations." *Journal of Politics* 49:401–440.

Beyle, Thad. 1999. "The Governors." In Virginia Gray, Russell Hanson, and Herbert Jacob, eds., *Politics in the American States,* 7th ed. Washington, DC: Congressional Quarterly Press, pp. 191–231.

Bland, Robert, and Wes Clarke. 1999. "Budgeting for Capital Improvements." In Roy Meyers, ed., *Handbook of Government Budgeting.* San Francisco: Jossey-Bass, pp. 653–677.

Bland, Robert, and Irene Rubin. 1997. *Budgeting: A Guide for Local Governments.* Washington, DC: International City/County Management Association.

Book of the States. 1998. Lexington, KY: Council of State Governments.

Break, George. 1980. *Financing Government in a Federal System.* Washington, DC: Brookings.

Bretschneider, Stuart, and Wipen Gorr. 1999. "Practical Methods for Projecting Revenues." In Roy Meyers, ed., *Handbook of Government Budgeting.* San Francisco: Jossey Bass, pp. 308–331.

Bronfenbrenner, Martin, Werner Sichel, and Wayland Gardner. 1990. *Macroeconomics,* 3rd ed. Boston: Houghton Mifflin.

Brudney, Jeffrey, and F. Ted Hebert. 1987. "State Agencies and Their Environments: Examining the Influence of Important External Actors." *Journal of Politics* 49:186–206.

Buchanan, James, and Marilyn Flowers. 1987. *The Public Finances,* 6th ed. Homewood, IL: Dorsey.

Budge, Ian, and Richard Hofferbert. 1990. "Mandates and Policy Outputs: U.S. Party Platforms and Federal Expenditures." *American Political Science Review* 84:111–132.

Budget Account Structure. 1995. Washington, DC: General Accounting Office.

Budget Deficit: Outlook, Implications, and Choices. 1990. Washington, DC: General Accounting Office.

Budget Issues: Analysis of Long-Term Fiscal Outlook. 1997. Washington, DC: General Accounting Office.

Budget Issues: Capital Budgeting for the Federal Government. 1988. Washington, DC: General Accounting Office.

Budget Issues: Capital Budgeting in the States. 1986. Washington, DC: General Accounting Office.

Budget Issues: Capping of Outlays is Ineffective for Controlling Expenditures. 1990. Washington, DC: General Accounting Office.

Budget Issues: Earmarking in the Federal Government. 1995. Washington, DC: General Accounting Office.

Budget Issues: 1991 Budget Estimates: What Went Wrong. 1992. Washington, DC: General Accounting Office.

Budget Issues: Overview of State and Federal Debt. 1988. Washington, DC: General Accounting Office.

Budget Issues: Restructuring the Federal Budget: The Capital Component. 1989. Washington, DC: General Accounting Office.

Budget Issues: The Role of Depreciation in Budgeting for Certain Federal Investments. 1995. Washington, DC: General Accounting Office.

Budget Object Classification. 1994. Washington, DC: General Accounting Office.

"Budget Values." 1999. *Washington Post National Weekly Edition,* September 27, p. 24.

Campbell, Alan, and Seymour Sacks. 1967. *Metropolitan America.* New York: Free Press.

Chan, James. 1999. "The Bases of Accounting for Budgeting and Financial Reporting." In Roy Meyers, ed., *Handbook of Government Budgeting.* San Francisco: Jossey-Bass, pp. 357–380.

Chapman, Ronald. 1996. "Capital Financing: A New Look at an Old Idea." In Jack Rabin, W. Bartley Hildreth, and Gerald Miller, eds., *Budgeting: Formulation and Execution.* Athens, GA: Carl Vinson Institute of Government, pp. 292–296.

Changing Public Attitudes on Governments and Taxes (annual). Washington, DC: Advisory Commission on Intergovernmental Relations.

Characteristics of Federal Grant-in-Aid Programs to State and Local Governments. 1995. Washington, DC: Advisory Commission on Intergovernmental Relations.

Clarke, Wes. 1998. "Divided Government and Budget Conflict in the U.S. States." *Legislative Studies Quarterly* 23:5–22.

Clingermayer, James, and B. Dan Wood. 1995. "Disentangling Patterns of State Debt Financing." *American Political Science Review* 89:108–120.

Coe, Charles. 1989. *Public Financial Management.* Englewood Cliffs, NJ: Prentice-Hall.

Cohen, Jeffrey. 2000. *Politics and Economic Policy in the United States,* 2nd ed. Boston: Houghton Mifflin.

Collender, Stanley. 1999. *Guide to the Federal Budget: Fiscal 2000.* New York: Century Foundation.

Compendium of Budget Accounts. 1997. Washington, DC: General Accounting Office.

Comptroller General: Memo to the President of the Senate and the Speaker of the House of Representatives. 1998. Washington, DC: General Accounting Office (June 10).

Congressional Appropriations: An Updated Analysis. 1999. Washington, DC: Joint Economic Committee, U.S. Congress.

Cooper, Phillip. 1999. "Courts and Fiscal Decision Making." In Roy Meyers, ed., *Handbook of Government Budgeting.* San Francisco: Jossey-Bass, pp. 502–526.

Cozzetto, Don, Mary Kweit, and Robert Kweit. 1995. *Public Budgeting.* White Plains, NY: Longman.

Credit Reform. 1998. Washington, DC: General Accounting Office.

Davidson, Roger, and Walter Oleszek. 1998. *Congress and Its Members,* 6th ed. Washington, DC: Congressional Quarterly Press.

Debt Collecting: Improved Reporting Needed on Billions of Dollars in Delinquent Debt and Agency Collection Performance. 1997. Washington, DC: General Accounting Office.

"Declaration of Independence." 1991. In Richard Heffner, ed., *A Documentary History of the United States,* 5th ed. New York: Mentor, pp. 15–19.

Defense Budget: Capital Asset Projects Undergo Significant Change Between Approval and Execution. 1994. Washington, DC: General Accounting Office.

Deficit Reduction. 1994. Washington, DC: General Accounting Office.

Department of Transportation: Flexible Funding Within Federal Highway Programs. 1997. Washington, DC: General Accounting Office.

Derthick, Martha. 1975. *Uncontrollable Spending for Social Services Grants.* Washington, DC: Brookings.

Dilger, Robert. 1983. "Grantsmanship, Formulamanship, and Other Allocational Principles." *Journal of Urban Affairs* 5:269–286.

Donahue, John. 1989. *The Privatization Decision.* New York: Basic.

Downs, Anthony. 1959–60. "Why the Government Budget is Too Small in a Democracy." *World Politics* 12:541–563.

———. 1973. *Opening Up the Suburbs.* New Haven, CT: Yale.

Duncombe, Herbert and Florence Heffron. 1983. "Legislative Budgeting." In Jack Rabin and Thomas Lynch, eds., *Handbook on Public Budgeting and Financial Management.* New York: Marcel Dekker, pp 417–457.

Dye, Thomas. 1966. *Politics, Economics, and the Public.* Chicago and Rand McNally.

———. 1990. *American Federalism.* Lexington, MA: Lexington.

———. 1990. *American Federalism.* Lexington, MA: Lexington.

———. 1992. *Understanding Public Policy,* 7th ed. Englewood Cliffs, NJ: Prentice-Hall.

The Economic and Budget Outlook: An Update. 1999. Washington, DC: Congress Budget Office.

The Economic and Budget Outlook: Fiscal Years 2000–2009. 1999. Washington, DC: Congressional Budget Office.

Edelman, Murray. 1988. *Constructing the Political Spectacle.* Chicago: University of Chicago.

Edwards, George. 1980. *Implementing Public Policy.* Washington, DC: CQ Press.

Edwards, George and Ira Sharkansky. 1978. *The Policy Predicament.* San Francisco: Freeman.

Erikson, Robert, Norman Luttberg, and Kent Tedig. 1991. *American Public Opinion,* 4th ed. New York: Macmillan.

Euske, K. J. 1983. "Budgeting and Public Management." In Jack Rabin and Thomas Lynch, eds., *Handbook on Public Budgeting and Finance.* New York: Marcel Dekker, pp. 401–416.

Executive Guide: Leading Practices in Capital Decision-Making. 1998. Washington, DC: General Accounting Office.

Federal Debt: Answers to Frequently Asked Questions. 1996. Washington, DC: General Accounting Office.

Federal Grants. 1996. Washington, DC: General Accounting Office/Accounting and Information Management Division, GAO/AIMD 97-7.

Fenno, Richard. 1966. *The Power of Purse.* Boston: Little, Brown.

Financing State Government in the 1990s. 1993. Denver, CO: National Conference of State Legislatures/National Governors' Association.

Finney, Robert. 1994. *Basics of Budgeting.* New York: American Management Association.

Fiscal Discipline in The Federal System.
1987. Washington, DC: Advisory
Commission on Intergovernmental
Relations.

Fisher, Louis. 1975. *Presidential Spending
Power.* Princeton, NJ: Princeton.

————. 1985. "Ten Years of the Budget
Act: Still Searching for Controls."
Public Budgeting and Finance, 5:3–28.

————. 1993. *The Politics of Shared Power,*
3rd ed. Washington, DC:
Congressional Quarterly Press.

————. 1997. *Constitutional Conflicts between
Congress and the President,* 4th ed.
Lawrence: University Press of Kansas.

Fisher, Louis, and Philip Joyce. 1997.
"Introduction: Reflections on Two
Decades of Congressional Budgeting."
Public Budgeting and Finance 17:3–6.

Fisher, Ronald. 1988. *State and Local Public
Finance.* Glenview, IL: Scott, Foresman.

Forest Service Management. 1998.
Washington, DC: General Accounting
Office. Resources, Community, and
Economic Development Division,
GAO/RCED 99-2.

Foss, Gwen. 1997. *The Confused Quote
Book.* New York: Gramercy.

Fram, Alan. 2000. Congress Approves
Budget Deal, Nears Adjournment.
Palouse Living. Moscow, ID. Associated
Press. December 26, 2000, p. 1.

Friedman, Robert. 1990. "The Politics of
Transportation." In Virginia Gray,
Herbert Jack, and Robert Albritton,
eds., *Politics in the American States,*
5th ed. Glenview, IL: Scott,
Foresman/Little Brown, pp. 527–559.

Fromson, Brett. 1995. "Winning the
Derivative Gamble." *Washington
Post National Weekly Edition,*
March 20–26, p. 21.

"Fundamentals of Revenue Bond Credit
Analysis." 1996. Moody's Investors
Service. In Jack Rabin, W. Bartley
Hildreth, Gerald Miller, eds.,
Budgeting: Formulation and Execution.
Athens, GA: Carl Vinson Institute and
Government, pp. 361–374.

Furniss, Norman. 1974. The Practical
Significance of Decentralization.
Journal of Politics 36:958–982.

Gilmour, John. 1992. "Summits and
Stalemates: Bipartisan Negotiations in
the Postreform Era." In Roger
Davidson, ed., *The Postreform Congress.*
New York: St. Martin's Press.

*Glossary of Terms Used in the Federal Budget
Process* (Exposure Draft). 1993.
Washington, DC: General Accounting
Office.

Gold, Steven. *The Fiscal Crisis of the States.*
1995. Washington, DC: Georgetown
University.

Goldberg, M. Hirsh. 1994. *The Complete
Book of Greed.* New York: William
Morrow.

Gosling, James. 1992. *Budgetary Politics in
American Governments.* New York:
Longman.

————. 1997. *Budgetary Politics in American
Governments,* 2nd ed. New York:
Garland.

————. 2000. *Politics and the American
Economy.* New York: Addison Wesley
Longman.

Gottron, Martha, ed. 1982. *Budgeting for
America.* Washington, DC:
Congressional Quarterly.

Government-Sponsored Enterprises. 1990.
Washington, DC: General Accounting
Office.

Gowda, Vanita. 2000. "Too Many Visitors,
Too Little Money." *Governing*
(March):40–41.

Graften, Carl and Anne Permaloff. 1983.
"Budgeting Reforms in Perspective."
In Jack Rubin and Thomas Lynch,
eds., *Handbook on Public Budgeting and
Finance.* New York: Marcel Dekker,
pp. 89–124.

Gramlich, Edward. 1990. "The Economics
of Fiscal Federalism and It's Reform."
In Thomas Swartz and John Peck,
eds., *The Changing Face of Fiscal
Federalism.* Armonk, NY:
M. E. Sharpe, pp. 152–174.

————. 1998. *A Guide to Benefit-Cost Analysis,* 2nd ed. Prospect Heights, IL: Waveland.

Grant Programs. 1998. Washington, DC: General Accounting Office, pp. 98–137.

Green, Gary, Arnold Fleischmann, and Tsz Man Kwong. 1996. "The Effectiveness of Local, Economic Development Policies in the 1980s." *Social Science Quarterly* 77:609–625.

Greider, William. 1982. *The Education of David Stockman and Other Americans.* New York: E. P. Dutton.

Grizzle, Gloria. 1986. "Does Budget Format Really Govern the Action of Budgetmakers?" *Public Budgeting and Finance* 6:60–70.

Grizzle, Gloria and William Klay. 1994. "Forecasting State Sales Tax Revenues: Comparing the Accuracy of Different Methods." *S & L Government Review.* 26, No. 3 (Fall):142–152.

Gupta, Dipak. 1994. *Decisions by the Numbers.* Englewood Cliffs, NJ: Prentice-Hall.

Hale, George, and Scott Douglas. 1977. "The Politics of budget Implementation: Financial Manipulation in State and Local Government." *Administration and Society,* vol. 9: pp. 367–368.

Hale, George, and Marian Palley. 1981. *The Politics of Federal Grants.* Washington, DC: Congressional Quarterly.

Hamilton, Christopher, and Donald Wells. 1990. *Federalism, Power, and Political Economy.* Englewood Cliffs, NJ: Prentice-Hall.

Hartley, Thomas, and Bruce Russett. 1992. "Public Opinion and the Common Defense: Who Governs Military Spending in the United States?" *American Political Science Review* 86:905–915.

Havemann, Joel. 1976. *The Federal Budget: Reform's First Round.* Washington, DC: National Journal Reprints.

Havens, Harry. 1992. *Budget Process: Use and Impact of Recsission Procedures* (testimony). Washington, DC: General Accounting Office.

Hay, Leon. 1980. *Accounting for Governmental and Nonprofit Entities,* 6th ed. Homewood, IL: Irwin.

Hedge, David. 1983. "Fiscal Dependency and The State Budget Process." *Journal of Politics* 45:198–208.

Heilbroner, Robert, and Peter Bernstein. 1989. *The Debt and the Deficit.* New York: Norton.

Heins, A. James. 1963. *Constitutional Restrictions on State Debt.* Madison: University of Wisconsin.

Hendrick, Rebecca, and John Forrester. 1999. "Budget Implementation." In Roy Meyers, ed., *Handbook of Government Budgeting.* San Francisco: Jossey-Bass, pp. 568–596.

Hicks, Alexander, and Duane Swank. 1992. "Politics, Institutions, and Welfare Spending in Industrialized Democracies, 1960–82." *American Political Science Review* 86:658–674.

High-Risk Series: An Update. 1999. Washington, DC: General Accounting Office.

Hildreth, W. Bartley. 1991. "Federal Financial Management." In Thomas Lynch, ed., *Federal Budget and Financial Management Reform.* New York: Quorum, pp. 151–170.

Historical Statistics of the U.S.: Colonial Times to 1957. 1960. Washington, DC: U.S. Department of Commerce.

Historical Tables: Budget of U.S. Government. FY 1999. 1998. Washington, DC: U.S. Government Printing Office.

Hoaglin, David, Richard Light, Bucknam McPeek, Frederick Mosteller, and Michael Stoto. 1982. *Data for Decisions.* Cambridge, MA: Abt.

Holder, William. 1996. "Financial Accounting, Reporting, and Auditing." In J. Richard Aronson and Eli Schwartz, eds., *Management Policies in Local Government Finance,* 4th ed., Washington, DC: International City/County Management Association pp. 169–200.

Hosansky, David. 1995. "The Other War over Mandates." *Governing* (April): 26, 28.

Howard, S. Kenneth. 1973. *Changing State Budgeting.* Lexington, KY: Council of State Governments.

Hyde, Albert, and William Jarocki. 1978. "Revenue and Expenditure Forecasting: Some Comparative Trends." In Albert Hyde and Jay Shafritz, eds., *Government Budgeting.* Oak Park, IL: Moore, pp. 532–548.

Hyde, Albert, and Jay Shafritz, eds. 1978. *Government Budgeting.* Oak Park, IL: Moore.

Ingram, Helen. 1977. "Policy Implementation Through Bargaining: The Case of Federal Grants-In-Aid." *Public Policy* 25:499–526.

Intergovernmental Relations. 1992. Washington, DC: General Accounting Office. HRD-92-87FS.

Isaak, Alan. 1985. *Scope and Methods of Political Science,* 4th ed. Homewood, IL: Dorsey.

Janis, Irving. 1982. *Groupthink.* Boston: Houghton Mifflin.

Jones, Charles. 1976. In Herbert Jacob and Kenneth Vines, eds., *Regulating the Environment in Politics in the American States,* 3rd ed. Boston: Little, Brown. pp. 388–427.

Jorion, Philippe. 1995. *Big Bets Gone Bad.* San Diego: Academic.

Kamlet, Mark, and David Mowery. 1985. "The First Decade of the Congressional Budget Act: Legislative Imitation and Adaptation in Budgeting. *Policy Sciences.* Vol. 18, no. 4 pp. 313–334.

Kessler, Glenn, and Eric Pianin. 2001. "A Run-In with Reality." *Washington Post National Weekly Edition,* January 29–February 4, p. 12.

Kettl, Donald. 1988. *Government by Proxy.* Washington, DC: Congressional Quarterly Press.

———. 1992. *Deficit Politics.* New York: MacMillan.

———. 1993. *Sharing Power.* Washington, DC: Brookings.

Key, V. O. 1940. "The Lack of a Budgetary Theory." *American Political Science Review* 34: pp. 1137–1144.

Kham, Aman. 1996. "Cash Management: Basic Principles and Guidelines." In Jack Rabin, W. Bartley Hildreth, and Gerald Millers, eds., *Budgeting: Formulation and Execution.* Athens, GA: Carl Vinson Institute of Government. pp. 313–322.

Kiewiet, D. Roderick, and Mathew McCubbins. 1991. *The Logic of Delegation.* Chicago: University of Chicago.

Kiewiet, D. Roderick, and Kristin Szakaly. 1992. Constitutional Limitations on Borrowing: An Analysis of State Bonded Indebtedness. Paper presented at the Annual Meeting of American Political Science Association, Chicago.

Kingdon, John. 1995. *Agendas, Alternatives, and Public Policies,* 2nd ed. New York: Harper-Collins.

Kirkman, James. 1989. Government-Sponsored Enterprises. Statement made before Subcommittee on Oversight House Ways and Means Committee, U.S. House. General Accounting Office. AFMD-89-16.

Kohut, Andrew, and Robert Toth. 1998. "A World of Difference." *Washington Post National Weekly Edition.* January 5. p. 22.

Lee, Robert. 1997. "A Quarter Century of State Budgeting Practices." *Public Administration Review* 57:133–140.

Lee, Robert, and Ronald Johnson. 1989. *Public Budgeting Systems,* 4th ed. Gaithersburg, MD: Aspen.

———. 1994. *Public Budgeting Systems,* 5th ed. Gaithersburg, MD: Aspen. Chapter 1.

————. 1998. *Public Budgeting Systems,* 6th ed. Gaithersburg, MD: Aspen.

Legislative Authority Over the Enacted Budget. 1992. Denver: National Conference of State. Legislatures.

LeLoup, Lance. 1978. "The Myth of Incrementalism: Analytic Choices in Budgetary Theory." *Polity* 10:488–509.

————. 1988. *Budgetary Politics,* 4th ed. Brunswick, OH: King's Court.

Leonard, Paul. 1996. "Debt Management." In J. Richard Aronson and Eli Schwartz, eds. *Management Policies in Local Government Finance,* 4th ed. Washington, DC: International City/County Management Association. pp. 313–338.

Levenbach, Hans, and James Cleary. 1981. *The Beginning Forecaster.* Belmont, CA: Lifetime Learning.

Lewis, Verne. 1952. "Toward a Theory of Budgeting." *Public Administration Review* 12:43–54.

Lindblom, Charles. 1959. "The Science of Muddling Through." *Public Administration Review* 19:79–88.

Line Item Veto: Estimating Potential Savings. 1992. Washington, DC: General Accounting Office.

Lowery, David. 1985. "The Keynesian and Political Determinants of Unbalanced Budgets: U.S. Fiscal Policy from Eisenhower to Reagan." *American Journal of Political Science* 29:428–460.

Lowery, David, and William Berry. 1983. "The Growth of Government in the United States: An Empirical Assessment of Competing Explanations." *American Journal of Political Science* 27:665–694.

Lowi, Theodore. 1979. *The End of Liberalism,* 2nd ed. New York: Norton.

Lyden, Fremont, and Marc Lindenberg. 1983. *Public Budgeting in Theory and Practice.* New York: Longman.

Lynch, Thomas. 1995. *Public Budgeting in America,* 4th ed. Englewood Cliffs, NJ: Prentice-Hall.

Makolo, Philomene. 1983. "National Development Through Budgeting." In Jack Rabin and Thomas Lynch, eds., *Handbook on Public Budgeting and Finance.* New York: Marcel Dekker, pp. 125–160.

Mansfield, Edwin. 1983. *Statistics for Business and Economics,* 2nd ed. New York: Norton.

Maraniss, David, and Michael Weisskopf. 1996. *Tell Newt to Shut Up!* New York: Touchstone.

Marmor, Theodore, Jerry Mashaw, and Philip Harvey. 1990. *America's Misunderstood Welfare State.* New York: Basic.

Maxwell, James, and J. Richard Aronson. 1977. *Financing State and Local Governments,* 3rd ed. Washington, DC: Brookings.

Mazmanian, Daniel, and Paul Sabatier. 1983. *Implementation and Public Policy.* Glenview, IL: Scott, Foresman.

McConnell, Grant. 1966. *Private Power and American Democracy.* New York: Knopf.

McKenna, Christopher. 1980. *Quantitative Methods for Public Decision Making.* New York: McGraw-Hill.

Meyers, Roy. 1994. *Strategic Budgeting.* Ann Arbor: University of Michigan Press.

————. 1997. "Late Appropriations and Government Shutdowns: Frequency, Causes, Consequences, and Remedies." *Public Budgeting and Finance* 17:25–34.

Mikesell, John. 1995. *Fiscal Administration,* 4th ed. Belmont, CA: Wadsworth.

Mill, John. 1974. *On Liberty.* London: Penguin.

Mohr, Lawrence. 1988. *Impact Analysis for Program Evaluation.* Chicago: Dorsey.

Moody, Scott, ed. 1998. *Facts and Figures on Government Finance,* 32nd ed. Washington, DC: Tax Foundation. 1250 H Street NW, Suite 750, Washington, DC, 20005.

Moore, Thomas. 1989. *Handbook of Business Forecasting.* New York: Harper and Row.

Mosher, Frederick, and Orville Poland. 1964. *The Costs of American Government.* New York: Dodd, Mead.

Motza, Maryann. "Corruption and Budgeting." In Jack Rabin and Thomas Lynch, eds., *Handbook on Public Budgeting and Finance.* New York: Marcel Dekker, pp. 509–538.

Mullins, Daniel, and Philip Joyce. 1996. "Tax and Expenditure Limitations and State and Local Fiscal Structure: An Empirical Assessment." *Public Budgeting and Finance* 16:75–101.

"Municipal Finance Criteria." Standard and Poor's 1996. In Jack Rabin, W Bartley Hildreth, and Gerald Miller, eds., *Budgeting: Formulation and Execution.* Athens, GA: Carl Vinson Institute of Government, pp. 341–360.

Murray, Charles. 1984. *Losing Ground: American Social Policy, 1950–1980.* New York: Basic.

Musgrave, Richard, and Peggy Musgrave. 1980. *Public Finance in Theory and Practice,* 3rd ed. New York: McGraw-Hill.

Nachmins, David. 1979. *Public Policy Evaluation.* New York: St. Martin's.

Nakamura, Robert, and Frank Smallwood. 1980. *The Politics of Policy Implementation.* New York: St. Martin's.

Nelson, Michael. 1999. *The Evolving Presidency.* Washington, DC: Congressional Quarterly Press.

Neustadt, Richard. 1954. "Presidency and Legislation: The Growth of Central Clearance." *American Political Science Review* 48:641–671.

Nice, David. 1985. "State Party Ideology and Policy Making." *Policy Studies Journal* 13:780–796.

———. 1987. "State-Financed Property Tax Relief to Individuals: A Research Note." *Western Political Quarterly* 40:179–185.

———. 1988. "The Item Veto and Expenditure Restraint." *Journal of Politics* 50:487–502.

———. 1991. "The Impact of State Policies to Limit Debt Financing." *Publius* 21:69–82.

———. 1994. *Policy Innovation in State Government.* Ames: Iowa State University.

Nice, David, and Patricia Fredericksen. 1995. *The Policies of Intergovernmental Relations,* 2nd ed. Chicago: Nelson-Hall.

Novick, David. 1992. "What Program Budgeting Is and Is Not." In Albert Hyde, ed., *Government Budgeting,* 2nd ed. Pacific Grove, CA: Brooks/Cole, pp. 342–348.

Oates, Wallace. 1996. "Fiscal Structure in the Federal System." In J. Richard Aronson and Eli Schwartz, eds., *Management Policies in Local Government Finance,* 4th ed. Washington, DC: International City/County Management Association. pp. 58–76.

Office of Management and Budget: Changes Resulting from the OMB 2000 Reorganization. 1996. Washington, DC: General Accounting Office. General Government Division/Accounting and Information Management Division, pp. 96–150.

Ooms, Van Doorn, Ronald Boster, and Robert Fleegler. 1999. "The Federal Budget and Economic Management." In Roy Meyers, ed., *Handbook of Government Budgeting.* San Francisco: Jossey-Bass, pp. 197–226.

Oppenheimer, Bruce. 1997. "Indicating Congressional Power: The Paradox of Republican Control." In Lawrence Dodd and Bruce Oppenheimer, eds., *Congress Reconsidered,* 6th ed. Washington, DC: Congressional Quarterly Press, pp. 371–389.

"Oregon and Washington Public Knowledge About Government." 1997. *Linkages* 13:1–2.

Ornstein, Norman, Thomas Mann, and Michael Malbin. 2000. *Vital Statistics on Congress.* Washington, DC: AEI Press.

O'Toole, Laurence. 1999. Research on Policy Implementation: Assessment and Prospect. Paper presented at the National Public Management Research Conference, Texas A&M University, College Station, TX; December 2–4.

Parker, Steven. "Budgeting as an Expression of Power." In Jack Rabin and Thomas Lynch, eds., *Handbook on Public Budgeting and Finance.* New York: Marcel Dekker, pp. 61–88.

Pearlstein, Steven. 2001. "Predicting the Unpredictable." *Washington Post National Weekly Edition.* June 22–28, pp. 19–20.

Performance Budgeting. 1993. Washington, DC: General Accounting Office.

Peters, B. Guy. 1996. *American Public Policy,* 4th ed. Chatham, NJ: Chatham House.

Peterson, George. 1976. "Finance." In William Gorham and Nathan Glazer, eds., *The Urban Predicament.* Washington, DC: Urban Institute. pp. 35–118.

Pianin, Eric. 1998. "Narrowing the Field of Battle." *Washington Post National Weekly Edition,* July 6, pp. 11–12.

———. 2000. "Binges are Part of the Regular Fare." *Washington Post National Weekly Edition,* October 30, p. 30.

Pitsuada, Bernard. 1988. "The Executive Budget: An Idea Whose Time has Passed." *Public Budgeting and Finance* (Spring.): 85–94.

Plato. 1975. *The Laws.* London: Penguin.

Posner, Paul. 1998. *The Politics of Unfunded Mandates.* Washington, DC: Georgetown University.

Pressman, Jeffrey, and Aaron Wildavsky. 1979. *Implementation,* 2nd ed. Berkeley: University of California.

Prompt Payment: State Laws are Similar to the Federal Act but Less Comprehensive. 1989. Washington, DC: General Accounting Office.

Public Pensions. 1996. Washington, DC: General Accounting Office.

Quade, E. S. 1975. *Analysis for Public Decision.* New York: Elsevier.

Rabin, Jack, W. Bartley Hildreth, and Gerald Miller. 1996. *Budgeting: Formulation and Execution.* Athens, GA: Carl Vinson Institute of Government.

Reed, B. J., and John Swain. 1997. *Public Finance Administration,* 2nd ed. Thousand Oaks, CA: Sage.

Reischauer, Robert. 1990. "Taxes and Spending Under Gramm-Rudman-Hollings." *National Tax Journal* 43:223–232.

Rogers, Jacqueline, and Marita Brown. 1999. "Preparing Agency Budgets." In Roy Meyers, ed., *Handbook of Government Budgeting.* San Francisco: Jossey-Bass, pp. 441–461.

Rogers, Robert, and Philip Joyce. 1996. "The Effect of Underforecasting on the Accuracy of Revenue Forecasts by State Governments." *Public Administration Review* 56:48–56.

Rosenthal, Alan. 1990. *Governors and Legislatures: Contending Powers.* Washington, DC: Congressional Quarterly Press.

———. 1998. *The Decline of Representative Democracy.* Washington, DC: Congressional Quarterly Press.

Ross, Russell, and Fred Schwengel. 1982. "An Item Veto for the President." *Presidential Studies Quarterly* 12:66–79.

Rossi, Peter, and Howard Freeman. 1982. *Evaluation,* 2nd ed. Beverly Hills, CA: Sage.

Royse, David, and Bruce Thyer. 1996. *Program Evaluation.* Chicago: Nelson-Hall.

Rubin, Irene. 1990. "Budget Theory and Budget Practice: How Good the Fit?" *Public Administration Review* 50:179–189.

———. 1997. *The Politics of Public Budgeting,* 3rd ed. Chatham, NJ: Chatham House.

———. 1998. *Class, Tax, and Power.* Chatham, NJ: Chatham House.

Saiz, Martin, and Susan Clarke. 1999. "Economic Development and Infrastructure Policy." In Virginia Gray, Russell Hanson, and Herbert Jacob, eds., *Politics in the American States,* 7th ed. Washington, DC: Congressional Quarterly Press, pp. 474–505.

Savas, E. S. 1982. *Privatizing the Public Sector.* Chatham, NJ: Chatham House.

Schattschneider, E. E. 1960. *The Semisovereign People.* New York: Holt, Rinehart, and Winston.

Schick, Allen. 1966. "The Road to PPB: The Stages of Budget Reform." *Public Administration Review* 26:243–258.

———. 1980. *Congress and Money.* Washington, DC: Urban Institute.

———. 1981. "The Three-Ring Budget Process: The Appropriations, Tax, and Budget Committees in Congress." In Thomas Mann and Norman Ornstein, eds., *The New Congress.* Washington, DC: American Enterprise Institute, pp. 288–328.

———. 1990. *The Capacity to Budget.* Washington, DC: Urban Institute.

———. 1995. *The Federal Budget.* Washington, DC: Brookings.

School Finance: State Efforts to Reduce Funding Gaps Between Poor and Wealthy Districts. 1997. Washington, DC: General Accounting Office.

Schroeder, Larry. 1996. "Forecasting Local Revenues and Expenditures." In J. Richard Aronson and Eli Schwartz, eds., *Management Policies in Local Government Finance,* 4th ed. Washington, DC: International City/County Management Association, pp. 99–124.

Schwartz, Eli. 1996. "Inventory and Cash Management." In J. Richard Aronson and Eli Schwartz, eds., *Management Policies in Local Government Finance,* 4th ed. Washington, DC: International City/County Management Association, pp. 389–410.

Schwarz, John. 1998. *American's Hidden Success,* revised ed. New York: Norton.

Schulman, Paul. 1980. "Nonincremental Policy Making: Toward an Alternative Paradigm." In Charles Levine, ed., *Managing Fiscal Stress.* Chatham, NJ: Chatham House, pp. 139–166.

Seckler-Hudson, Catheryn. 1953. "Performance Budgeting in Government." *Advanced Management.* (March):5–9, 30–32.

Sharkansky, Ira. 1968a. "Agency Requests, Gubernatorial Support, and Budget Success in State Legislatures." *American Political Science Review* 62:1220–1231.

———. 1968b. *Spending in the American States.* Chicago: Rand McNally.

———. 1970. *The Routines of Politics.* New York: Van Nostrand Reinhold.

Shuman, Howard. 1992. *Politics and the Budget,* 3rd ed. Englewood Cliffs, NJ: Prentice-Hall.

Significant Features of Fiscal Federalism, Volume 1. 1995. Washington, DC: Advisory Commission on Intergovernmental Relations.

Simmons, R. C. 1976. *The American Colonies.* New York: Norton.

Singer, Neil. 1976. *Public Microeconomics,* 2nd ed. Boston: Little, Brown.

Skidmore, Max. 1999. *Social Security and Its Enemies.* Boulder, CO: Westview.

Smith, Steven, and Christopher Deering. *1990. Committees in Congress,* 2nd ed. Washington, DC: Congressional Quarterly Press.

Sobel, Russell, and Randall Holcombe. 1996. "The Impact of State Rainy Day Funds in Easing State Fiscal Crises During the 1990–1991 Recession." *Public Budgeting and Finance* 16:28–48.

Social Service Privatization. 1997. Washington, DC: General Accounting Office. GAO/HES-98-6.

Stapleford, John, and Roger Figuro. 1983. "Economic Impact of Budgeting." In Jack Rabin and Thomas Lynch, eds., *Handbook on Public Budgeting and Financial Management.* New York: Marcel Dekker, pp. 565–584.

Statistical Abstract. 1998. Washington, DC: Census.

Statistical Abstract. 1999. Washington, DC: Census.

Steiss, Alan. 1989. *Financial Management in Public Organizations.* Pacific Grove, CA: Brooks/Cole.

Stewart, Charles. 1987. "Does Structure Matter? The Effects of Structural Change on Spending Decisions in the House, 1871–1922." *American Journal of Political Science* 31:584–605.

———. 1989. *Budget Reform Politics.* Cambridge: Cambridge University.

Straussman, Jeffrey. 1986. "Courts and Public Purse Strings: Are Portraits of Budgeting Missing Something?" *Public Administration Review* 46:345–351.

Swan, Wallace. "Theoretical Debates Applicable to Budgeting." In Jack Rabin and Thomas Lynch, eds., *Handbook on Public Budgeting and Finance.* New York: Marcel Dekker, pp. 3–60.

Swindell, David, and Mark Rosentraub. 1998. "Who Benefits from the Presence of Professional Sports Teams? The Implications for Public Funding of Stadiums and Arenas." *Public Administration Review* 58:11–20.

"Symposium: The Politics and Administration of Privatization." 1996. *Policy Studies Journal* 24:629–678.

Taylor, Graeme. 1977. "Introduction to Zero-Base Budgeting." *The Bureaucrat* 6:33–55.

Thomas, Clive, and Ronald Hrebenar. 1990. "Interest Groups in the States." In Virginia Gray, Herbert Jacob, and Robert Albritton, eds., *Politics in the American States,* 5th ed. Glenview, IL: Scott, Foresman/Little, Brown, pp. 123–158.

———. 1999. "Interest Groups in the States." In Virginia Gray, Russell Hanson, and Herbert Jacob, eds., *Politics in the American States,* 7th ed. Washington, DC: Congressional Quarterly Press, pp. 113–143.

Thompson, Joel. 1987. "Agency Requests, Gubernatorial support, and Budget Success in State Legislatures Revisited." *Journal of Politics* 49:756–779.

Thurber, James. 1992. "New Rules for an Old Game: Zero-Sum Budgeting in the Postreform Congress." In Roger Davidson, ed., *The Postreform Congress.* New York: St. Martin's, pp. 257–278.

———. 1997. "Centralization, Devolution, and Turf Protection in the Congressional Budget Process." In Lawrence Dodd and Bruce Oppenheimer, eds., *Congress Reconsidered,* 6th ed. Washington, DC: Congressional Quarterly Press, pp. 325–346.

"Trends in Public Knowledge Concerning State Revenue and Expenditures." 1996. *Partners* 2:1.

Unfunded Mandates. 1998. Washington, DC: General Accounting Office. GAO/GGD-98-30.

Vogler, David. 1993. *The Politics of Congress,* 6th ed. Madison, WI: William C. Brown.

Vogt, A. John. 1996. "Budgeting Capital Outlays and Improvements." In Jack Rabin, W. Bartley Hildreth, and Gerald Miller, eds., *Budgeting: Formulation and Execution.* Athens, GA: Carl Vinson Institute of Government, pp. 276–291.

Walker, Jack. 1969. "The Diffusion of Innovations Among the American States." *American Political Science Review* 63:880–899.

Welfare Reform: Implementing DOT's Access to Jobs Program. 1998. Washington, DC: General Accounting Office.

White, Barry. 1999. "Examining Budgets for Chief Executives." In Roy Meyers, ed., *Handbook of Government Budgeting.* San Francisco: Jossey-Bass, pp. 462–484.

White, Joseph. 1994. "(Almost) Nothing New Under the Sun: Why the Work of Budgeting Remains Incremental." *Public Budgeting and Finance* 14:113–134.

White, Joseph, and Aaron Wildavsky. 1991. *The Deficit and the Public Interest.* Berkeley: University of California.

Wildavsky, Aaron. 1974. *The Politics of the Budgetary Process,* 2nd ed. Boston: Little, Brown.

———. 1980. *How to Limit Government Spending.* Berkeley: University of California.

———. 1986. *Budgeting,* revised, ed. New Brunswick, NJ: Transaction.

———. 1992. *The New Politics of the Budgetary Process,* 2nd ed. New York: Harper-Collins.

Wildavsky, Aaron, and Naomi Caiden. 1997. *The New Politics of the Budgetary Process,* 3rd ed. New York: Longman.

Wilensky, Harold. 1975. *The Welfare State and Equality.* Berkeley: University of California Press.

Winters, Richard. 1999. "The Politics of Taxing and Spending." In Virginia Gray, Russel Hanson, and Herbert Jacob, eds, *Politics in the American States,* 7th ed. Washington, DC: Congressional Quarterly Press, pp. 304–348.

Wolkoff, Michael. 1999. "State and Local Government Budgeting: Coping with the Business Cycle." In Roy Meyers, ed., *Handbook of Government Budgeting.* San Francisco: Jossey-Bass, pp. 178–196.

World Almanac. 1996. Mahwah, NJ: K-III Reference Corp.

———. 1999. Mahwah, NJ: PRIMEDIA Reference.

Wright, Gerald, Robert Erikson, and John McIver. 1987. "Public Opinion and Policy Liberalism in the American States." *American Journal of Political Science* 31:980–1001.

Wyszomirski, Margaret. 1982. The De-Institutionalization of Presidential Staff Agencies. *Public Administration Review* 42:448–458.

Year-End Spending. 1998. Washington, DC: General Accounting Office. AIMD-98-185.

Index